Pattern, Construction, System

Construction Grammar and Systemic Functional Grammar take different approaches to the study of lexico-grammar, based on language as a cognitive and as a social phenomenon respectively. This is the first book to bring the two approaches together, using corpus-based Pattern Grammar as an underlying descriptive framework, in order to present a comprehensive and original treatment of verb-based patterns in English. It describes in detail two processes: deriving over 800 verb argument constructions from 50 verb complementation patterns; and using those constructions to populate systemic networks based on 9 semantic fields. The result is an approach to the lexis and grammar of English that unifies disparate theories, finding synergies between them and offering a challenge to each. Pattern Grammar, Construction Grammar, and Systemic-Functional Grammar are introduced in an accessible way, making each approach accessible to readers from other backgrounds. This title is also available as open access on Cambridge Core.

SUSAN HUNSTON is Professor of English Language at the University of Birmingham. Her notable publications include *Corpora in Applied Linguistics*, 2nd edition (2022, CUP), *Interdisciplinary Discourse* (with Thompson, 2020, Routledge), and *Pattern Grammar* (with Francis, 2000, John Benjamins). She is a Fellow of the Academy of Social Sciences.

Pattern, Construction, System

A Unified Approach to Grammar and Lexis

Susan Hunston

University of Birmingham

CAMBRIDGE
UNIVERSITY PRESS

CAMBRIDGE
UNIVERSITY PRESS

Shaftesbury Road, Cambridge CB2 8EA, United Kingdom

One Liberty Plaza, 20th Floor, New York, NY 10006, USA

477 Williamstown Road, Port Melbourne, VIC 3207, Australia

314–321, 3rd Floor, Plot 3, Splendor Forum, Jasola District Centre, New Delhi – 110025, India

103 Penang Road, #05–06/07, Visioncrest Commercial, Singapore 238467

Cambridge University Press is part of Cambridge University Press & Assessment, a department of the University of Cambridge.

We share the University's mission to contribute to society through the pursuit of education, learning and research at the highest international levels of excellence.

www.cambridge.org
Information on this title: www.cambridge.org/9781009629027

DOI: 10.1017/9781009629065

First published 2025

Cover image: anilyanik/DigitalVision Vectors/Getty Images.

A catalogue record for this publication is available from the British Library

A Cataloging-in-Publication data record for this book is available from the Library of Congress

ISBN 978-1-009-62902-7 Hardback

For Rosie
and
For Leo

Contents

Figures

Tables

Acknowledgements

The research for this book was supported by the Leverhulme Trust, project number EM-2022-022.

I would like to thank the research assistants on the project, Caroline Ellis, Abbie Ip (Tsz Yuet Ip), and Kelly Su (Ze Su), for their invaluable help. I would also like to thank University of Birmingham website developers Cerys Lewis and Mohammad Afraz Ahmed.

I acknowledge the following sources of copyright material and am grateful for the permission granted. Figure 2.1 is reproduced from Perek and Patten (2019) 'Towards an English constructicon using patterns and frames' *International Journal of Corpus Linguistics* 24(3):354-384 (figure 3), by permission from the publisher. Figure 2.2 is reproduced from Diessel (2020) 'A dynamic network approach to the study of syntax' *Frontiers in Psychology* 11 (figure 28), by permission from the author. Table 3.3 is derived from information contained in Francis et al. (1996) *Collins Cobuild Grammar Patterns 1: Verbs* HarperCollins. Permission has been requested from the publisher. Figures 5.1 and 5.2 are reproduced from Thompson (2014) *Introducing Functional Grammar* Routledge, by permission from the publisher. Figure 5.3 is adapted from Halliday and Matthiessen (2014) *Halliday's Introduction to Functional Grammar* Routledge, by permission from the publisher. Figure 5.4 is adapted from Neale (2002) 'More delicate transitivity: extending the process type system for English to include full semantic classifications' PhD thesis, Cardiff University, by permission from the author.

In addition, I acknowledge the following sources. Table 4.1 uses information on the website pdev.org.uk. Table 4.3 uses information on the website framenet.icsi.berkeley.edu.

Funding from the University of Birmingham made it possible for this book to be published open access, making the digital version freely available for anyone to read and reuse under a Creative Commons licence.

1 Introduction

1.1 Prologue

The argument of this book can be stated very simply in terms of three key ideas.

Firstly, verbs in English are used with complementation patterns. Often, the complementation patterns are linked to the verb meaning. For example, when LIE is used in the sense of 'being in a horizontal position' it is used with a preposition or with an adjective: *... lying on the ground*; *... lying at the end of the bed*; *... lay awake*. When it means 'be in a position in a competition' it is used with an ordinal number or with *in*: *... lying second*; *... lying in second place*. When it is used in the sense of 'say something untrue' it is used without complementation, or with *about* or *to*: *He lied*; *He lied about his past*; *He lied to his employers*. Part of knowing the grammar of English is knowing what complementation patterns a verb is used with, and dictionaries aimed at learners of English often include information about complementation in their entries. In the Collins COBUILD dictionaries, the grammar coding is called 'grammar patterns'. The approach to coding lexis in this way is known as Pattern Grammar.

Secondly, language can be said to be composed of constructions, that is, pairings of form and meaning. A description of a construction can capture something that is idiosyncratic usage, such as the 'let alone' construction: *I shouldn't even have talked to him, let alone been friendly*. They also account for much more regular sentence patterns, such as the 'caused motion' construction: *They pushed the piano into the classroom*. The meaning of a construction overrides the canonical meaning of any individual word used in it. For example, LAUGH does not mean anything like PUSH, but *The bank manager laughed me straight out of the room* is an instance of the 'caused motion' construction. Knowing a language means having a store of constructions and using them conventionally, or at least in a way that other language users understand. Describing a language means itemising its constructions and showing how they are related to one another. This approach to language description is known as Construction Grammar.

Thirdly, the language resources that a community uses can be expressed in terms of choices of form and meaning. For example, an event may be represented, or construed, as an occurrence in the 'external' world or as a construct in the 'internal' world of thought: *Bandits killed the villagers*; *They surmised that the villagers had been killed by bandits*. Differences between verbs are modelled as choices between features. For example, the difference between *Tom enjoyed the concert* and *The concert entertained Tom* is the 'direction' of the process of sensing emotion. The difference between *Harold made some cakes* and *Harold burnt the cakes* is the difference between creating something and having an effect on something that already exists. There are also differences in the participants involved in a process. In *Harold burnt the cakes*, 'the cakes' is the Goal of the process, and the clause answers the question 'what did Harold do to the cakes?'. However, in *Harold crossed the room*, 'the room' is not the Goal but is described as the Scope of the process. The question 'what did Harold do to the room?' does not make sense. This approach to contrasts in language description derives from Systemic Functional Grammar (SFG).

These approaches have developed independently of each other. This book brings them together.

1.2 The Background to This Book

The aim of this book is to bring together three approaches to form and meaning that have developed separately from each other but which in many ways support each other. The three approaches are: Pattern Grammar; Construction Grammar; and Systemic-Functional Linguistics. They are brought together in a study that starts with fifty verb complementation patterns, reinterprets these patterns as constructions, and organises these constructions into networks inspired by SFG. The progression through the stages of the research is summarised in Figure 1.1.

The starting point is the extensive corpus-driven lexicography carried out in the 1990s as part of the COBUILD project (Moon 2007). The research that led to the publication of the 1995 Collins COBUILD English Dictionary (CCED) was based on the 200 million word Bank of English corpus (Sinclair 1995: viii). This corpus was considered large for its time, and whereas it sacrificed balance for size (McEnery and Hardie 2012: 6), it included major types of written and spoken English, predominantly from the UK but also from the USA and Australia. The approach to lexicography was innovative (Moon 2009); not only did it prioritise observation of large amounts of data over introspection, but the explanations of words given in the dictionary reflected their usage. The introduction to the dictionary states: '. . . it is a feature of all COBUILD dictionaries that the definitions (or explanations, as we often call them) are written in

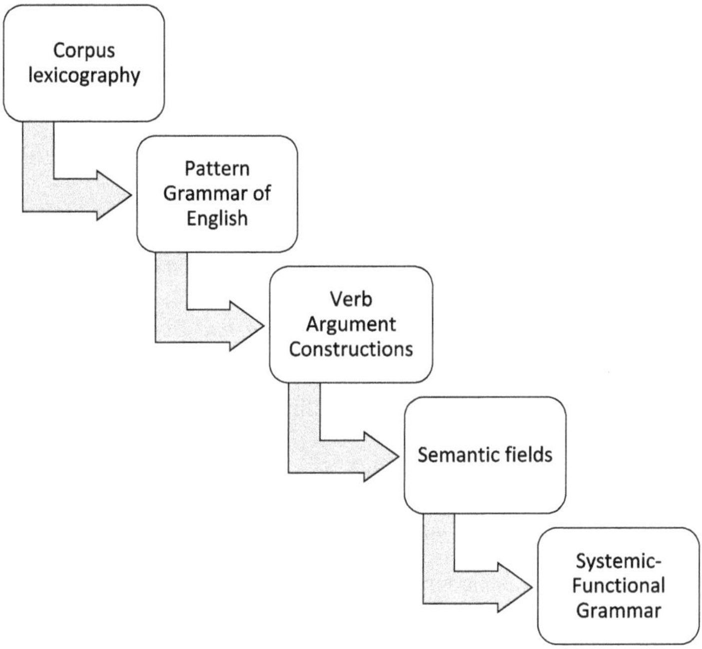

Figure 1.1 The research journey from pattern to construction to system

full sentences, using vocabulary and grammar that occur naturally with the word being explained' (Sinclair 1995: xviii).

As an example, here are the explanations of three senses of the verb INTEND in CCED, with a gloss of the usage of the part underlined:

- Sense 1: If you **intend** to do something, you have decided or planned to do it.
  - (the verb has a human subject and is followed by a to-infinitive clause)
- Sense 2: If something **is intended** for a particular purpose, it has been planned to fulfil that purpose.
  - (the verb is used in the passive and is followed by the preposition *for*)
- Sense 3: If you **intend** a particular idea or feeling in something that you say or do, you want to express it or want it to be understood.
  - (the verb has a human subject and is followed by a noun phrase that indicates an idea or a feeling)

Moon (2009: 9) describes the approach as an 'emphasis on form and downplay of independent meaning'. An important part of the emphasis on form was the development of a coding schema which detailed what might be called the 'grammatical behaviour' of each sense of each word. This can be exemplified using the three senses of INTEND:

- Sense 1: If you **intend** to do something . . .
  - Grammar codes: **V to-inf**; **V -ing**; **V that**
  - Examples: *she intended to do . . .* ; *I didn't intend coming . . .* ; *we had always intended that the new series . . .*
- Sense 2: If something **is intended** for a particular purpose . . .
  - Grammar codes: ***be* V-ed *for* n**; ***be* V-ed to-inf**; ***be* V-ed *as* n**
  - Examples: *this money is intended for the development . . .* ; *columns are usually intended to add grandeur . . .* ; *Hatfield had been intended as a leisure complex . . .*
- Sense 3: If you **intend** a particular idea or feeling in something that you say or do . . .
  - Grammar codes: **V n**; **V n n**; **V n to-inf**; **V n prep**
  - Examples: *he didn't intend any sarcasm*; *he hadn't intended it that way*; *I didn't intend it to be . . .* ; *he intended it as a put-down comment . . .*

As a consequence of this lexicographic enterprise, the CCED comprised a grammatical analysis of around 70,000 words. The next stage of grammatical analysis was the listing of each pattern associated with verbs (87 patterns), nouns (63 patterns), and adjectives (49 patterns), together with all the words in the dictionary having that pattern code (Francis et al. 1996, 1998). For example, the pattern **V to-inf** lists 202 verbs, including of course INTEND. All these patterns and the associated words can be found on the grammar patterns website (http://grammar.collinsdictionary.com/grammar-pattern), which is an updated web version of the publications Francis et al. (1996, 1998).

The study in this book does not reanalyse a corpus, but instead takes as its primary data 52 of the 87 verb patterns, and their associated verbs, identified in Francis et al. (1996) and to be found on the grammar patterns website. Those patterns are interpreted as Verb Argument Constructions. From the 52 patterns, 809 constructions are identified. The next stage is to select a number of commonly studied semantic fields (such as Causation and Communication) and to find all the constructions that contribute to those fields. Those constructions are then organised in networks inspired by SFG.

This process can be illustrated as follows. One of the verb complementation patterns identified in Francis et al. (1996) is the pattern **V *after* n**, where a verb is followed by a prepositional phrase beginning with *after*. Instances of 'verb + *after*' are considered to be an example of this pattern only when the choice of preposition is dependent on, or governed by, the verb. Example (1) is an example of the pattern because the choice of *after powerful storage systems* is dependent on the verb *is hankering*, whereas example (2) is not an example of this pattern, because the choice of *after my flight* is not dependent on the verb *arrive*.

(1) ... and even the automotive industry is hankering after increasingly powerful energy storage systems. (enTenTen21)

(2) I'm concerned there won't be anywhere to camp when I arrive after my 3+ day flight. (enTenTen21)

The pattern **V *after* n** and the verbs identified as occurring with it (Francis et al. 1996: 151–153) are reinterpreted as constituting four constructions:

- The 'hanker after something' construction (= A person wants something very much).
- The 'follow after someone' construction (= A person follows another person, often with negative intentions).
- The 'chase after something' construction (= A person tries to get something that is difficult to get).
- The 'clean up after someone' construction (= A person helps someone, especially by correcting their mistakes).

In each construction, a number of verbs are found in the verb slot:

- *hanker after, hunger after, lust after, thirst after, yearn after*
- *chase after, follow after*
- *chase after, go after, run after*
- *clean up after, clear up after, run around after, tidy up after*

The first of these constructions ('hanker after') expresses a meaning of 'wanting something in the future'. It is one of a range of constructions that express similar meanings, i.e.

- 'dream about something'
- 'hanker after something'
- 'jump at the chance of something'
- 'yearn for something'
- 'dream of something'
- 'aspire to something'

Examples (1) to (6) illustrate these constructions:

(1) ... the kind of treatment I'd always dreamed about when I was an actress. (BNC)

(2) A lot of people hanker after making a big scientific discovery ... (BNC)

(3) I had jumped at the chance of a part-time job in the City. (BNC)

(4) [It] makes you yearn for the return of black-and-white photography. (BNC)

(5) [He] had made her dare to dream of a permanent partnership. (BNC)

(6) [They] . . . aspire to more senior positions. (BNC)

These constructions all express an emotion in relation to the future. In this they contrast with the expression of emotion towards the past (the 'repent of something' construction, example (7)) or a more general time frame (the 'delight in something' construction, example (8)).

(7) . . . nor was it her habit . . . to repent of what she did. (BNC)

(8) The river draws many visitors who delight in the beautiful scenery . . . (BNC)

In these constructions, the reason for the emotion is implicit in the noun phrase following the preposition. In example (8), we may deduce that the visitors delight in the scenery because it is beautiful. In example (3), we may deduce that a part-time job in the City is particularly desirable, without being told why. Other constructions that express emotion make the rationale more explicit, in that the object of emotion is in a noun phrase and the reason in a prepositional phrase. This is true of the 'admire someone for something' construction (example (9)) and the 'pride oneself on something' construction (example (10)).

(9) I also admire Bethany . . . for efforts to try and improve the estate. (BNC)

(10) Ministers pride themselves on their attention to detail . . . (BNC)

There are, then, at least 10 constructions that express an emotion towards something. Within these10, contrasts may be observed: reacting to future, past, or general situations; leaving the cause of the emotion implicit or expressing it in a prepositional phrase; expressing a positive emotion ('delight'); or a negative one ('repent'). These alternatives can be shown as a network. Figure 1.2 shows a very simplified partial network for the meaning 'expressing emotion towards something' (more detailed networks are shown in Chapter 7).

A taxonomy of the type shown in Figure 1.2 is termed in this book a 'meaning network'. An alternative way of showing the same information is to specify the choices available to the language user in expressing this meaning. Figure 1.3 shows these choices: the speaker chooses between three time references and between positive or negative polarity, and chooses whether or not to make a reason explicit. This arrangement of the relevant choices is termed in this book a 'systemic network'.

In this book, only a sample of the patterns and constructions studied are shown. The full set of 52 patterns and 809 constructions can be seen on the Transitivity-Net website (transitivity-net.bham.ac.uk). That website shows also the full set of meaning networks and systemic networks, most of which are shown in this book also.

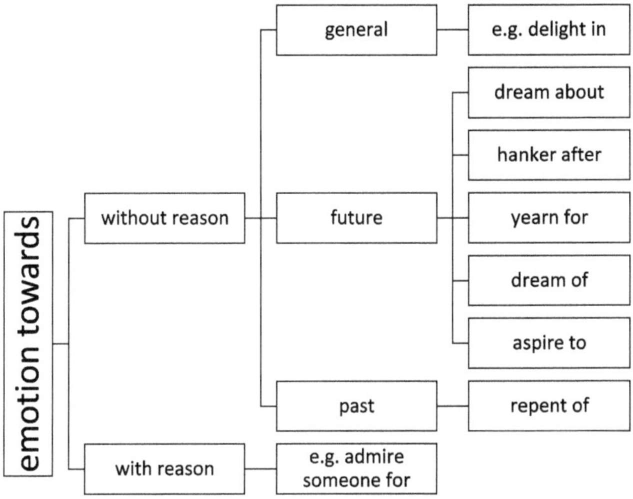

Figure 1.2 A simplified meaning network for 'expressing emotion towards something'

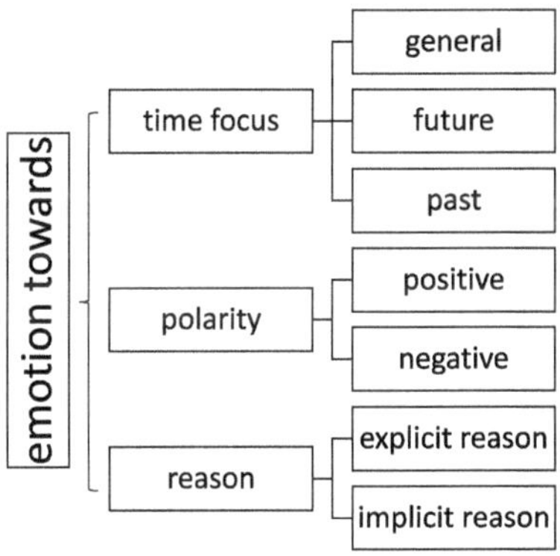

Figure 1.3 A simplified systemic network for 'expressing emotion towards something'

This book, then, considers three distinct approaches to language description (pattern, construction, and system), raising the question of why these particular approaches have been selected, and why the enterprise of 'unifying' them has been attempted. The simple answer is that all three are usage-based, and all three posit lexis and grammar as comprising a single entity, in opposition to approaches that envisage a lexicon that is separate from syntax (a view associated with Chomsky, though see Andor 2015). Grammar patterns consist of lexical items in combination with grammatical units such as clauses or prepositional phrases. They account for the grammatical behaviour of words. Constructions similarly consist of both lexical and grammatical items and in some cases at least consist of grammatical frames with lexical slots (Haspelmath 2023). Systemic Functional Grammar considers lexis and grammar to form a continuum; accounts can focus on the more general 'grammar-like' descriptions or the more specific 'lexis-like' ones (Halliday 1973: 55).

In spite of having this in common, the three approaches have developed independently, belong to different traditions of language study, and have different views of what it is that a grammarian does. This may be explained as follows:

- Pattern Grammar is a descriptive framework based on corpus observation, specifically corpus lexicography. By implication, the job of the grammarian working with pattern grammar is to provide a coherent model of what is observed, consistent with approaches such as Sinclair (2004) and Hoey (2005).
- Construction Grammar aligns itself with Cognitive Linguistics, which studies language as a mental construct. The job of the construction grammarian is to model speakers' mental representations of language (Goldberg 2006).
- Systemic-Functional Linguistics sees language as a social entity. The job of the Systemic Functional Grammarian is to build models that best reflect community language resources (Halliday 1978).

'Language', then, can be reified as three objects: language in the mind; language in society; and language in corpus. These perspectives could be seen as incompatible, but this book argues that it is useful to draw out their compatibilities.

Although the approaches have different origins, connections are beginning to be made between the three. There are clear similarities between Pattern Grammar and Construction Grammar, such that articulating the contribution of Pattern Grammar to the notion of construction is an obvious next step (e.g. Ellis et al. 2016; Perek and Patten 2019). Connections are also beginning to be made between Construction Grammar and Systemic Functional Grammar (Laffut 2006; Lin and Peng 2006; Yang 2023). Both approaches regard lexis and grammar as indivisible. In addition, both Construction Grammar and Systemic Functional Grammar prioritise language as a meaning-making resource and take seriously the connection between meaning and form. Perhaps most strikingly, both regard themselves as constituting a theory that accounts for a language in its entirety, not just lexis and grammar. The whole of language consists of constructions: 'it's constructions all the way down' (Goldberg 2006:18); and/or the whole of language consists of systems: 'it is systems all the way down' (Matthiessen 2023: 31). Each draws on corpora in support of its model of language, particularly to add quantitative information to the description (e.g. Matthiessen 2006; Stefanowitsch and Gries 2003; Ellis et al. 2016; Gries 2019).

The purpose of this book is to bring all three together and to find compatibility between views of language as a mental and as a social phenomenon. In terms of personal history, I am an 'insider' in terms of Pattern Grammar and an 'outsider' in terms of both Construction Grammar and Systemic Functional Grammar. In terms of the two theories of language, this book takes an agnostic stance, regarding models of language as abstractions from what is, and accepting of the viability of alternative models. In other words, it is argued that models of language can sit alongside each other, each offering useful insights, and it is not necessary to decide that one is 'right' and the other 'wrong'. Is language a mental or a social phenomenon? It is both. Does language consist of constructions or of systems? It consists of both. Can a dialogue between two disparate traditions of language study be fruitful to both? And can observations from Corpus Linguistics assist that dialogue? I believe the answer is yes to both questions.

1.3 The Organisation of the Book

The two chapters following this introduction discuss the relationship between pattern and construction. Chapter 2 provides further background information on the two concepts and the connections between them. Chapter 3 is an account of the process of reinterpreting the verb patterns as constructions.

Chapter 4 demonstrates a further stage in the analysis: the annotation of semantic roles. This has been applied to a subset of the constructions only. The chapter explains and exemplifies this process, also discussing other approaches to semantic role annotation.

In the following four chapters, attention turns to SFG and its role in this study. Chapter 5 provides background information on SFG and the questions it raises. Chapter 6 explains in detail how one semantic field, Causation, is treated in this study, showing how two kinds of networks (the Meaning Network and the Systemic Network) are derived. Chapters 7 and 8 perform the same exercise, though in less detail, for a further eight semantic fields: Cognition and Communication in Chapter 7; and Creation, Change, Location_change, and Possession_transfer (related to material processes); and Equivalence and Logical Relation (related to relational processes) in Chapter 8.

Chapter 9 concludes the study, discussing the issues it raises for both Construction Grammar and Systemic Functional Grammar.

1.4 A Note on Websites, Corpora, and Conventions

Readers may wish to take note of two websites that contain information of relevance to this book:

- The grammar patterns website, hosted by HarperCollins publishers, contains the output from the original Pattern Grammar study carried out in the 1990s by Gill Francis, Susan Hunston, and Elizabeth Manning. It is a digitised and revised version of the publications Francis et al. (1996, 1998). It can be found at: grammar.collinsdictionary.com/grammar-pattern.
- The Transitivity-Net website, hosted by the University of Birmingham, contains the output from the current study. It shows all the constructions and networks referred to in this book. It can be found at: transitivity-net.bham.ac.uk.

This book does not include analysis of a corpus. However, corpora are used as sources of illustrative examples; these corpora have been accessed via Sketch Engine (www.sketchengine.eu). Mostly, the British National Corpus has been used. Although this corpus is somewhat old and relatively small by modern standards, it is convenient to use because its small size means that searches are quickly performed. In some cases, examples come from the British Academic Written Corpus or the much larger English Web2021 corpus. A few examples come from the Bank of English corpus as it existed in the 1990s, when it stood at around 200 million tokens. Examples are annotated with the corpus they come from, as follows:

- BAWE. British Academic Written Corpus. 7 million tokens.
- BNC. British National Corpus. 96 million tokens.
- BoE. Bank of English. 200 million tokens.
- enTenTen21. English Web 2021. 52 billion tokens.

Throughout this book, the following conventions are used:

- Verb complementation patterns are shown in bold, with the verb shown with capital V and other elements in lower case. Word classes and clause types are shown in regular type, and specific words are shown in italics. For example, **V *to* n that** means 'Verb + *to* + noun phrase + that-clause'.
- Construction names are shown in inverted commas e.g. the 'causative *into*' construction.
- Numbered examples are shown in regular type. Example phrases that are not numbered are shown in italics if they come from a corpus and in inverted commas if they are invented.
- Lemmas are shown in capital letters e.g. INTEND.

2 Background to Pattern Grammar and Construction Grammar

2.1 Introduction

This chapter provides an introduction to two of the concepts that are central to this study: Pattern Grammar and Construction Grammar. The chapter consists of an overview of each, followed by a discussion of how they are related to one another.

2.2 Pattern Grammar

Pattern Grammar was initiated by Gill Francis and developed as a means of recording the grammatical patterning of individual entries in the Collins COBUILD English Dictionary – CCED (Sinclair 1995). It was based on an insight articulated by Sinclair (1987: 109), that when a lexicographer investigates a word in a corpus using concordancing software, the various senses of the word are observable as different patternings i.e. sequences of lexical and grammatical elements. As an example of the interdependence of grammatical form and meaning, Table 2.1 shows examples of different senses of the verb DECIDE and the observed patterning.

Sinclair (1991: 7) concluded that 'there is ultimately no distinction between form and meaning', and that it was consequently important to record the detail of the patterning of each sense of each word. Of course, learners' dictionaries generally do record grammatical information, but Francis observed that traditional notation has two disadvantages: it tends to use technical terminology that a learner may not know; and it tends to lack important detail (Francis 1993: 140–141). The advantage of the detailed corpus-based lexicography used in the COBUILD project was that every recurring pattern associated with each sense of each word could be recorded, using a simple but flexible scheme. Although each word in the dictionary is coded in this way, this book is concerned only with verb patterns, so this discussion will be restricted to them. When the dictionary was published in 1995, a total of 152 verb complementation patterns had been identified (Francis et al. 1996: 625–630). (Some of these patterns are used with very few verbs; some are variations of other patterns and can be

Table 2.1 *DECIDE pattern and meaning (examples from the BNC and enTenTen21)*

Example	Pattern	Notation	Meaning
Michael decided to change his name.	Subject is animate. Verb is followed by a to-infinitive clause.	**V to-inf**	Michael determines a course of action.
Jen decided that the best thing to do was to leave.	Subject is animate. Verb is followed by a that-clause.	**V that**	Jen reaches a conclusion about a situation.
Lucy decided on the steak and kidney pie.	Subject is animate. Verb is followed by 'on' and a noun phrase.	**V *on* n**	Lucy makes a choice between available foods.
Ecca hesitated, but her new friend's smile decided her.	Subject ('behaviour') is inanimate. Verb is followed by an animate noun phrase.	**V n**	A circumstance enables Ecca to make up her mind.

subsumed in them. There are 87 patterns deemed substantial enough to be covered in a named section in Francis et al. 1996.) The patterns might be divided into five types:

1. The verb is followed by a single element comprising a phrase or clause type e.g. 'verb + noun phrase' (**V n**); 'verb + that-clause' (**V that**); 'verb + -ing clause' (**V -ing**). Examples are 'built a castle', 'said that he was sad', and 'liked drinking black coffee'.
2. The verb is followed by two elements comprising phrase or clause types e.g. 'verb + noun phrase + noun phrase' (**V n n**); 'verb + noun phrase + that-clause' (**V n that**); 'verb + noun phrase + -ing clause' (**V n -ing**). Examples are 'baked her mother a cake', 'told him that she was sad', and 'saw the child crossing the road'.
3. The verb is followed by a prepositional phrase beginning with a specific preposition e.g. 'verb + *at* + noun phrase' (**V *at* n**); 'verb + *into* + noun phrase' (**V *into* n**); 'verb + *on* + noun phrase' (**V *on* n**). Examples are 'look at the picture', 'look into the crime', and 'decide on a puppy'.
4. The verb is followed by a noun phrase and a prepositional phrase e.g. 'verb + noun phrase + *at* + noun phrase' (**V n *at* n**); 'verb + noun phrase + *into* + noun phrase' (**V n *into* n**); 'verb + noun phrase + *on* + noun phrase' (**V n *on* n**). Examples are 'took the applicant at her word', 'bullied him into crime', and 'decided her on a puppy'.
5. The verb is used in a clause beginning with an anticipatory *it* or a dummy subject *there* e.g. '*it* + verb + adjective + that-clause' (***it* v-link adj that**);

'*there* + verb + noun phrase + prepositional phrase' (***there*** **v-link v prep**). Examples are 'it seemed unbelievable that he was sad' and 'there was a book on the table'.

It will be noted that these codes give information only about the form of the elements in the pattern. For example, as shown in Table 2.1, the subject of DECIDE is always animate, and one might say either human or human-like. Not only is this information not given in the pattern notation, but in fact it is assumed that all verbs occur with Subjects, so that the presence of a Subject is not dependent on which verb is used, and so the patterns do not indicate the presence of a noun phrase before the verb. (See Hanks 2013, discussed in Chapter 4, for an alternative approach.)

In those cases where the code indicates a class of thing (phrase or clause) rather than a specific word, the code can subsume substantial detail. Most strikingly, the term 'noun phrase', indicated by '**n**', includes not only single nouns, pronouns, and multi-word noun phrases, but also '-ing' clauses. For example, the pattern 'verb + *as* + noun phrase' (**V *as* n**) also covers instances of 'verb + *as* + -ing clause', such as . . . *qualify as being in priority need* (Francis et al. 1996: 161). In some cases, however, a phrase type needs to be specified in more detail. The pattern 'verb + noun phrase + *into* + -ing clause' (**V n *into* -ing**) departs from the norm in specifying an '-ing' clause, because the verbs used in that pattern are different from those in the equivalent **V n *into* n** pattern. Specific phrase types are used also when they contribute to the meaning of a verb. The pattern 'verb + reflexive pronoun + prepositional phrase' (**V pron-refl prep**) indicates that the noun phrase following the verb is a particular kind of pronoun (e.g. 'He found himself in a dark forest'). Although in other patterns, the noun phrase can be a pronoun (e.g. an example of **V n n** would be 'He baked himself a cake'), in the case of FIND the reflexive pronoun is integral to the meaning of the phrase. Similarly, the pattern 'verb + amount + *of* + noun phrase' (**V amount *of* n**) indicates that whatever follows the preposition must represent an amount, however, that is expressed (e.g. 'She thought highly / a great deal of her friend'). Again, this usage distinguishes this meaning of THINK.

The next stage in the Pattern Grammar project was the collection of all the entries in the CCED (Sinclair 1995) that have the same pattern. For example, all the verbs with the patterns **V to-inf**, **V that** and **V *on* n** were collected. Unsurprisingly, this is not a random list of verbs; rather, the verbs can be grouped according to shared meaning. For example, the verbs with the pattern **V *on* n** can be arranged into over 30 'meaning groups'. Some examples are:

- The 'comment on something' group e.g. *comment, discourse, dwell, generalise, lecture, preach, pronounce, remark, rule, speak, talk,* and *write.*

- The 'reflect on something' group e.g. *brood, cogitate, meditate, reflect,* and *speculate.*
- The 'beat on something' group e.g. *bang, beat, grate, hammer, press, stamp,* and *tread.*
- The 'depend on someone or something' group e.g. *bank, count, depend, hinge, lean, rely, ride,* and *turn.*
- The 'focus on something' group e.g. *(eyes) alight, centre, (eyes) fall, (eyes) fix, focus,* and *(eyes) rest.*

The patterns and the meaning groups identified are listed in Francis et al. (1996: 215–229) and on the grammar patterns website (grammar.collinsdictionary.com/grammar-pattern). The description of the meaning groups, and the examples given, allow for more details of phraseology to be given. For example, in the description of the 'depend on something' group some verbs are used with an animate subject ('a person relies on something or someone') and some with an inanimate one ('an event turns on a contingency'). In the 'focus on something' group, it is noted that a subset of the verbs listed have 'eyes' as the subject ('her eyes rested on the photograph').

Francis et al. (1996) list 87 'main' verb patterns, that is, those used with sufficient different verbs to warrant a mention in the contents page of the book. Each pattern subsumes its passive equivalent and its phrasal verb equivalent. For example, the pattern entry for **V *on* n** includes the passive pattern ***be* V-ed *on*** (e.g. *His car was fired on*) and the phrasal verb pattern **V P *on* n** (e.g. *Big American firms were muscling in on the market*). In some cases, there are minor patterns, accounting for very few verbs, that are listed as add-ons to the main ones. For example, the pattern entry for **V *on* n** includes **V *on* n *as* n/-ing/ adj** (e.g. *look on someone as selfish*) and **V *on* n to-inf** (e.g. *bank on someone to do something*). This explains the discrepancy between the recorded numbers of patterns: 87 listed in the contents page and 152 in the index.

Pattern Grammar has been criticised, justifiably, for its lack of detail as regards the semantic sets that the participants belong to (Hanks 2013), for its lack of quantitative information (Stefanowitsch and Gries 2003) and for its lack of engagement with semantic theory (Perek and Patten 2019). The meaning groups themselves might be said to be something of a compromise between comprehensive coverage and manageable proportion. For example, one of the 32 groups listed under the pattern **V *on* n** is the 'pounce' group (Francis et al. 1996: 220). The description picks out three subgroups, but does not allocate verbs to the subgroups:

- 'physically attacking someone' e.g. 'pounce on a victim' and 'fire on a village';
- 'criticising someone' e.g. 'turn on someone' and 'round on someone';
- 'stopping someone's activities' e.g. 'crack down on crime'.

These subgroups are very different from each other, raising questions as to whether they belong together. In addition, some of the 16 verbs listed as belonging to the 'pounce' group do not fit comfortably into any of the subgroups. Examples are the verbs DUMP and PREY. The phrase 'dump on someone' has the specific sense of 'talk about one's own unhappiness to an excessive extent', while 'prey on someone' has the specific sense of 'exploit a vulnerable person'. They do, however, fit with the overall group description of 'attacking or harming someone or treating them in a bad or hostile way'. The 'pounce' group could have been divided into several more specific groups, but to some extent having many groups with one or two verbs negates the value of the groups themselves. Even with such broad groupings, there are in all the patterns some verbs that just do not fit, and these are listed in a 'miscellaneous' or 'verbs with other meanings' group.

The important advantage of the Pattern Grammar resource is its comprehensiveness. Every single sense of every single word in the CCED is coded for the grammar patterns it is used with, leading to many thousands of word+pattern combinations. With a very few exceptions, Francis et al. (1996) list all the verbs in that dictionary that have been coded with a given pattern. The main exceptions are the patterns **V** (intransitive verb without complementation e.g. 'The car stopped') and **V n** (transitive verb e.g. 'The horse jumped the fence'). There are so many verbs with these patterns that Francis et al. (1996) list only the most frequent. Aside from these two patterns, the comprehensiveness makes it a useful resource for others wishing to reinterpret the patterns in terms of constructions (e.g. Ellis et al. 2016; Perek and Patten 2019).

2.3 Construction Grammar

Construction Grammar has an extensive literature, which describes several variations on the common approach (Croft and Cruse 2004: 257–290; Fillmore 2013; Hilpert 2014; Hoffman 2016; Michaelis 2024). For the most part, the version that is prioritised here is that articulated by Goldberg (2006), Hilpert (2014), and Haspelmath (2023). This section will consider three aspects of Construction Grammar: what a construction is; how constructions are investigated; and the concept of the constructicon.

Goldberg's definition of constructions is that they are 'learned pairings of form with semantic or discourse functions' (Goldberg 2006: 5). They are said to exist at all levels of language: 'from morphemes to abstract sentence patterns' (Hoffman 2016: 2), and to account for, essentially, everything that a speaker knows about the structure, phraseology and usage of a language (Hilpert 2014: 2). Some definitions specify that a construction should be 'non-compositional', that is, its meaning is not predictable from the meaning of its constituents (e.g. Goldberg 1995: 4). However, Hilpert (2014:12–13) argues that this criterion is no longer widely used. More recently, Haspelmath (2023: 8) proposes an alternative definition of a construction that is somewhat controversial, but which fits well with the verb argument constructions discussed in this book:

> A construction is a conventional schema for creating or motivating well-formed expressions in which there is at least one open slot that can be filled by one of several expressions that belong to the same form-class.

This slot-and-filler definition excludes both single-word and fixed-phrase constructions, which have no open slot, as well as very generalised constructions such as the interrogative or the past tense. The definition also excludes the requirement that a construction be 'learnt' or 'known', instead requiring it to be 'a conventional schema'. This means that a construction can be discovered in a corpus, as a regularly occurring schema, without the requirement to demonstrate that speakers have a representation of the construction in their minds. This is in line with the approach of Boas (2008) and Goldberg and Herbst (2021). The definition also makes it clear that the construction itself is an abstraction that generates instances, not the instances themselves.

Many well-known studies of constructions focus on the idiosyncratic, sometimes disparagingly known as 'butterfly collecting' (Hilpert 2014:14). Perek (2021) notes commonly cited examples of constructions such as: the 'let alone' construction from Fillmore et al. (1988) (e.g. 'I don't like fish, let alone oysters'); the 'what's X doing Y' construction from Kay and Fillmore (1999) (e.g. 'What's my name doing on this list'); and the 'just because … doesn't mean … ' construction from Bender and Kathol (2001) (e.g. 'Just because she works for Trump doesn't mean she's a racist'). In line with Haspelmath's definition, few if any studies discuss single words in terms of constructions. Similarly, although constructions can be general grammatical principles, such as tense or mood formations (e.g. the 'past tense' construction; the 'interrogative' construction), these again are rarely studied (Perek 2021). On the other hand, there is an extensive tradition of studies of argument constructions (Goldberg 1995; Boas 2008; Hilpert 2014; Diessel 2020; Goldberg and Herbst 2021, Chapter 2). These are the most relevant to the constructions proposed in this book. Examples that are based on verb valency include the 'resultative' construction, the 'ditransitive' construction, and the 'caused_motion' construction. An example based on adjective valency is the 'nice of you (to do)' construction (Goldberg and Herbst 2021).

Studies of argument constructions focus on specifying the meaning of the construction and the constraints on which verbs (or nouns, or adjectives) are licensed to occur in it, as well as extensions to it, such as metaphorical uses. It is argued that a construction is often used with words in a given semantic set (Boas 2008). For example, the 'ditransitive' construction is used with verbs that mean 'transfer possession'. However, one of the main points made in the literature is that the construction itself has a meaning which is not dependent on the meaning of the verbs found in it. Speakers are often creative with constructions, because the meaning of a construction overrides the usual meaning of its component parts. Goldberg (2006: 73) offers some examples, such as 'Pat sneezed the foam off the cappucino', which is an instance of the 'caused motion' construction because of its form ('verb something somewhere'), even though SNEEZE is an unusual verb to use in this context. Another example is 'She kissed him unconscious', which exemplifies the 'resultative' construction, again because of its form ('verb someone state'), although again KISS does not usually mean 'bring about a result'. An example given by Goldberg and Herbst (2021: 293) is the use of adjectives such as *big, sick, rich, American*, and *cold* in the '(it was) nice of you (to do)' construction. The meaning of the construction means that these adjectives are interpreted with an evaluative, not descriptive, meaning. Hilpert (2014) refers to this as 'coercion', citing Michaelis (2004). He summarises the principle as 'constructions may override word meanings, creating non-compositional constructional meanings in the process' (Hilpert 2014: 17).

Boas (2008) notes that there are problematic limits to this creativity, however. For example, he notes that whereas an example like 'He talked himself blue in the face' is possible, a similar 'He spoke himself blue in the face' is not. This suggests that the idea that a construction will license the use of all verbs in a semantic class must be treated with caution. Boas (2008) proposes that the semantic classes involved should be more narrowly defined to take account of this. An interesting example in English is the verb SUGGEST which, conventionally in British English, is not used in the 'tell someone to do' construction as TELL, ORDER, ADVISE, and COUNSEL are. This implies that SUGGEST does not belong to a set meaning 'impose an action on someone by talking'. The example is interesting because SUGGEST is changing in this regard, such that examples such as (1) and (2) appear to be increasing in acceptability.

(1) I called my midwife and was suggested to go to the hospital. (enTenTen21)

(2) . . . many people suggested me to wear loose and comfortable clothes at that time . . . (enTenTen21)

This implies that SUGGEST is moving from outside a semantic set to inside it.

According to Haspelmath, then, constructions have empty slots that can be filled by a range of words, and the range and relative frequency of these words can be identified from corpus studies. This offers a way of deriving the meaning of a construction based on usage evidence rather than intuition (Boas 2008; Goldberg and Herbst 2021). This approach forms the basis of work by Gries and Stefanowitsch (Stefanowitsch and Gries 2003; Gries and Stefanowitsch

2004; Gries 2019). They use the term 'collostruction' to mean the collocation between constructions and words, and 'collexeme' to mean a word that occurs significantly in a construction. Put simply, these studies explain ways of identifying what is a 'typical' word in the empty slot in a verb argument construction, and by extension what the canonical or prototypical meaning of the construction is. For example, Stefanowitsch and Gries (2003: 225) study the 'into-causative' construction (e.g. 'He tricked me into giving him my phone') and identify TRICK as the verb most strongly attracted to that construction. A possible consequence of this is that when other verbs are used in this construction, such as TALK or DEBATE, the construction still implies a level of trickery or deceit. Gries and Stefanowitsch (2004) study alternations and discover, for example, that whereas GIVE is the verb most strongly associated with the 'ditransitive' construction, the alternative 'to-dative' construction has BRING as its prototypical collexeme. The most typical usages, then, would be 'Mary gave John a book' but 'John brought the book to Mary'.

An important aim of those working in Construction Grammar is not only to list the constructions in a language but to represent the links and dependencies between those constructions: that is, to devise a constructicon. Numerous constructicon projects, relating to several different languages, are now in progress (e.g. Lyngfelt et al. 2018; Herbst and Uhrig 2019; Ziem et al. 2019; Sass 2024). Their aim is to build networks that will account for all constructional features of a language: in traditional terms, all of its grammar, lexis, and phraseology. This is an ambitious goal and understandably some constructicons set themselves more modest interim goals. The constructicon of Czech reported by Sass (2024), for example, prioritises what might be called 'lexical' constructions, leading to a 'construction dictionary' as the intermediate step to a full constructicon.

Here, I will focus on two projects which aim to build constructicons of English. They have been selected because, like the study reported in this book, their starting point is an inventory of verb complementation patterns. The projects are led by (1) Perek and Patten (2019; see also englishconstructicon.bham.ac.uk) and (2) Herbst and Ulrig (2019).

The aim of Perek and Patten's project is to build a constructicon for English that is 'more comprehensive' than current alternatives (e.g. Fillmore et al. 2012; Perek and Patten 2019: 355). To do this they exploit two resources that they describe as comprehensive in complementary ways: FrameNet (Ruppenhofer et al. 2016), which 'is based on sound semantic principles derived from a specific theory of word meaning'; and the Grammar Pattern books (Francis et al. 1996, 1998), which 'contain a wealth of information about the combinatorial properties of a large number of English nouns, verbs, and adjectives' (Perek and Patten 2019: 361–362). The authors exploit that fact that in FrameNet the frames are arranged in hierarchies, using concepts such as 'inheritance'. Perek and Patten (2019: 359) illustrate this with an example of the Transfer Frame, which is inherited by the Giving and Receiving Frames. In turn, the Giving Frame is inherited by the Lending and Supply Frames, and the Offering Frame uses parts of the Giving Frame also. There is, therefore, a hierarchy of frames, with Transfer as the most general and Lending, Supply, and Offering as the most specific.

Perek and Patten (2019) also make use of the fact that all the verbs recorded as occurring with a specific pattern are to be found in electronically stored lists, as are all the verbs recorded as occurring with specific Frames. By matching the lists, it is possible to add semantic information from FrameNet to the patterns. That is, instead of the subjectively derived 'meaning groups', they propose Frame-inspired groupings. Perek and Patten illustrate their approach with the verb complementation pattern **V that**. They identify several general frames that use this pattern: Communication, Mental_activity, Perception, and Emotion. Of these, Communication accounts for most of the verbs with the pattern **V that**. Figure 2.1, from Perek and Patten (2019: 372), shows the relevant frames, with numbers showing the number of verbs identified in each.

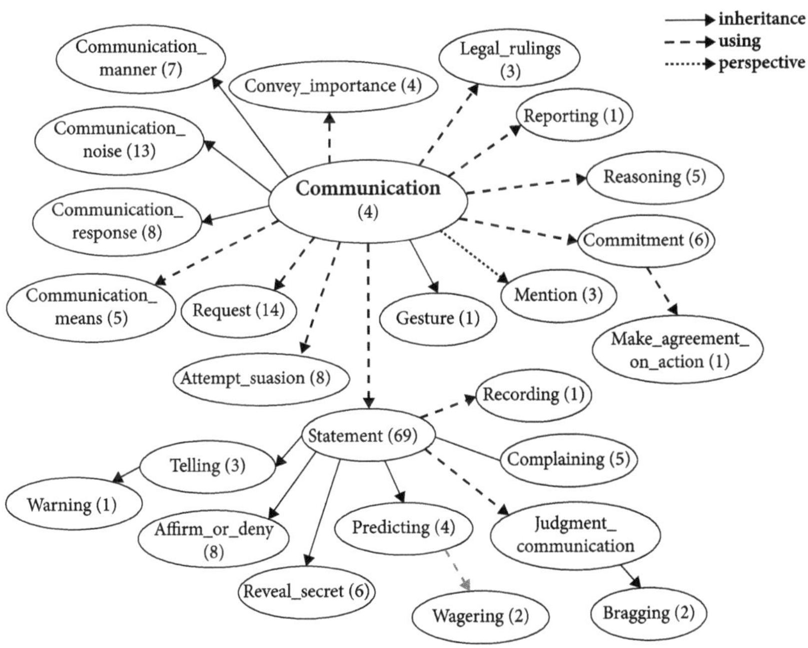

Figure 2.1 The Communication network of frames in the 'V that' pattern. (reproduced from Perek and Patten 2019: 372)

FrameNet lists 24 frames that inherit from or use the Communication Frame, either directly or via another frame. For example, Communication_manner, Communication_noise, and Communication_response all inherit directly from Communication. However, Make_agreement_on_action uses the Commitment Frame, which in turn uses Communication. Perek and Patten place each of the Communication verbs listed under the **V that** pattern in Francis et al. (1996) into one of the 24 frames. They add a further frame, Wagering, proposing that it uses the Predicting Frame, which inherits from Statement.

Perek and Patten (2019: 380) conclude that using FrameNet in this way can 'turn patterns into a structured set of form-meaning pairs at varying levels of semantic granularity', but point out that considerable manual work is needed to merge the two resources into a constructicon. To some extent, the work reported in this book replicates Perek and Patten's work, though it does not use FrameNet, for reasons outlined in Chapter 4. It could be argued that this makes the work in this book less rigorous in terms of semantic theory. On the other hand, the less cumbersome process of arriving at constructions from patterns means that more constructions can be described, and the next step of populating system networks can be achieved.

The starting point for Herbst and Uhrig's (2019) project is the Erlangen Valency Patternbank; this is an inventory of valency patterns for verbs, nouns, and adjectives found in the *Valency Dictionary of English* (Herbst et al. 2004). The valency patterns are similar to the grammar patterns described earlier, and are similarly based on a large-scale corpus lexicography project, but offer more specific detail, for example in relation to collocation as well as grammatical form. As a consequence, a large proportion of verb valency patterns (46 per cent) are specific to a single verb (Herbst and Uhrig 2019: 175). Herbst and Uhrig's aim is to build a constructicon of argument constructions that will be usable by a more general constructicon of English. They note that an argument construction must both describe the form and meaning of the construction and list the items that can occur in it (Herbst and Uhrig 2019: 177), which could be said to be the criteria used also in the study described in this book. Their paper discusses a number of issues of relevance to this study also, such as how specific or how general to make a construction, how to name a construction in a way that most adequately captures its form and meaning, and how to represent the connection between closely related constructions. They also discuss what the representation of a construction should be in a constructicon, concluding that 'it is perfectly obvious that the exact format of an entry must be adapted to the needs of the particular user group envisaged' (Herbst and Uhrig 2019: 179).

Attempts to compile constructicons, such as these, raise the more general question of how constructions are related to one another, or how the relationship between constructions might be described. This matter is discussed in detail by Diessel (2020), who emphasises the need to account for Construction Grammar within psychological theory and frames his argument accordingly. He agrees with Boas that 'argument-structure constructions are organized around particular verbs, or narrow verb classes' (Diessel 2020: 5). He proposes 'constructional relations' of two kinds: 'similarity' and 'contrast'. Similarity relations between constructions, he argues, are similar to lexical relations, in that they form a network of varying kinds of connections, such as hyponymy, synonymy, or collocation. He concludes: 'Taken together, this research suggests that argument-structure constructions are organized in construction families with overlapping structural and/or semantic properties similar to lexical expressions in the mental lexicon' (Diessel 2020: 11).

This is illustrated with a cluster of five constructions expressing possession transfer, each one of which is linked to every other one. The five are:

i. The transitive e.g. 'Sally gave some money'.
ii. The ditransitive e.g. 'Sally gave Jim some money'.
iii. The directional oblique, subdivided into (iv) and (v).
iv. The to-dative e.g. 'Sally gave some money to Jim'.
v. The 'provide *with*' e.g. 'Sally provided Jim with money'.

As all the examples are transitive, they all inherit the characteristics of construction (i). Constructions (iv) and (v) are sub-types of construction (iii). The double object construction (ii) includes all three arguments (Sally, Jim, and money), and the three also appear in constructions (iv) and (v) as alternations of the double object. These relations are shown in Figure 2.2.

The issue of how constructions are related to one another is also a central concern in Goldberg and Herbst (2021). They base their discussion on the 'nice of you' construction (e.g. 'It was nice of you to bring the cake'), and in keeping with similar studies they itemise in detail the constraints on the elements of the

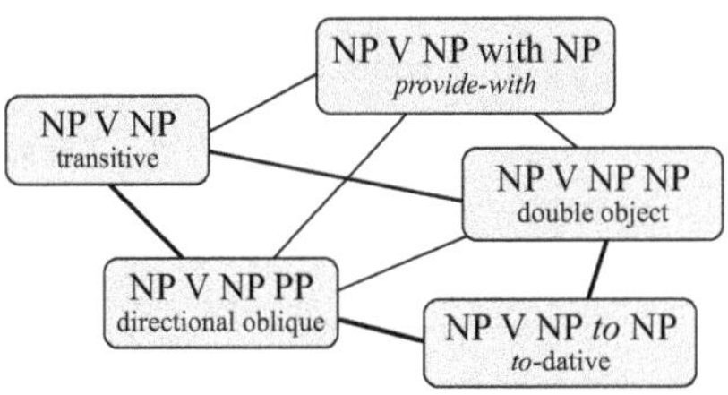

Figure 2.2 Verb argument construction families (from Diessel 2020: 11)

construction. These include restrictions on the to-infinitive clause, which must construe an action rather than a state, and which is unlikely to be passive. The study is corpus-based, with a quantification of the adjectives used. Comparisons are drawn between US and British usage ('nice of you' versus 'good of you'), and the study has a diachronic dimension, with changes in frequency over time noted and accounted for. Importantly, connections are drawn between this construction and other related ones, as itemised in the following:

i. The fragment 'adj of you to' (without *it*), used as a greeting e.g. 'Nice of you to come'.
ii. The fragment 'adj of me' (without *it* or a to-infinitive clause), used as self-criticism e.g. 'Silly of me'.
iii. The similar in form 'difficult to-infinitive' e.g. 'It is difficult to imagine a better example'.
iv. The more general 'adjective to-infinitive' e.g. 'She was impossible to talk to'.
v. The more general 'adjective that-clause' e.g. 'They were surprised that he arrived so early'.

This leads to the discussion of construction relations, and how they might be represented. The authors argue that the situation is neither simple nor random: '... language is not generated by a small set of elegant principles' but also '... constructions do not comprise an unstructured list' (Goldberg and Herbst 2021: 286). They draw an analogy with 'bricolage' in art, which is neither totally ordered not totally disordered. There are no straightforward taxonomies of constructions, but some partial networks might be proposed. Figure 2.3, for example, is an attempt to represent Goldberg and Herbst's observations about relations between the adjective argument constructions mentioned.

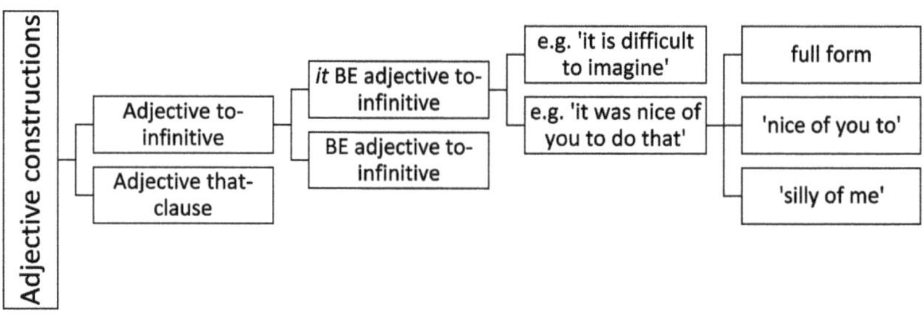

Figure 2.3 Adjective argument constructions (re-imagined from Goldberg and Herbst 2021)

2.4 Pattern Grammar and Construction Grammar Compared

Sinclair's work on Corpus Linguistics and the initial work on Construction Grammar grew up independently of each other, yet it is striking how similar their approaches to language are. Sinclair's work on corpus lexicography led to his proposal of the Unit of Meaning as the place where meaning is located. The Unit of Meaning is a variable phrase, typically consisting of a node wordform or lemma, its associated collocations, word classes and lexical sets, and a discourse function or semantic prosody (Sinclair 1991, 2004). Units of Meaning are remarkably similar to many of the constructions discussed in the literature. The famous 'naked eye' example (Sinclair 2004: 30–35) accounts for phrases such as 'invisible to the naked eye', 'too faint to be seen with the naked eye', or 'barely visible to the naked eye'. Sinclair summarises this as a sequence that mixes meaning with lexical and grammatical items: 'visibility + preposition *to* or *with* + *the naked eye*' (Sinclair 2004: 33). This could equally well be expressed as 'the "visible to the naked eye" construction', similar to 'the "accident waiting to happen" construction'.

From the point of view of Pattern Grammar, there are some equally obvious overlaps. In some cases, the same or very similar phenomena are discussed, with different terminology. Examples include the **V n *into* -ing** pattern and the 'causative "into" construction' (Stefanowitsch and Gries 2003), and the ***it* v-link ADJ to-inf** pattern and the 'nice of you' construction (Goldberg and Herbst 2021). Points about the 'meaning' of patterns and the coercion of meaning when the patterns are used creatively are made in Hunston and Francis (2000) and are consistent with the discussions mentioned earlier. It is not surprising, therefore that both Ellis et al. (2016) and Perek and Patten (2019) take the comprehensive listings in Francis et al. (1996) as a resource for 'populating' studies of constructions.

For many years, however, whereas it was noted that patterns and constructions were somewhat similar, they tended to be seen as 'in competition' with each other rather than 'in collaboration'. More recently, the potential contribution of Pattern Grammar to Construction Grammar has been discussed in Hunston and Su (2019) and Hunston (2019, 2022). In these publications, it is proposed that the meaning groups themselves can be interpreted as candidate constructions, thus aligning Pattern Grammar and Construction Grammar. For example, the **V *on* n** pattern, whose meaning groups are shown in Section 2.2, can be reinterpreted as a set of constructions, which might include:

- a '[person] [produce language] *on* [topic]' construction e.g. *He spoke on the evils of race and colour prejudice* ... (BNC)
- a '[person] [rely/bank] *on* [situation]' construction e.g. *[They] relied on their own expertise*. (BNC)

- a '[eyes] [alight/fall/fix/rest] *on* [entity]' construction e.g. . . . *her eyes rested on a distant tree . . .* (BNC)
- a [person] [form of attack] *on* [person]' construction e.g. *Nicholson rounded on him, his eyes blazing.* (BNC)

Such constructions might be defined at greater or lesser levels of detail. For example, the final construction listed, from the 'pounce on something' meaning group, could be interpreted with each verb + pattern combination constituting a separate construction, or as the generalised construction shown. This line of argument is followed in Chapter 3.

To the suggestion that patterns and constructions are aligned, though, a number of caveats must be made. The pattern-based constructions proposed in this book meet only some definitions of a construction. Most of them, for example, are not non-compositional. That is, their meaning is entirely deducible from their constituent parts. They represent only one kind of construction, with no mention of a wide range of more idiomatic constructions such as 'accident waiting to happen', or 'the more . . . the more . . . ', or 'let alone', or 'what's . . . doing'. They also do not cover more abstract constructions, such as the negative or the interrogative. Finally, the constructions referred to in this book, and listed on the Transitivity-Net website (transitivity-net.bham.ac.uk), are only proposed constructions. They have been derived through a subjective reinterpretation of verb complementation patterns, which themselves are the product of a large-scale corpus study. The constructions have not arisen through a statistical study, neither can it be known whether they exist as mental constructs in the minds of speakers of English. Testing out the proposed constructions through measurement or psycholinguistic experimentation, remains a task for the future.

2.5 Conclusion

This chapter has introduced Pattern Grammar and Construction Grammar as distinct but overlapping approaches to language description. The argument has been made that the corpus analysis work that led to the Pattern Grammar resource can be placed at the service of Construction Grammar, facilitating a more comprehensive approach to deriving constructions and to modelling the connections between them. This implies a difference in status between the two approaches, with Construction Grammar the more theoretically developed of the two, and Pattern Grammar simply helping out. This observation will be returned to in Chapter 9 of this book.

Chapter 3 continues the focus on patterns and constructions, with an account of the development of constructions from patterns, and the use of networks to model a hierarchy of constructions.

3 From Pattern to Constructions

Chapter 2 argued that grammar (or valency) patterns, as identified through a lexicography project, could be a useful resource for identifying verb argument constructions, noting that other researchers such as Ellis et al. (2016), Herbst and Uhrig (2019), and Perek and Pattern (2019) have reached the same conclusion. This chapter describes the process used to derive candidate constructions from the Pattern Grammar resource and proposes that taxonomy networks can be used to depict the relationship between those constructions. It further argues that the 'size' of a construction is not fixed, but that more general and more specific constructions, as indicated by the taxonomy networks, can be proposed.

3.1 Background

A precursor to the argument in this book can be found in Hunston and Su (2019), though that paper dealt with the patterning of adjectives while this book takes verbs as its starting point. Working specifically with the semantic area of evaluation (Martin and White 2005; Hunston 2011), Hunston and Su hypothesise an alignment between pattern and construction, arguing that 'each of the meaning-pattern combinations identified in Francis et al. (1996, 1998) can be regarded as a construction' (Hunston and Su 2019: 567). They use the adjective meaning groups in Francis et al. (1998) as a basis for identifying constructions, though in practice they depart from the groups themselves quite substantially.

For example, there are a large number of adjectives that are complemented by a that-clause (the pattern **ADJ that**) and that indicate an emotive reaction to a target. In Francis et al. (1998) these are divided into several meaning groups ('surprised', 'angry', 'horrified', 'glad', and 'anxious'), whereas Hunston and Su (2019: 575) suggest there is one construction: 'person is reaction that-situation'. In contrast, the pattern **ADJ *for* n** (*grateful for, fearful for, good for, convenient for*, etc.) is interpreted as six constructions, based on the function of the preposition; the adjectives recorded for this pattern are listed under 13 meaning groups that do not align with the proposed constructions. In some cases, the mapping of construction to meaning groups is straightforward: the 'proxy *for*' construction, for instance, unites adjectives meaning 'afraid' (*afraid*, *concerned*, *fearful*, and *worried*) and those meaning either 'happy' or 'sad' (e.g. *delighted*, *glad*, and *happy*; *sad* and *sorry*), which Francis et al. (1998) split into two groups. In other cases, the picture is more complex: the 'specifying *for*' construction (e.g. *suitable for children*, *ready for action*, *necessary for success*, and *convenient for the airport*) brings together adjectives from four different meaning groups. This is because the proposed constructions focus on the function of the preposition whereas the original meaning groups prioritised the meaning of the adjectives.

Hunston and Su (2019) proceed to group the constructions under seven 'analyses', each labelled with functional roles, such as 'Target' and 'Evaluator'. For example, the second analysis comprises constructions with the elements Evaluator-Hinge-Evaluation-Target. Eight constructions are listed, each based on a different pattern: Person is *happy about* a situation; Person feels *guilty at* a situation; Person is *interested in* something; Person is *dismissive of* something; Person is *keen on* something; Person is *happy with* a situation; Person is *happy to* do something; Person is *annoyed that* a situation existed. As in this book, the constructions are named after one of the adjectives used with it. Hunston and Su (2019: 581) go on to argue that a taxonomy of evaluation constructions could be proposed, based on the notion of delicacy (Halliday 1985; Wible and Tsao 2020). The eight constructions above, for example, are all more specific versions of either a 'Person + BE + Affect + Preposition + Entity' construction or a 'Person + BE + Affect + Clause' construction.

The research reported in this chapter applies the same principles to verb complementation patterns, but here there is no focus on a single area of meaning, so there is a much wider area of expression to consider. A total of 54 verb patterns have been reinterpreted. These exclude the intransitive pattern **V**, patterns with *it* and *there*, and a few patterns that are used with very few verbs, such as **V n *towards* n**. Table 3.1 lists the patterns and shows the number of constructions identified for each. Three columns of patterns are shown in Table 3.1. The first column lists patterns composed of phrases and clauses but not prepositional phrases. The second column lists patterns consisting of the verb and a prepositional phrase. The third column lists patterns with a verb, a noun phrase, and a prepositional phrase. The full set of constructions can be found on the Transitivity-Net website: transitivity-net.bham.ac.uk. The process of identifying constructions, and the issues that arise in that process, are the subject of this chapter. The chapter also develops the notion of taxonomy and system. The question of element annotation is reserved for Chapter 4.

Table 3.1 *List of patterns and the number of constructions identified in each*

Patterns	No. of constructions	Patterns	No. of constructions	Patterns	No. of constructions
V n (Cognition)	9	V about n	16	V way prep/adv	23
V n (Communication)	10	V after n	4	V n about n	8
V n (Material)	41	V against n	12	V n against n	8
V n (Relational)	19	V around n	7	V n as adj	6
V adj	12	V as adj	2	V n as n	10
V -ing	16	V as n	8	V n at n	8
V to-inf	25	V at n	17	V n by n	6
V that	21	V between pl-n	4	V n for n	21
V wh	20	V by amount	3	V n from n	26
V n n	20	V by -ing	3	V n in n	24
V n adj	17	V for n	21	V n into n	18
V n -ing	11	V from n	16	V n into -ing	6
V n to-inf	27	V in n	19	V n of n	8
V n that	8	V into n	18	V n on n	20
V n wh	8	V of n	12	V n out of n	13
		V off n	2	V n to n	37
		V on n	30	V n with n	29
		V onto n	4		
		V out of n	7		
		V over n	15		
		V through n	7		
		V to n	42		
		V towards n	5		
		V with n	36		

3.2 Meaning Groups and Constructions: The Example of 'V *into* n'

To recap: Francis et al. (1996) group all the verbs recorded as occurring with a given complementation pattern into 'meaning groups'. The general purpose of this is to demonstrate that form is linked to meaning, and that the verbs that share complementation patterns tend also to share aspects of meaning (Hunston and Francis 2000: 83). The more specific purpose is to identify the range of meanings made by each pattern and to organise the long list of verbs found to occur with that pattern into something that makes sense and is usable in language learning and teaching. As noted in Chapter 2 and Section 3.1, the resource has been used by constructions researchers as a starting point for identifying constructions (Ellis et al. 2016; Hunston and Su 2019; Perek and Patten 2019), though there is clearly no one-to-one correspondence between construction and meaning group. Rather, the pattern-based meaning groups are a useful resource, a preliminary organisation of a mass of data, available for further use.

In this section, the question of meaning group and construction will be discussed in relation to the pattern **V *into* n** (verb + *into* + noun phrase). It is obvious that this pattern participates in at least two constructions with radically different meanings, exemplified by 'He turned into a frog' [= became a frog] and 'She bumped into a tree' [= made physical contact with a tree]. The difference in form between the two is the verb: TURN and BUMP. There is, therefore, a 'turn into' construction that is markedly different from, on the one hand, a 'turn left/right' construction with the same verb and on the other hand, from a 'physical contact' construction with the same preposition. If, however, the form is 'grow into', as in 'He grew into a handsome man', to what extent is this the same construction as 'turn into' and to what extent is it different? Both mean a process of becoming, at the end of which the Subject 'he' is identifiable as the object of the preposition: 'a frog' or 'a handsome man'. In one case the process implies supernatural involvement, while in the other case it implies gaining maturity.

Arguably, then, it is the case that each verb+ *into* form is an individual construction, but that some level of generality has to be imposed if the constructions are to do more than replicate a dictionary. The position taken in this book is that there are two superordinate constructions – the 'change/turn/grow into something' construction and the 'bump/barge/crash into something' construction. There are also more specific constructions, including 'turn into', 'grow into', and 'bump into'.

To demonstrate more comprehensively how issues such as this play into deriving constructions from the pattern, 3 of the 13 meaning groups from Francis et al.'s (1996) account of the pattern **V *into* n** are discussed further here. (This example was suggested by Peter Uhrig, personal communication). The groups are: the 'CRASH' group; the 'INFILTRATE' group; the 'TURN' group. Table 3.2 gives the relevant information from each meaning group: its mnemonic name, the rubric for the group, and the verbs listed in the group. The three groups have been selected as examples because they illustrate different decisions made in reinterpreting meaning groups as constructions. It should be recalled that in this book, non-technical names for constructions are used, based on a selected verb from the construction, such as the 'turn into' construction or the 'crash into' construction. This does not imply that the construction is used with the one verb only. It is proposed that the 'turn into' construction, for instance, is used with 34 verbs, or is the superordinate for 34 more specific constructions, while the 'crash into' construction is used with 9 verbs, or is the superordinate for 9 more specific constructions. It should also be recalled that a verb may appear in more than one construction, used in slightly different senses or with different collocates. For example, 'He barged into the railings' means physical contact has taken place whereas 'He barged into the room' does not.

Table 3.2 *Three meaning groups from the pattern* ***V* into *n***

Name of group	Description of group	Verbs in the group
THE 'CRASH' GROUP (Francis et al. 1996: 205)	These verbs are concerned with collisions. The prepositional phrase indicates the thing or person that someone or something hits.	*bang*, *barge*, *bump*, *cannon*, *crash*, *plough*, *run*, *slam*, and *smash*
THE 'INFILTRATE' GROUP (Francis et al. 1996: 207–208)	These verbs indicate that someone or something enters a place, group, or thing, physically or metaphorically.	*ascend*, *assimilate*, *barge*, *bleed*, *book*, *break*, *check*, *cram*, *creep*, *cross*, *crowd*, *crumble*, *dive*, *empty*, *fall*, *filter*, *fit*, *flash*, *get*, *go*, *hack*, *infiltrate*, *integrate*, *jam*, *marry*, *move*, *pack*, *pile*, *plug*, *push*, *put*, *roll*, *slot*, *splash*, *throng*, *tumble*, and *withdraw*
THE 'TURN' GROUP (Francis et al. 1996: 204)	These verbs are concerned with becoming. The prepositional phrase indicates what something becomes. We include here *segue* and *shade*, which indicate either that something becomes something else or that it is next to or followed by something else.	*amalgamate*, *ball*, *blook*, *blossom*, *broaden*, *build*, *change*, *coalesce*, *condense*, *convert*, *curl*, *decompose*, *degenerate*, *develop*, *erupt*, *escalate*, *evolve*, *fizzle*, *form*, *gel*, *germinate*, *grow*, *merge*, *metamorphose*, *mushroom*, *mutate*, *ossify*, *segue*, *shade*, *transmute*, *turn*, *blow up*, *curl up*, and *shape up*

We return now to the meaning groups shown in Table 3.2.

THE 'CRASH' GROUP is treated in this book, and on the Transitivity-Net website, as a single construction, named the 'crash into' construction, with the description: 'An entity collides with another entity' ('entity' here meaning a person or a thing). On the Transitivity-Net website it is construction six in the pattern **V *into* n**. The verbs listed for the construction are identical with the list of verbs in the meaning group shown in Table 3.2. The verbs BANG, BARGE, CRASH, SLAM, and SMASH are close synonyms. The verbs CANNON, PLOUGH, and RUN are more problematic: in other contexts they are not associated with this meaning, but 'cannon into something', 'plough into something', and 'run into something' do mean that a collision has taken place. It could be argued that 'bump into something' implies a less catastrophic collision, but physical contact still takes place, and the difference is one of degree.

The description of THE 'INFILTRATE' GROUP itself includes a list of subgroups (entering a place, group, or thing, which might be a physical location or figurative), suggesting a more eclectic mix of verbs and the possibility of more than one construction mapped on to this meaning group. In response, it is interpreted as seven distinct constructions, as follows (the numbers such as Cx1 refer to number given to this construction on the Transitivity-Net website):

- Cx1 the 'crowd into' construction. Many people move into a space so that the space is full. Verbs: *cram*, *crowd*, *jam*, *pack*, *pile*, and *throng*. Note that the Subject of the verb is plural.
- Cx2 the 'barge into' construction. A person moves into a space. Verbs: *barge*, *break*, *cross*, *dive*, *push*, and *withdraw*.
- Cx3 the 'filter into' construction. A substance moves into a space. Verbs: *bleed*, *empty*, and *filter*.
- Cx15 the 'integrate into' construction. A person joins a community. Verbs: *assimilate*, *infiltrate*, *integrate*, and *intrude*.
- Cx16 the 'get into' construction. A person joins a social or physical entity. Verbs: *book*, *check*, *get*, *hack*, *marry*, and *tumble*.
- Cx17 the 'fit into' construction. An entity is consistent with a category. Verbs: *fall* and *fit*.
- Cx18 the 'creep into' construction. An entity starts to exist somewhere. Verbs: *creep* and *flash*.

Even with these seven proposed constructions, the question of how general or specific a construction should be remains. Of the above, construction 16 is probably the most diverse and least satisfactory. It takes a broad, abstract view of the meaning (joining an entity), but risks overstating the similarities between the more specific constructions: 'book/check into a hotel'; 'hack into a computer'; 'get/tumble into a situation'; 'marry into a family'.

THE 'TURN' GROUP is, arguably, equally diverse, but in this book and the Transitivity-Net website it is treated as a single construction (Cx7). The construction is described as 'An entity changes to become something else' and the example given is *Though the tenants didn't like living there, they grew into a community in the course of their campaigns.* A total of 34 verbs are listed in the construction. In each case, there is a meaning of 'become something different', although, as previously illustrated, more precisely focused constructions could be proposed. These could be:

- General change, with no specifics added: *change into*, *convert into*, *mutate into*, and *turn into*.
- Become a larger entity: *broaden into*, *build into*, *escalate into*, *grow into*, *mushroom into*, and *blow up into*.
- Change into a more advanced or mature entity: *bloom into*, *blossom into*, *develop into*, *evolve into*, *germinate into*, *grow into*, and *shape up into*.
- Conversely, change into something less advanced or mature: *degenerate into*, *fizzle into*, and *ossify into*.

- Change to a different structure: *condense into*, *decompose into*, *metamorphose into*, *mutate into*, and *transmute into*.
- Several things combine to form one thing: *amalgamate into*, *coalesce into*, *form into*, *gel into*, and *merge into*.
- Change shape: *ball into a fist*, *curl into a ball*, *curl up into a ball*.
- Gradually change: *segue into* and *shade into*.
- Suddenly change: *erupt into*.

The main difficulty here is that each verb+preposition instance has a quite specific meaning, and the list as a whole could be divided up in different ways. For example, the 'become a larger entity' construction (second bullet point above), could be divided into sequences implying a negative affect (*build into*, *escalate into*, *mushroom into*, and *blow up into*), and those suggesting a positive change (*broaden into* and *grow into*). An alternative would be to pick out *mushroom into* and match it with *balloon into* in a construction that in abstract terms is something like '[entity] + [verb from noun indicating something that increases in size quickly] + *into* + [ensuing larger entity]'. The solution adopted here is to take a compromise position and to propose a fairly general superordinate construction. This issue of taxonomy will be returned to in Section 3.4.

3.3 The Most Difficult Pattern: 'V n'

Before moving on to the representation of construction networks, it is as well to say something about the most difficult pattern dealt with in this study: the **V n** pattern (verb + noun phrase). This pattern encompasses all transitive verbs (Verb + Object), and it includes also the Verb + Complement sentence pattern. The difficulty of this pattern arises simply because of the sheer volume of verbs that occur in it, the vast range of meanings expressed, and the variety of relations between the verb and the noun phrase that follows it. Halliday (1994), for example, identifies several kinds of relation between Subject and Object, as shown in examples (1)–(7):

(1) The lion caught the tourist. Actor-Process-Goal (Halliday 1994: 109);
(2) I believe you. Senser-Process-Phenomenon (Halliday 1994: 118);
(3) John made a statement. Sayer-Process-Verbiage (Halliday 1994: 141);
(4) You haven't signed your name. Actor-Process-Scope (Halliday 1994: 149);
(5) Your story sounds complete nonsense. Carrier-Process-Attribute (Halliday 1994: 120);
(6) The deadliest spiders are the funnelwebs. Identified-Process-Identifier (Halliday 1994: 122);
(7) Peter has a piano. Possessor-Process-Possessed (Halliday 1994: 133).

Halliday and Matthiessen (2014) propose distinctions between process types. The primary distinctions are between 'material', 'relational', 'mental', and 'verbal' processes (see Chapter 5), but there are also subcategories. Their examples mainly come from verbs that are used intransitively (the pattern **V**), and those that are used transitively (the pattern **V n**). For example, they distinguish 'types of doing-&-happening' (Halliday and Matthiessen 2014: 228ff.), noting that these can be 'creative' or 'transformative', with cross-cutting distinctions between physical and abstract. Creative processes are divided into 'general' and 'specific'. Transformative processes are divided into 'elaborating', 'extending', and 'enhancing'. The elaborating processes are further divided into 15 types, of which these are examples: change a state (e.g. burn/freeze/harden something); change the make-up of something (e.g. blow up/prune/smash something); change a surface (e.g. polish/wipe/sweep something); change the size of something (e.g. compress/grow/stretch something); change a shape (e.g. coil/deform/flatten something). For each category, example verbs are given, divided into those that are used intransitively, transitively, or both. This potentially provides the basis for identifying constructions, though a relatively small number of verbs are considered.

There is, then, a vast amount of material to be considered in this pattern. To help with the issue of volume, in this book, the pattern **V n** has been subdivided into four, based on Halliday's primary process types, i.e.: **V n (Relational)**; **V n (Material)**; **V n (Cognition)**; **V n (Communication)**. This reduces the number of constructions in each category and, as we shall see, the complexity of the pattern networks.

Another difficulty is that Francis et al. (1996) break with their practice of listing all verbs identified as occurring with a pattern, and in the case of **V n** (and the intransitive **V**), list only the most frequent verbs. This was necessary because of space constraints. In this book, the coverage is even less comprehensive, and some verbs have been discarded because they could not be accounted for by a construction. The result of both these decisions is that some of the constructions give the impression of being quite incomplete in terms of the verbs that could be said to belong to them. For example, construction 1 in the **V n (material)** pattern is the 'build something' construction, described as 'A person or entity brings a physical entity into being'. The construction lists only seven verbs: *blow bubbles*; *build a building*; *lay a trap*; *leave a mark*; *make a meal*; *rule a line*; *start a fire*. This admittedly feels quite random, with *build* and *make* having a very general use but the others having a very restricted collocation. There are, surely, many more verbs in English that mean 'bring into being'. Many of these, however, did not make the cut in Francis et al. (1996), while others that are frequent enough to have been included, such as *start*, may be so frequent because they have a range of other uses (*start running*, *start to think*, *the day started*, etc.) rather than because their 'create' use is frequent.

The commentary on the 'build something' construction above illustrates another noticeable aspect of the **V n** pattern: it is often necessary to specify collocates in order to make sense of the verbs in a construction. Here are a few examples:

- **V n (relational)** Cx8: the 'develop a fault' construction. A person or entity gains a quality. Verbs: *adopt an attitude*; *affect an interest*; *assume a manner*; *develop a fault*; *develop an illness*; *gain weight*; *gain speed*; *gather speed*; *lose weight; lose speed*; *recover consciousness*.
- **V n (relational)** Cx11: the 'follow a route' construction. A person or entity moves relative to a place or entity. Verbs: *clear an object*; *cover a distance*; *cross a line*; *describe a circle*; *follow a route*; *jump a fence*; *run a distance; travel a distance*; *travel a place*; *walk a distance*; *walk a route*.
- **V n (communication)** Cx9: the 'make a suggestion' construction. A person produces an utterance. The verb and the noun phrase following indicate the type of utterance. Verbs: *add a remark*; *ask a question*; *call a name*; *draw a comparison*; *make a suggestion*; *offer advice*; *pass a comment*; *put a question*; *withdraw a remark*.

The pattern **V n (material)** is particularly problematic in terms of the range of things it covers, and it could well be argued that constructions have been 'merged' inappropriately, just to reduce the complexity. Here are two examples:

- **V n (material)** Cx4: the 'repair something' construction. The description is: 'A person or entity changes the state of a physical thing'. The verbs listed in this construction on the Transitivity-Net website are arranged in five groups, each of which refers to a different kind of physical change. The first group consists of verbs indicating destruction: *break*, *destroy*, *fight*, *hurt*, *shoot*, and *strike*. The second group consists of verbs with the opposite meaning: *fix*, *mend*, and *repair*. The third group consists of verbs indicating making a change in appearance: *mark*, *paint*, and *decorate*. The fourth group consists of: *change*, *close* and *open*. The fifth group is a random collection: *cook food*, *prepare food*, *sign a document*, and *work metal*.
- **V n (material)** Cx26: the 'start work' construction. The description is: 'A person starts, stops, or continues an activity'. Again, the listed verbs are divided into groups. The first set of verbs indicates 'stop': *abandon a process*; *drop an activity*; *finish an activity*; *stop an activity*. The second set indicates 'start': *begin talks*; *attempt a task*; *open a meeting*; *start work*. The third set indicates 'continue': *continue an activity*; *maintain a process*; *repeat an action*. The final two verbs indicate that an activity does not take place are: *avoid an activity* and *prevent an event*.

It is probably then the case that specifying constructions from the **V n** pattern brings into the sharpest focus the question of 'what a construction is'. It may indeed be the case that each construction should consist of a small number of verbs and quite specific argument collocates. There is certainly scope for splitting the constructions shown on the Transitivity-Net website.

3.4 From Constructions to Construction Network

The first task in this project, then, was to derive a set of Verb Argument Constructions from each verb complementation pattern. The decisions about demarcating one construction from another (what constitutes 'the same' form and meaning) make it clear that a simple list is not adequate for recording constructions. Some constructions are more like each other than others are. There is, for example, a more significant difference between 'turn into a frog' and 'bump into a tree' than between 'crowd into a space' and 'cross into a space'. This is hardly a novel observation. As noted in Chapter 2, researchers who build constructicons aim not only to identify sets of constructions but also to show how they relate to one another (Lyngfelt et al. 2018; Herbst and Uhrig 2019). This chapter has the more modest aim of showing how the constructions derived from a single pattern relate to one another. To do this, the concept of the network is adopted from Systemic Functional Grammar (Matthiessen 2023). The aim is to represent all the constructions proposed from a given verb complementation pattern as a network. Identifying the nodes of the network gives information about how the constructions are the same as or different from one another. That is, the nodes express the parameters of difference found within a single pattern. The process of moving from pattern to construction to network will now be illustrated in three examples: **V n adj**; **V n *to* n**; **V *after* n**.

A Simple Example: V n adj

The first example is the pattern **V n adj** (verb + noun phrase + adjective). It has been chosen for its relative simplicity. In Francis et al. (1996: 280–285), the pattern is described, as all the verb patterns are, in terms of traditional structural categories, with meaning groups then identified within each structure. For the pattern **V n adj**, the structures and meaning groups are shown in Table 3.3. It will be noted that one group (group 2.2) is divided into several subgroups, and that where the verb-adjective collocation is restricted, the relevant adjective is shown in the list of verbs. Meaning groups 2.2 (vii) and 2.5 list 'other' verbs, that is, verbs that occur with the pattern but which do not fit into any other group. Additional information given by Francis et al. (1996), and not repeated here, is the sense number of each verb as given in the Collins COBUILD English

Table 3.3 *Structures, meaning groups, and verbs in the pattern* ***V n adj*** *(adapted from Francis et al. 1996: 280–285)*

Structure	Meaning group	Verbs
I Subject-Verb-Object e.g. *He wished both of them dead.*	1.1 'like'	5 verbs: *like*, *need*, *prefer*, *want*, and *wish*
	1.2 'imagine'	2 verbs: *imagine* and *picture*
II Subject-Verb-Object-Object Complement e.g. *The doctor caught her asleep.*	2.1 'consider' and 'call'	24 verbs: *account*, *believe*, *brand*, *call*, *certify*, *confess*, *consider*, *count*, *declare*, *deem*, *diagnose*, *find*, *hold*, *judge*, *label*, *pass*, *presume*, *profess*, *pronounce*, *prove*, *rate*, *report*, *rule*, and *think*
	2.2 'make'	
	2.2 (i) 'pull open'	26 verbs: *blast (open)*, *blow (open)*, *clamp (shut)*, *close*, *ease*, *force*, *jam*, *kick*, *lever*, *nail (shut)*, *open (wide)*, *prize (open)*, *pry*, *pull*, *push*, *shove*, *shut (tight)*, *slam (shut)*, *slide*, *spread (wide)*, *tape (shut)*, *tear (open)*, *tug*, *wedge*, *wrench (open)*, and *yank*
	2.2 (ii) 'squash flat'	20 verbs: *batter (flat)*, *blot (dry)*, *cram (full)*, *draw (close)*, *jerk (loose)*, *leave (dead)*, *pat (dry)*, *plane (flat)*, *pull (free)*, *scrub (clean)*, *set (free)*, *shake (loose)*, *shoot (dead)*, *squash (flat)*, *squeeze (dry)*, *stuff (full)*, *sweep (clean)*, *towel (dry)*, *wipe (clean)*, and *wrench (loose)*
	2.2 (iii) 'hold steady'	4 verbs: *have*, *hold*, *keep*, and *leave*
	2.2 (iv) 'drive mad'	8 verbs: *batter (unconscious)*, *beat (unconscious)*, *drive (mad)*, *jolt (awake)*, *knock (unconscious)*, *scare (stiff)*, *send (mad)*, and *strike (blind)*
	2.2 (v) 'turn down low'	4 verbs: *pitch*, *crank up*, *turn down*, and *turn up*
	2.2 (vi) 'paint yellow'	4 verbs: *colour*, *paint*, *spray*, and *turn*
	2.2. (vii) other verbs	4 verbs: *get*, *make*, *render*, and *slice*
	2.3 'find'	3 verbs: *capture*, *catch*, and *find*
	2.4 'bury alive'	3 verbs: *burn*, *bury*, and *skin*
	2.5 other verbs	3 verbs: *be born*, *picture*, and *serve*
III Subject-Verb-Object-Complement e.g. *Shares ended the day slightly higher.*	3.1 'begin'	4 verbs: *begin*, *end*, *finish*, and *start*

Dictionary (Sinclair. 1995). Francis et al. (1996) also give examples for several of the verbs in each meaning group, which are not repeated here.

Altogether, Table 3.3 shows 110 verbs divided into 14 meaning groups. In some cases, reinterpreting these as constructions is relatively straightforward. For example, meaning group 1.2, with the two verbs IMAGINE and PICTURE, can easily be considered a construction. In other cases, decisions have to be made, as they were when the original meaning groups were described. For example, meaning group 2.2 (i) contains:

- A set of verbs indicating 'a person [cause] something open': BLAST, BLOW, EASE, FORCE, KICK, LEVER, PRIZE, PRY, PULL, PUSH, SHOVE, SLIDE, TEAR, TUG, WRENCH, and YANK. (In each case the adjective is *open*.)
- A partially overlapping set of verbs indicating 'a person [cause] something closed': CLAMP, EASE, FORCE, KICK, NAIL, PULL, PUSH, SHOVE, SLAM, SLIDE, and TAPE. (In each case the adjective is *closed* or *shut*.)
- A set of verbs indicating 'a person [close/open] something [to a degree]': OPEN, SHUT, and SPREAD. (The adjective is *wide* or *tight*.)
- A set of verbs indicating 'a person [forcibly maintain] something [open/closed]': JAM, NAIL, TAPE, and WEDGE. (The adjective is *open*, *closed* or *shut*.)

It is a matter of judgement as to whether these are treated as one construction or as four 'smaller' constructions. In this instance, the constructions follow the meaning group, and one 'larger' construction is proposed, though of course these could be divided up.

For the pattern **V n adj**, a total of 17 constructions are proposed, that is, slightly more than the number of meaning groups. Table 3.4 shows these constructions, giving the construction name, its description, a sample list of verbs and an example taken from the British National Corpus. The construction name and description allow restrictions on form and/or meaning to be recorded. For example, construction 6 has a reflexive pronoun in the place of the noun phrase. Construction 13 specifies that the affected entity is food. In the case of all the constructions, the description specifies whether the Subject in the construction is a person, an entity, or possibly either. Construction 14, for example, specifies 'a financial entity'. (See Chapter 4 for further discussion of this point.)

It is immediately apparent from Table 3.4 that while the 17 proposed constructions can be represented as a simple list, they could also be sensibly divided into groups. One clear group is the set of constructions that indicate causation. Constructions 7–13 all mean that one person or entity causes another entity to exist in a particular state or to have a particular quality. Constructions 15–17 could be added to these, though in those cases the caused state is

Table 3.4 *Proposed constructions from the pattern* ***V n adj***

Cx number	**1**	**2**	**3**	**4**
Cx name	the like something quality construction	the want something quality construction	the believe something quality construction	the imagine something quality construction
Cx description	A person likes something to have a particular quality.	A person wants something to have a particular quality.	A person thinks that something has a particular quality.	A person imagines a possible entity to have a particular quality.
Sample verbs	like, prefer	need, want, wish	believe, consider, find, presume, think	imagine, picture
Example	*He likes his coffee strong.*	*She wants her garden wild.*	*. . . many considered them too weak . . .*	*She imagined him haggard and afraid.*
Cx number	**5**	**6**	**7**	**8**
Cx name	the call something quality construction	the profess oneself quality construction	the make something quality construction	the push something open construction
Cx description	A person says that something has a particular quality.	A person says of themselves that they have a particular quality.	A person or entity changes something so that it has a particular quality.	A person or entity moves something so that it is open or closed.
Sample verbs	brand, call, declare, label, pronounce, report	confess, find, profess, pronounce, prove	get, make, render	blast, close, force, kick, jam, open, pull, push, tug, yank
Example	*Other people pronounced them wanton . . .*	*She professed herself reluctant to remain indoors.*	*The pain of the spasms had made him impervious to . . .*	*The wind had . . . slammed the door shut.*

Table 3.4 (*cont.*)

Cx number	**9**	**10**	**11**	**12**
Cx name	the wipe something clean construction	the keep something safe construction	the crank the volume up higher construction	the colour something red construction
Cx description	A person or entity changes something so that it has a particular quality.	A person or entity maintains something in a particular state.	A person changes the volume of something.	A person or entity changes the colour of something.
Sample verbs	squash (flat), towel (dry), cram (full), pull (loose), wipe (clean)	have, hold, keep, leave	crank up, pitch, turn down, turn up	colour, paint, spray, turn
Example	*She wiped the surface clean.*	*You have to keep the powder dry.*	*She cranked the volume up higher.*	*Children learn to colour the sky blue.*
Cx number	**13**	**14**	**15**	**16**
Cx name	the serve food cold construction	the begin the day higher construction	the leave someone alive construction	the capture someone alive construction
Cx description	A person serves a meal either hot or cold.	A financial entity begins or ends a period of time at a particular level.	A person does or does not kill someone.	A person finds a person in a particular state.
Sample verbs	Serve	begin, end, finish, start	leave (alive), shoot (dead)	capture, catch, find
Example	*It can be served hot or cold.*	*Shares ended the day lower.*	*He shot him dead.*	*. . . most of the soldiers had been captured alive.*
Cx number	**17**			
Cx name	the bury someone alive construction			
Cx description	A person causes harm to someone while they are alive.			
Sample verbs	burn, bury, skin			
Example	*They were buried alive.*			

represented by the verb rather than by the adjective, and the acted upon participant is a person. Another group is the set of constructions that indicate construal, that is they mean that a person 'brings a situation into being' through thought or speech. These are constructions 1–6. This act of construal could be said to be a kind of figurative causation – a situation is brought about figuratively, by saying or thinking something, rather than literally, by doing something. This leaves construction 14, which remains something of an outlier. These observations are summarised in Table 3.5. In this table, the constructions are identified simply by a number and a verb, rather than by the full construction name. The full name and description can be found in Table 3.4.

As previously explained, the connections between these constructions can be shown as a network, see Figure 3.1. In this figure, construction 14 is subsumed under 'causation', just to neaten the figure. The layout is in a sense arbitrary, moving as it does from left to right rather than from top to bottom, but it follows the convention used in Systemic Functional Grammar. Importantly, although the most specific, rightmost points of the network consist of the named constructions, each node in the network can also be described as a construction – a 'larger', or more general, construction. These constructions might be described as:

Table 3.5 *Groups of constructions derived from the pattern **V n adj***

Group	Subgroup	Constructions	Note
Construal	Cognition	Cx1 'like' Cx2 'want' Cx3 'believe' Cx4 'imagine'	A person brings a situation into being, metaphorically, through thought.
	Communication	Cx5 'call' Cx6 'profess self'	A person brings a situation into being, metaphorically, by saying something.
Causation	Acted upon participant is entity	Cx7 'make' Cx8 'push open/ shut' Cx9 'wipe clean' Cx10 'keep' Cx11 'crank up' Cx12 'colour' Cx13 'serve'	The action brings about a situation represented by the adjective.
	Acted upon participant is person	Cx15 'leave' Cs16 'capture' Cx17 'bury'	The action brings about a situation, with the adjective indicating a related circumstance.
Time		Cx14 'begin'	

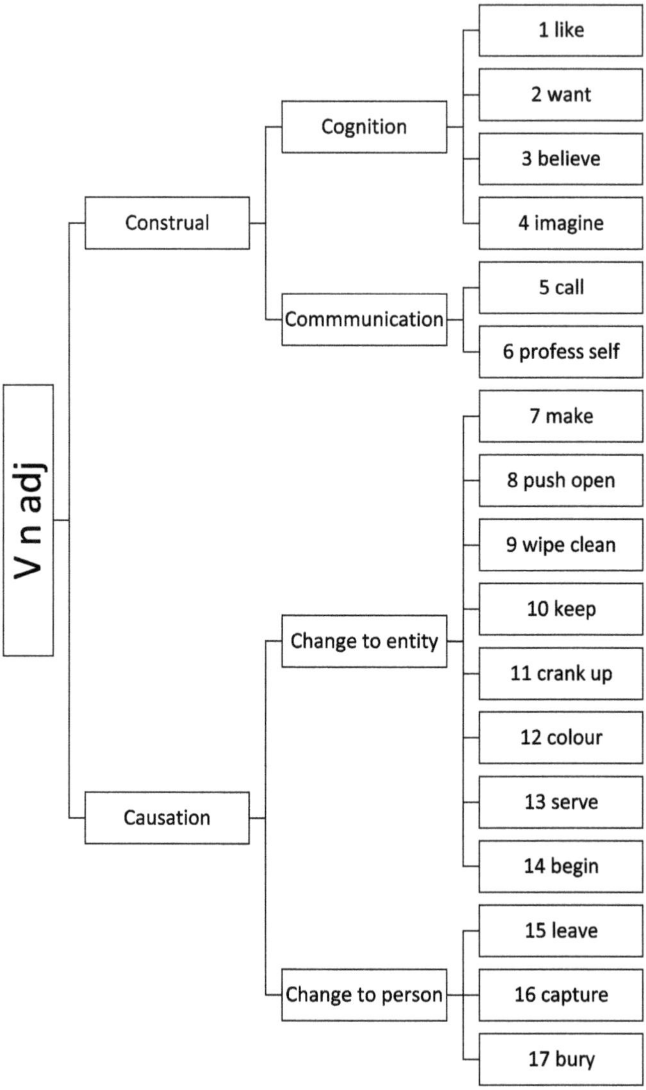

Figure 3.1 A network for the constructions derived from the pattern **V n adj**

- V n adj = the 'make/construe entity quality' construction
  - The 'construe entity quality' construction
    - The 'cognise entity quality' construction
    - The 'communication entity quality' construction

- The 'cause entity quality/state' construction
  - The 'cause entity quality/state' construction
  - The 'act_on person quality/state' construction

It is thus the case that from the pattern a construction network is proposed comprising levels of generality. From left to right in Figure 3.1, we move from more general constructions to more specific ones.

Figure 3.1 replicates the network that appears on the Transitivity-Net website. It is worth noting, though, that a further stage could identify still more specific constructions that lie between some of the rightmost constructions proposed here and the individual verb constructions. As an example, consider the 'call something quality' construction (Cx5). A total of 11 verbs are listed as occurring in this construction: BRAND, CALL, CERTIFY, DECLARE, DIAGNOSE, LABEL, PASS, PRONOUNCE, PROVE, REPORT, and RULE. There are, then, 11 distinct constructions that are here grouped together. It would be possible to take the network further to the right to show how they relate to one another. A 'prose' version of the network might look like this:

- The entry point to the network is the **V n adj** pattern, where **V** represents an act of communication. They can be divided into: illocutionary (where the words bring a change in the world) and non-illocutionary (where the words reflect a situation in the world).
  - Illocutionary: CERTIFY, DECLARE, PASS, PRONOUNCE, and RULE. These can be divided into actions that are conventionally written and those that are conventionally spoken.
    - Conventionally written: CERTIFY and PASS
    - Conventionally spoken: DECLARE, PRONOUNCE, and RULE
  - Non-illocutionary: BRAND, CALL, DIAGNOSE, LABEL, PROVE, and REPORT. These can be divided into actions calling on expertise and those not calling on expertise.
    - With expertise: DIAGNOSE and PROVE
    - Without expertise: BRAND, CALL, LABEL, and REPORT. These can be divided into communications that indicate attitude and those that do not.
      - Attitudinal: BRAND, LABEL, and CALL. These form a cline from negative to more neutral
      - Non-attitudinal: REPORT

Figure 3.2 shows this diagrammatically.

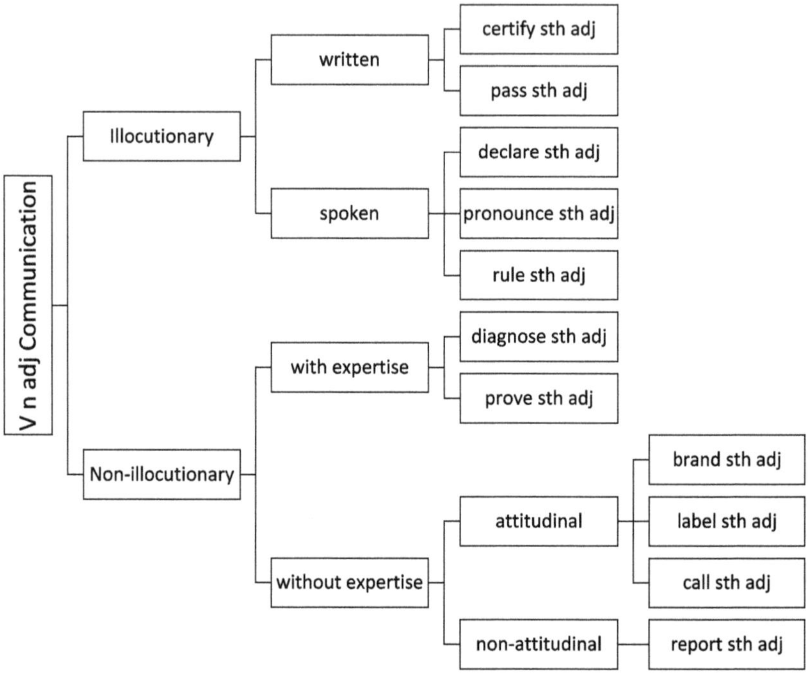

Figure 3.2 Further degrees of delicacy in the network for the constructions derived from **V n adj**

A More Complex Example: V n to *n*

The second example to be given here is the pattern **V n *to* n** (verb + noun phrase + *to* + noun phrase). This is an example of a pattern comprising an Object noun phrase and a prepositional phrase; patterns of this kind were an important innovation in Francis's original work (Francis 1993). This pattern is described in Francis et al. (1996) as having three structures:

- Structure I: Subject-Verb-(Direct) Object-(Indirect) Object. Example: *We explained the situation to him.*
- Structure II: Subject-Verb-Object-Object Complement. Example: *She changed her name to Caroline.*
- Structure III: Subject-Verb-Object-Adjunct. Example: *She banished him to the upstairs room.*

There are a few points that need to be made about these structures. Firstly, the notation in Francis et al. (1996) is slightly different from that given above. In that book the distinction between 'Direct Object' and 'Indirect Object' is not made, but novel terms 'Prepositional Object' and 'Prepositional Complement' are used. In the examples given above, 'to him' (Structure I) is labelled as a Prepositional Object and 'to Caroline' (Structure II) is labelled as a 'Prepositional Object Complement'. These terms might be glossed as 'like an ordinary Object (etc.) but a prepositional phrase'. Secondly, integral to Francis's work is that the optional Adjunct element (see Structure III) is not excluded from the description of verb complementation if the form of the Adjunct (in this case, a prepositional phrase beginning with *to*) is dependent on the verb.

Francis et al. (1996: 418–433) identify 10 meaning groups with Structure I, one group with Structure II, and 19 groups with Structure III, giving a total of 30 meaning groups. For this book, these groups have been reinterpreted as 37 constructions and these are organised, as in the case of **V n adj**, as a network. At the most general, or leftwards extreme of the network is a distinction based on the type of process indicated by the construction. Inspired by the process types proposed by Halliday (Halliday and Matthiessen 2014), but changing the terminology somewhat, these processes are: Action, Communication, Cognition, and Relation. Because the networks can become too dense to see clearly, the practice adopted here is to show detail in separate figures. Figure 3.3 shows the constructions subsumed by Communication, Cognition, and Relation only. In the case of Communication, a further distinction is made between communicating about information (e.g. 'break the news to someone') and communicating about action: telling someone to do something (e.g. 'challenge someone to a duel') or promising to do something (e.g. 'promise help to someone'). In the case of Cognition, a distinction is made between constructions where the Cognizer is the Subject (e.g. 'person prefers tea to coffee' Cx30) and those where some other entity is the Subject (e.g. 'person drew my attention to the problem' Cx33).

For clarity, the constructions shown in Figure 3.3 are expressed more fully than those in Figure 3.1. It should be remembered that in each case several verbs can be assigned to a construction. For example, construction 34 (a person compares one thing to another) occurs with verbs such as *anchor*, *connect*, *correlate*, *index*, *liken*, *link*, *match (up)*, *relate*, and *tie*, as well as with *compare*. As previously noted, more specific constructions could be proposed from this list.

Construction 34 illustrates a further point: although networks are a convenient way to express relationships between constructions, they do tend to stress, or even exaggerate, the differences between alternatives. It could well be argued that construction 34 indicates an act of Cognition (someone thinks that two things are similar) as well as a process of Relation (one thing is similar to another). The same could be said of construction 35. The

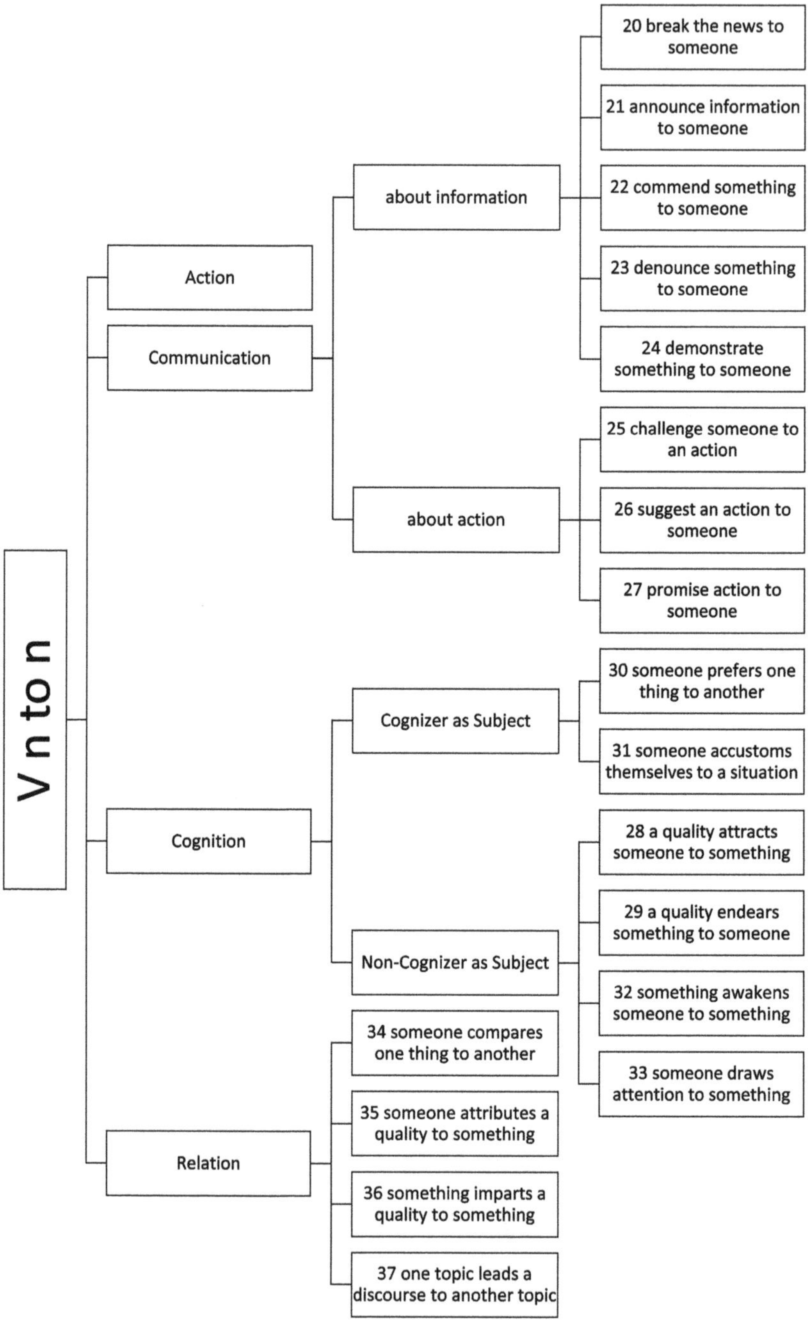

Figure 3.3 Communication, Cognition, and Relation process-based constructions from the pattern **V n *to* n**

network representation does not allow for a construction to be 'partly this and partly that'. However, overlaps of this kind are considered further in Chapter 4.

The 'Action' processes that occur with the pattern **V n *to* n** are rather more complex and interesting. They are shown in Figure 3.4. First, a distinction can be drawn between the actions of 'transfer', 'change', and 'cause' (Figure 3.4a). An example of transfer is 'give something to someone' (Cx1), an example of change is 'change one thing to another' (Cx9), and an example of cause is 'incite someone to an action' (Cx17). A second relevant distinction appears to be between literal and figurative actions. In the case of 'transfer' (Figure 3.4b) and 'cause' (Figure 3.4d), the constructions reflect this distinction. Literal transfer is exemplified by 'give something to someone' (Cx1), while figurative transfer is exemplified by 'grant respect to someone' (Cx5). There is one literal cause construction – 'deport someone to a place' (Cx12) – while the other constructions express figurative rather than literal movement, such as 'promote someone to a role' (Cx15). Again, the network configuration requires that fuzzy boundaries be treated as clear. For example, constructions such as Cx17 ('incite someone to action') and Cx18 ('condemn someone to an ordeal') are treated as figurative, though the results may be physical enough, because the acts of inciting and condemning are generalised accounts of complex situations and not as literal as the act of deportation. In the case of 'change' constructions (Figure 3.4c), the figure may raise questions, because the same numbered constructions are shown as both literal and figurative. This is because this distinction is not made in respect of these constructions on the Transitivity-Net website. However, it makes sense to distinguish between, for example, 'choke someone to death' (Cx11), where the

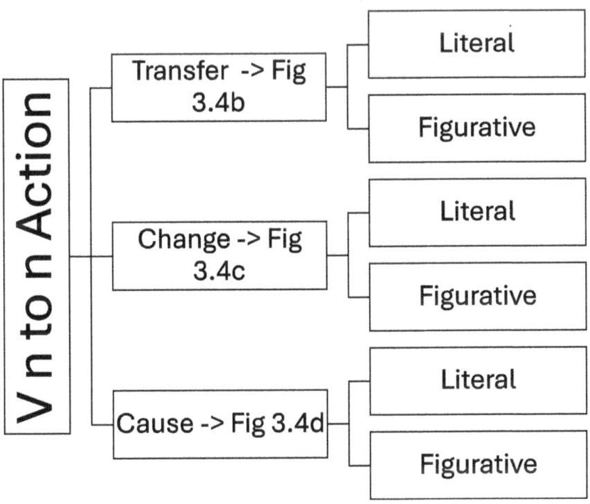

Figure 3.4a Action process-based constructions from the pattern **V n *to* n**

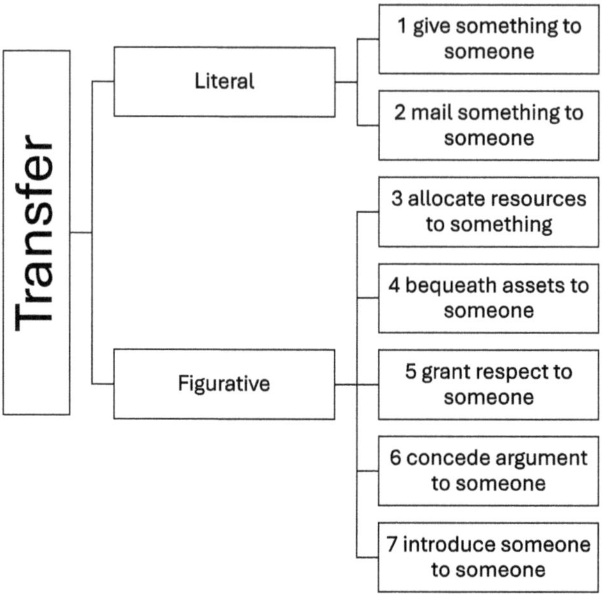

Figure 3.4b Action process-based constructions, the transfer network

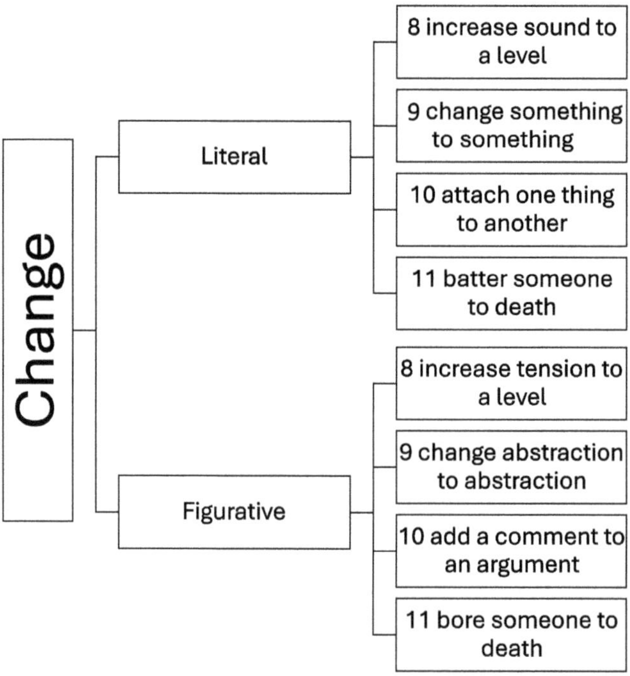

Figure 3.4c Action process-based constructions, the change network

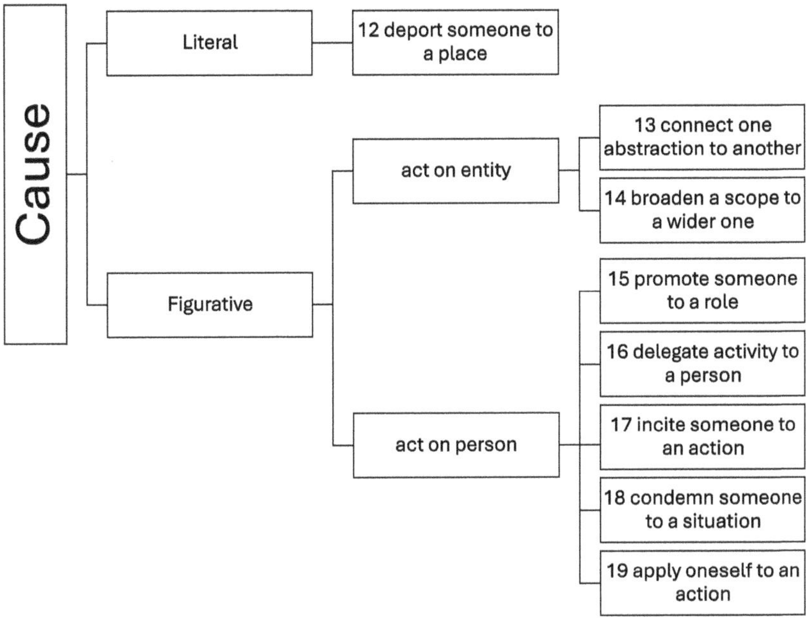

Figure 3.4d Action process-based constructions, the cause network

victim actually dies, and 'bore someone to death' (also Cx11), where the most usual interpretation is that the victim remains alive. Within figurative cause actions another distinction is made: between acting on an abstract entity and acting on a person. Constructions 17 and 18 exemplify acting on a person, while constructions 13 and 14 (e.g. 'attach a condition to a ruling' and 'broaden the scope of the enquiry to the whole organisation') exemplify acting on an entity.

As with the pattern **V n adj**, the constructions that are identified can be expressed as more general than the 37 listed, and indeed as more specific. It has already been noted that constructions 8–11 can be (and probably should be) divided into two more specific constructions each. Going up the hierarchy, or leftwards in the network, the more general constructions might be expressed as:

- The 'person transfers_possession to person' construction.
- The 'person/entity changes entity to a state' construction.
- The 'person/entity causes person/entity to new situation' construction.
- The 'person communicates something to someone' construction.
- The 'person cognizes one thing to another thing' construction.
- The 'entity causes person to mental state' construction.
- The 'person forms_relation one thing to another thing' construction.

The Indeterminacy of Networks: V after *n*

The discussions of the previous two patterns have made the point that the proposed networks are to an extent arbitrary, in the sense that in many cases alternative versions might be proposed. This point is made more strongly in respect to the final example, the pattern **V *after* n**. Four constructions only are proposed for this pattern:

- Cx1 the 'yearn after something' construction. Description: A person wants something very much. Verbs: HANKER, HUNGER, LUST, THIRST, and YEARN. Example: *He's never hankered after the travelling life.* (BNC)
- Cx2 the 'follow after someone' construction. Description: A person follows another person, probably with negative intentions. Verbs: CHASE and FOLLOW. Example: *I've been threatened, spat on, chased after . . .* (BNC)
- Cx3 the 'chase after something' construction. Description: A person tries to get a physical or abstract entity that is difficult to get. Verbs: CHASE, GO, and RUN. Example: *All these years you've spent chasing after something you can't have.* (BNC)
- Cx4 the 'clean up after someone' construction. Description: A person helps someone, especially by correcting their mistakes and/or doing something they should have done. Verbs: CLEAN UP, CLEAR UP, RUN AROUND, and TIDY UP. Example: *He always expected other people to clean up after him.* (BNC)

The network shown on the Transitivity-Net website prioritises the distinction between processes: cognition ('yearn after') as opposed to action (the other constructions). Then a distinction is made between literal actions ('follow after someone') and figurative ones ('chase after' and 'clean up after'). This is shown in Figure 3.5. An alternate network would begin with what might be called the two meanings or functions of *after*: indicating an aim or desire ('yearn after' and 'chase after a desired thing'); indicating space or time ('follow after someone' and 'clean up after someone'). Figure 3.5b shows this alternative. The point is that neither of these is transparently 'correct' but that both model one perspective on the relationship between the constructions.

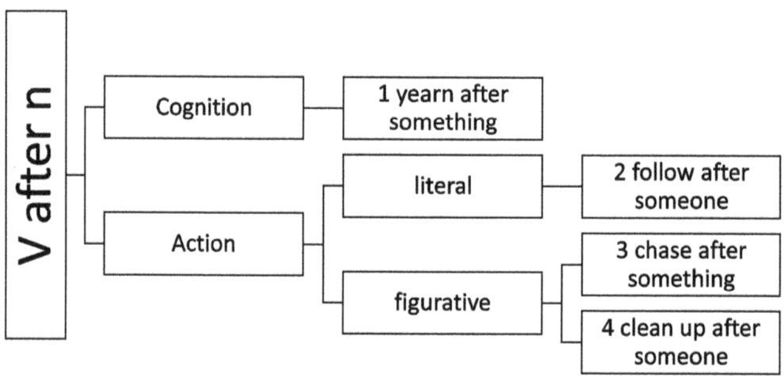

Figure 3.5a Alternative networks for constructions derived from **V *after* n**

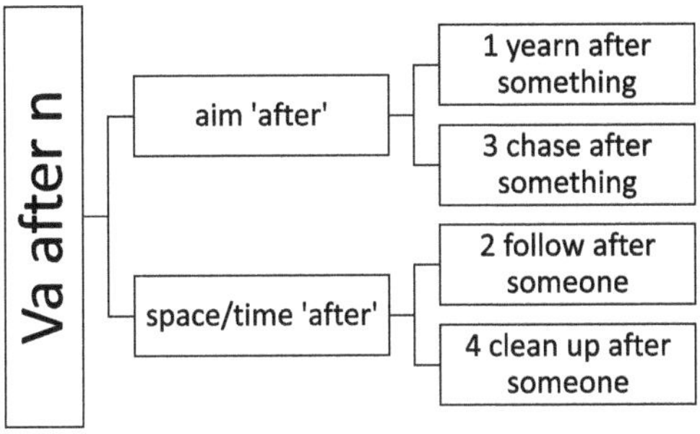

Figure 3.5b Alternative networks for constructions derived from **V *after* n**

3.5 The Construction Networks as Heuristic: Identifying Distinctions

In this study, then, the constructions drawing on each pattern are modelled in a network. As well as the 'end-point' constructions, the nodes of the network can be interpreted as 'more general' constructions. The networks are a way of organising the constructions neatly, but they also act as a heuristic to discover what language resources are relevant to each set of constructions. The distinctions that are made in deriving the networks give an insight into how constructions with the same complementation form might differ because of the configuration of the other elements in the construction.

To give a sense of the range of distinctions that have been proposed, two verb complementation patterns will be given as examples.

Example: V n that

The first example is the pattern **V n that** (verb + noun phrase + that-clause). Eight constructions are identified from this pattern. They are:

- Cx1: speaker informs/notifies/teaches/tells someone that . . .
- Cx2: speaker reassures/guarantees/promises someone that . . .
- Cx3: speaker warns/cautions someone that . . .
- Cx4: speaker persuades/convinces someone that . . .
- Cx5: speaker bets/wagers someone that . . .
- Cx6: evidence shows/decides/tells someone that . . .
- Cx7: cognizer deludes/flatters/kids themselves that . . .
- Cx8: thought hits/strikes someone that . . .

The network accounting for these is shown in Figure 3.6. In forming the network, the following distinctions are made:

- A distinction in the process: communication (Cx1–Cx6) or cognition (Cx7 and Cx8) (Figure 3.6). Note that construction 6 is ambiguous in this respect. On the one hand, the evidence acts like a speaker, 'telling' or 'showing' someone that something is the case. This is, however, a metaphoric representation of what is 'really' happening: a person is forming a thought based on the available evidence. Thus the evidence communicates to a cognizer that something is the case. Because of the network format, the construction has to be classed as communication or cognition: for the purposes here, the surface form of 'telling' takes precedence. Chapter 4 discusses instances such as this further and shows examples of dual coding.
- A distinction in the source of the communication/cognition (Figures 3.6b and 3.6c). This may be a person (Cx1–Cx5, where the source is a speaker, also Cx7, where the source is the cognizer), or an entity (Cx6), or a thought/idea (Cx8).
- A distinction in whether the communication leads to a change or not (Figure 3.6b). In most cases, the giving of information does not necessarily lead to change: someone can be told something or warned of something without changing thoughts or actions. In the case of the verbs PERSUADE and CONVINCE (Cx4), however, there is a perlocutionary effect of the hearer changing their perception, and in the case of BET and WAGER (Cx5) there is a change in the situation of speaker and hearer – they have formed a contract.
- Finally, Cx1–Cx3 are distinguished by the presence or absence of affect (Figure 3.6b). Cx1 (INFORM) does not necessarily imply affect. Cx2 (REASSURE) implies positive affect and Cx3 (WARN) implies negative affect.

Figure 3.6a shows the network of constructions derived from the pattern **V n that**.

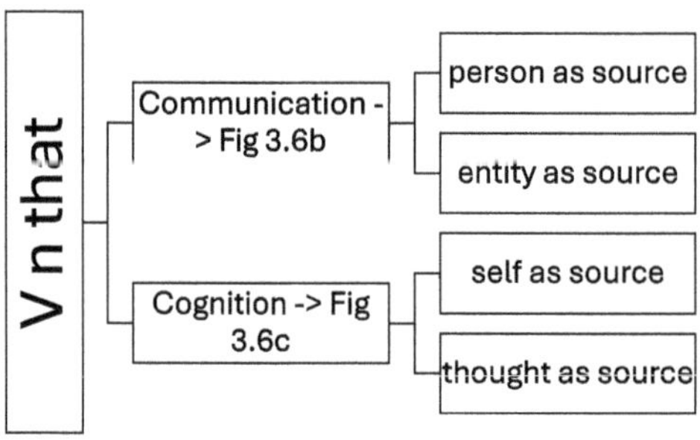

Figure 3.6a The network of constructions from the pattern **V n that**

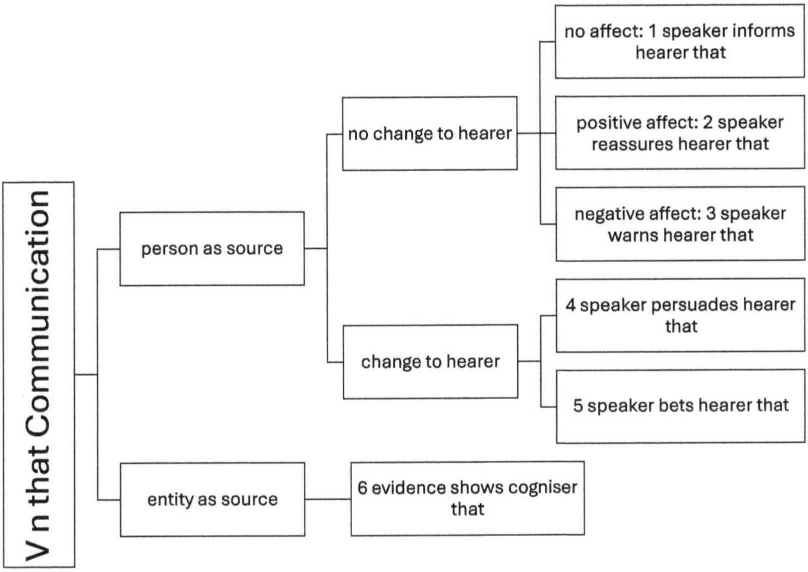

Figure 3.6b **V n that**: Communication constructions

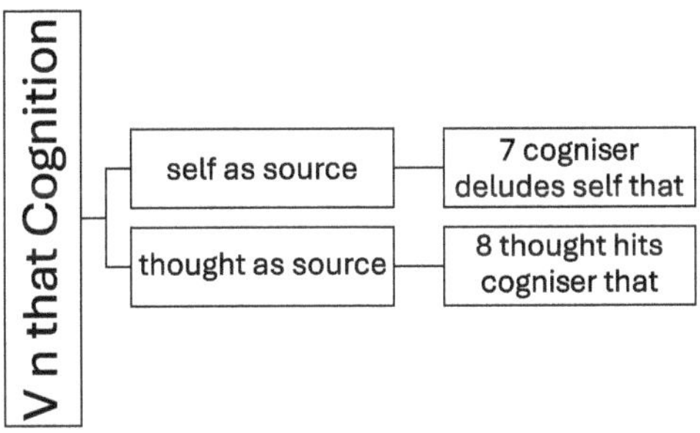

Figure 3.6c **V n that**: Cognition constructions

If this network were continued to the right, that is, making distinctions of greater delicacy, more parameters of difference could be identified. In construction 1, for example, there are seven verbs: INFORM, INSTRUCT, NOTIFY, REMIND, SHOW, TEACH, and TELL. These could be divided into groups:

- The 'give information' constructions: the 'inform someone that' construction; the 'notify someone that' construction; the 'tell someone that' construction.

- The 'give instruction' constructions: the 'instruct someone that' construction; the 'teach someone that' construction.
- The 'renew information' construction: the 'remind someone that' construction.
- The 'non-specific modality' construction: the 'show someone that' construction.

These distinctions use concepts such as 'general vs specific modality' (talking versus showing), the nature of the speech act involved (telling versus teaching), and the new/old status of the content (telling versus reminding).

Example: V n with *n*

The second example discussed here is the pattern **V n *with* n** (verb + noun phrase + *with* + noun phrase). A total of 29 constructions are proposed for this pattern. The network is shown in Figure 3.7. This network draws on the following distinctions.

- The first distinction made is based on the apparent meaning of the preposition *with* that arises out of the meaning of the construction. Three meanings are proposed: 'conjunction', 'transfer', and 'manner' (Figure 3.7a). 'Conjunction' means that *with* indicates two entities in relation to each other; for example, 'contrast one thing with another' (Cx1), or 'link one thing with another' (Cx6), or 'exchange blows with someone' (Cx5) (Figure 3.7b). 'Transfer' means that *with* indicates that something gains possession of something or that one thing is placed in proximity to another. Examples include 'furnish someone with something' (Cx11), 'sweeten a dish

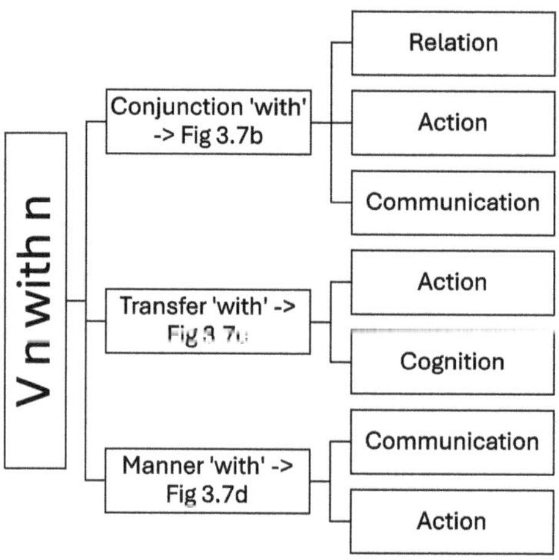

Figure 3.7a The network of constructions from the pattern **V n *with* n**

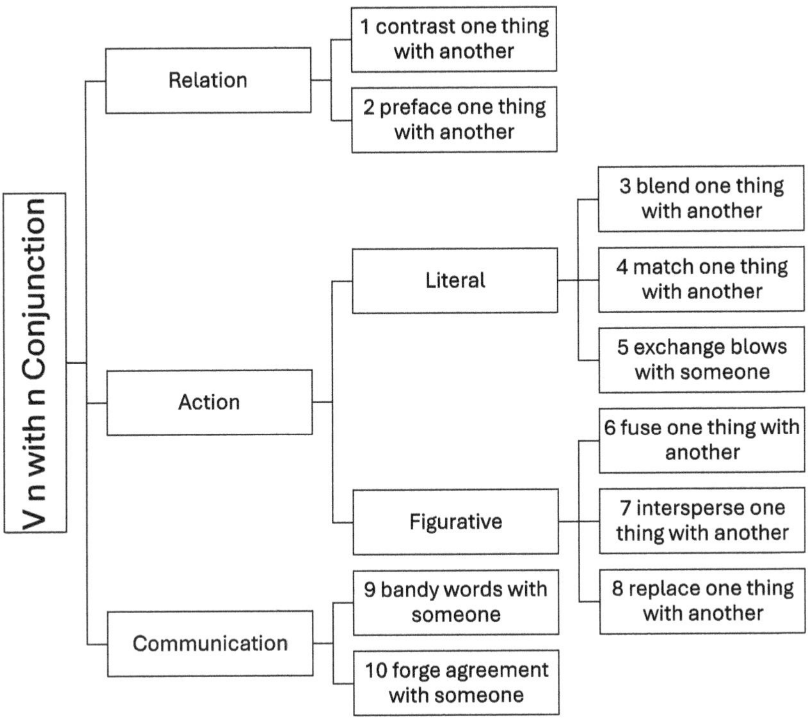

Figure 3.7b **V n *with* n**: Conjunction *with* constructions

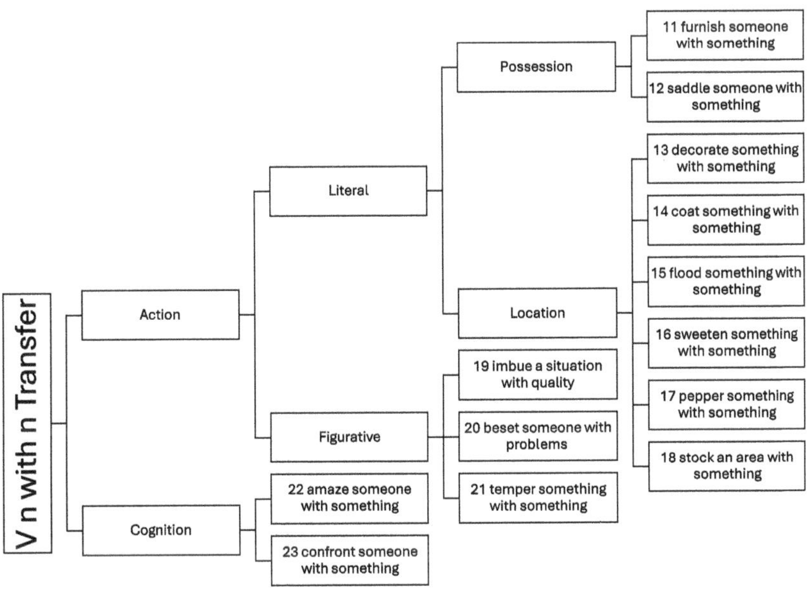

Figure 3.7c **V n *with* n**: Transfer *with* constructions

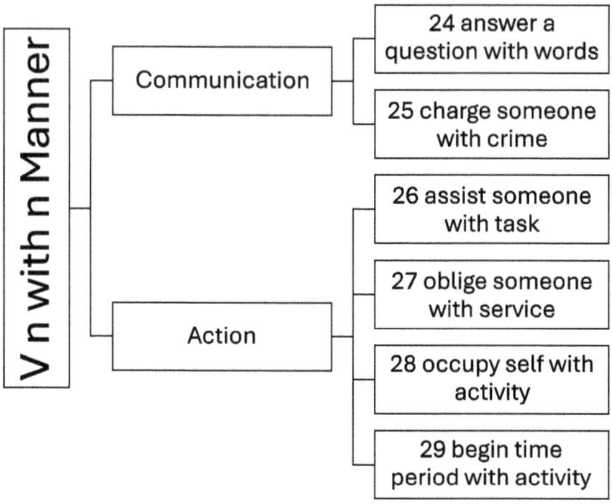

Figure 3.7d **V n *with* n**: Manner *with* constructions

with something' (Cx16), or 'imbue a situation with a quality' (Cx19) (Figure 3.7c). 'Manner' means that *with* indicates how something is done; for example, 'answer a question with a comment' (Cx24), or 'oblige someone with a service' (Cx27) (Figure 3.7d). All the constructions with this pattern are assigned to one or other meaning of *with*.

- The second distinction is made based on the nature of the process expressed by the construction. The process types are based on but not identical to those used by Halliday (Halliday and Matthiessen 2014). They are: 'relation'; 'action'; 'communication'; 'cognition'. An example of 'relation' is 'preface one thing with another' (Cx2). An example of 'action' is 'exchange blows with someone' (Cx5). An example of 'communication' is 'bandy words with someone' (Cx9). An example of 'cognition' is 'amaze someone with something' (Cx22). Each of the preposition meaning types has constructions with more than one process type. All the constructions with this pattern are assigned to one or other process type.
- The third distinction is between 'literal' and 'figurative' meaning constructions. Although all the constructions are either literal or figurative, the distinction is made only when there are constructions that differ along this dimension. In practice, this means that it is used only with a subset of the 'action' constructions. Literal actions include examples such as 'blend one thing with another' (Cx3), 'furnish someone with something' (Cx11), and 'stock an area with something' (Cx18). Figurative actions include examples such as 'fuse one thing with another', glossed as 'A person establishes

a connection between two abstract entities' (Cx6), 'imbue a situation with a quality' (Cx19), and 'beset someone with problems' (Cx20).
- The eight constructions that share the features of 'transfer', 'action' and 'literal' are further distinguished by whether the construction relates to 'possession' or to 'location'. The 'possession' constructions are: 'furnish someone with something' (Cx11) and 'saddle someone with something' (Cx12). The 'location' constructions are: 'decorate something with something' (Cx13); 'coat something with something' (Cx14); 'flood something with something' (Cx15); 'sweeten something with something' (Cx16); 'pepper something with something' (Cx17); 'stock an area with something' (Cx18).

3.6 Conclusion

This chapter has illustrated two processes: reinterpreting each of 54 verb complementation patterns as constructions and representing those constructions as a taxonomy or network. Both processes are, admittedly, subjective and open to challenge or revision, but they make use of concepts found elsewhere in the field, such as the distinction between process types, or between literal and figurative meaning. Examples of verb argument constructions and networks are given in this chapter. Constructions and networks for each of the 52 grammar patterns considered in this study can be found on the Transitivity-Net website.

As a conclusion to the chapter, it is worth considering again what is meant by 'construction' in this book, and to illustrate what kinds of form and meaning slots occur in those constructions, bearing in mind Haspelmath's (2023) account of a construction having 'at least one open slot'. Consider example (8):

(8) She struck me as a very bossy, short-tempered teacher. (BNC)

This is an instance of the grammar pattern **V n *as* n**, and it is an instance of the 'strike someone as' construction. There is one other verb in the same construction – *impress* – and this is one of 10 constructions proposed with the same pattern.

Example (8) consists of five elements, shown in Table 3.6. Row 1 shows the example. Row 2 shows the form of the construction: noun + verb + noun + *as* + noun. Row 5 explains the meaning of the construction as a whole. Row 3 describes the range of form and meaning available in each slot. NP1 construes any person or thing. NP2 construes only a person (something capable of an opinion). NP3 construes only a characteristic or identity, such as 'a very bossy, short-tempered teacher'. The verb may be only *strike* or *impress*. The preposition may only be *as*. Row 4 classifies the slots into four types: the preposition is a fixed item; the verb is a slot that is variable within a small range; NP1 is an

Table 3.6 *Slots in verb argument constructions*

Row	Noun (NP1)	Verb	Noun (NP2)	*as*	Noun (NP3)
1	she	struck	me	*as*	a very bossy short-tempered teacher
2	Noun phrase construing any person or thing.	One of a limited set of verbs: STRIKE, IMPRESS	Noun phrase construing a person only	*as*	Noun phrase construing a characteristic or identity only
3	Open slot	Variable slot	Restricted slot	Fixed item	Restricted slot

Example (1) consists of five elements, shown in Table 3.6. Row 1 shows the example. The header row shows the form of the construction: noun (NP1) + verb + noun (NP2) + as + noun (NP3). Row 2 describes the range of form and meaning available in each slot. NP1 construes any person or thing. NP2 construes only a person (something capable of an opinion). NP3 construes only a characteristic or identity, such as 'a very bossy, short-tempered teacher'. The verb may be only STRIKE or IMPRESS. The preposition may only be *as*. Row 3 classifies the slots into four types: the preposition is a fixed item; the verb is a slot that is variable within a small range; NP1 is an open slot; NP2 and NP3 are 'restricted' slots – they do not contain items that are listable like the verbs, but their meaning is more restricted than NP1.With these constructions, then, there is not a simple distinction between 'closed' and 'open' slots, but degrees of variation and fixedness. This would seem to be a characteristic, maybe even a distinguishing characteristic, of verb argument constructions. In summary, the meaning of the construction as a whole is: NP2 has an opinion about NP1, ascribing to NP1 the characteristic of NP3, based on NP1's appearance, speech or actions.

open slot; NP2 and NP3 are 'restricted' slots – they do not contain items that are listable like the verbs, but their meaning is more restricted than NP1. With these constructions, then, there is not a simple distinction between 'closed' and 'open' slots, but degrees of variation and fixedness. This would seem to be a characteristic, maybe even a distinguishing characteristic, of verb argument constructions.

Table 3.6 illustrates the presentation of constructions as a sequence of elements. In many traditions, those elements are labelled with their semantic roles. Chapter 4 discusses this issue and explains the process of semantic role labelling in this study.

4 Semantic Role Annotation

4.1 Introduction

One of the aims of the study described in this book was to undertake at least some annotation of semantic roles. Doing so requires a consideration of the available ways of doing this, and of the different purposes of the role annotation in different approaches. Similar debates are to be found in, for example, the valency grammar literature (Herbst and Götz-Votteler 2007; Herbst and Uhrig 2019). The term 'valency' has a longer history than 'pattern' and is the term preferred by some of the approaches discussed in this chapter. Herbst (2007: 20) distinguishes between syntactic and semantic valency. Syntactic valency is equivalent to 'grammar pattern', identifying the form of the arguments that accompany and categorise a verb or other lexical item (Matthews 2007: 3). Semantic valency relates to the meaning of those arguments. Götz-Votteler (2007) usefully sets out some options:

- identify the semantic roles, which constitute 'a more or less fixed set' such as Agent or Patient;
- identify the semantic components of the items occupying those roles, such as animacy;
- subclassify the arguments into semantic categories, such as 'person, animal, object, or force';
- describe the arguments in verb-specific terms, specifying subgroups, such as 'a group of people such as an army' as the Agent of the verb ATTACK.

Herbst and Uhrig (2019) describe a project to reinterpret valency patterns as constructions, and so to designate the valency patternbank of English into a constructicon of English. In this enterprise, the verbs and their arguments become elements or 'slots' in constructions.

In this chapter, four traditions of semantic element annotation are briefly described and compared. They are: Corpus Pattern Analysis – CPA (Hanks 2013), Systemic Functional Grammar – SFG (Halliday and Matthiessen 2014), Local Grammar – LG (Barnbrook 2002), and FrameNet (Fillmore et al. 2003). Following this survey, the approach to semantic annotation taken in this study is described.

When comparing approaches to semantic annotation, a number of parameters of difference may be identified (Hunston and Sui 2024). One such difference is between the semantic label as input to the identification of the unit and the semantic label as the output or consequence of the identification of the unit. For example, in CPA, category labels such as 'Human', 'Entity', or 'Proposition' are used to account for an example being identified as belonging to a given unit. That is, the labelling is part of the input to the unit. In FrameNet, on the other hand, the label indicates the role that the element plays in the Frame that the unit is part of. That is, the label is the output of the unit, explaining what the unit means. Example (1) illustrates this comparison. The CPA labels are 'Human' and 'Entity = valuable'; the annotation might be glossed as 'if you find the verb ACCEPT and noun phrases meaning "human being" and "a valuable entity", then you have found an example of this unit'. FrameNet identifies this example as belonging to the Receiving frame and labels the Frame Elements 'Recipient' and 'Theme'. The annotation might be glossed as 'if an example belongs to this frame, then its elements may be interpreted as having these roles'.

(1)				
		She	accepted	a glass of wine. (BNC)
	CPA	Human	accepted	Entity=valuable
	FrameNet	Recipient	accepted	Theme

A second difference is between schemas which allocate examples to specific contexts or meaning areas, and those which take a more general view of meaning. Local Grammar, for example, selects instances with specific rhetorical functions and allocates element labels commensurate with those functions. Systemic Functional Grammar, on the other hand, applies more general labels. Example (2) illustrates this comparison. The LG labels draw on the specific rhetorical function of the example, Apologiser and Apologisee (drawing on Su and Wei 2018), while the SFG labels simply treat the example as an instance of a verbal process (drawing on Halliday and Matthiessen 2014).

(2)				
	I	want to	apologise	to the rest of you.
	LG	Apologiser	Apologising	Apologisee
	SFG	Sayer	Process	Receiver

The reason for the different labelling systems is that each approach has a distinct purpose. Corpus Pattern Analysis aims to define precisely the various meanings a word can have, in terms that are similar to valency grammar (Herbst et al. 2004). In practical terms, the patterns can be used in automatic sense disambiguation: if an instance of the verb ACCEPT is found preceded by a noun phrase belonging to the class 'Human' and followed by a noun phrase belonging to the class 'Entity of a valuable kind' (see example (1)), then the verb belongs to this specific sense and no other. Systemic Functional Grammar seeks to establish the range of resources available to the speaker of a language (see Chapter 5). It distinguishes process types, such as 'verbal process', and establishes potential participant types as a way of establishing how that process type operates (see example (2)). FrameNet identifies the role that each element of a target utterance has within a situation or Frame; for example, the subject of the verb ACCEPT in example (1) is the Receiver in a situation in which one person gives something to another person. FrameNet specifies how Frames can be expressed. That is, it does not ask 'what meanings can this word make?', as CPA does, but asks 'what are the different ways that this meaning can be made?' Local Grammar does something similar, but focuses on rhetorical functions, such as apology (see example (2)), rather than situational Frames. This difference in purpose makes it difficult for one schema to exactly replicate the terminology from another schema.

4.2 Corpus Pattern Analysis

The CPA project led by Hanks (Hanks 2013) led to the compilation of the online Pattern Dictionary of English Verbs (PDEV) (accessed at pdev.org.uk). The purpose of the project was to distinguish word meanings by identifying 'patterns' consisting of structural elements and semantic sets. In Hanks's words: 'A pattern consists of a valency structure, together with sets of preferred collocations' (Hanks 2013: 92). Each pattern is associated with 'a particular meaning or implicature' (Hanks 2013: 92). A distinction is made between prototypical uses, or 'norms', and unusual or creative uses, or exploitations. Hanks distinguishes his approach from that of Hunston and Francis (2000), noting that 'their framework does not assign a central role to lexical collocations in determining what counts as a pattern' (Hanks 2013: 6). He points out, correctly, that this means that patterns, in the Francis et al. (1996, 1998) sense, do not distinguish between word meanings unless two meanings have different syntactic patterns. He gives the example of *fire a gun* and *fire an employee*, which in Pattern Grammar terms are both coded **V n**, but which in PDEV are accounted for by two separate patterns (Hanks 2013: 6):

- pattern 1 ([Human] **fire** [Firearm]) and
- pattern 5 ([Human1 = *Employer*] **fire** [Human2 = *Employee*])

(The representation of the PDEV patterns is somewhat simplified here. Single square brackets are used instead of double ones, and some alternatives, such as 'either a person or an institution can fire an employee' are omitted.)

Central to Hanks' work is the notion of lexical sets. In the *fire a gun/ employee* examples, for instances, the lexical sets 'Human' and 'Firearm' are used. This means that identification of the pattern is dependent on (a) the identification of the valency pattern **V n** and (b) the recognition that the

Subject and Object nouns belong to the class Human or the class Firearm. Discussing how lexical sets are arrived at, Hanks uses the example of the verb URGE (Hanks 2013: 117). One meaning of this verb occurs in examples such as (3).

(3) We urged our horses forward. (BNC)

Hanks notes that the most frequent noun in the object slot is *horse*, but that common sense dictates that other animals used as transport, such as camels, might also be urged, even if there is little corpus evidence to that effect. On the other hand, inanimate entities which human beings control, such as vehicles, cannot truly be urged, though examples can be found of somewhat whimsical uses such as example (4).

(4) He urged the ship onwards. (enTenTen21)

In Hanks' terms, example (4) would be an instance of exploitation, that is, a metaphoric extension of the central usage of URGE. There is, then, a fuzzy lexical set that contributes to this meaning of URGE and that might be given the name [Steed]. Hanks refers to the criterion that the urged entity should possess consciousness as 'intensional', distinguished from an 'extensional' criterion that simply lists all occurring collocates (Hanks 2013: 118).

In PDEV, the meaning of each pattern is explained by means of an implicature. This explains rather than defines the pattern. To illustrate this, Table 4.1 shows 7 selected patterns from the 21 patterns listed in the PDEV entry for the verb TELL. They have been chosen to illustrate a range of valency patterns and lexical sets. Because the implicatures are sometimes a little difficult to interpret, being expressed formulaically, a gloss has been added in some cases.

The valency or syntactic patterns shown in Table 4.1 are as would be expected. We see the grammar patterns **V n** (pattern 8), **V n *from* n** (pattern 14), **V n *of* n** (pattern 5), **V n that** (pattern 1), and **V n to-inf** (pattern 6). What is more interesting are the lexical sets specified for each pattern. In pattern 1 the Subject may be either a human being, or an institution, or an information source, and the Object may be a human being or an institution. In patterns 12, 14, and 21 the Subject may only be a human being. In pattern 8 the Subject may be an inanimate entity (such as *evidence*) or an event (such as *his departure*). The Object is the word *story*, with obligatory modifiers. Most interestingly, the implicature given for pattern 21 ('one child tells tales on another') specifies elements that are not present in the pattern itself: a teacher or other authority figure to whom the information is given; an action that the second child has done; and a rule that is broken by that action. It also includes the information that to 'tell tales on someone' is regarded as a wrong thing to do by other children.

Table 4.1 *Selected patterns of TELL from PDEV*

1	Pattern	[Human1 | Institution1 | Information_Source1] **tell** [Human2 | Institution2] [QUOTE] [THAT] [WH+]
	Implicature	[Human1 | Institution1 | Information_Source1] informs [Human2 | Institution2] [QUOTE] [THAT] [WH+]
	Gloss	Person tells person that something is the case. OR (e.g.) Newspaper tells people what events took place.
5	Pattern	[Human1 |Institution1 | Information_Source] **tell** [Human2 | Institution2] [of [Anything = *Topic*]]
	Implicature	[Human1 |Institution1 | Information_Source] informs [Human2 | Institution2] about some facts concerning [Anything = *Topic*]]
	Gloss	Person tells person of any topic.
6	Pattern	[Human1 | Institution1] **tell** [Human2 | Institution2] [to+INF]
	Implicature	[Human1 | Institution1] orders, instructs, or advises [Human2 | Institution 2] to +INF (V)
	Gloss	Person tells person to do something. OR (e.g.) Government tells Civil Service to do something.
8	Pattern	[Inanimate | Event] **tell** {story}
	Implicature	[Inanimate | Event] is a reason for believing {[MOD] story}
	Gloss	(e.g.) The evidence told the story of the crime. OR (e.g.) His departure told its own story.
12	Pattern	[Human] **tell** {joke}
	Implicature	[Human] says something that is intended to be funny.
14	Pattern	[Human] **tell** [Anything1] {from} [Anything2]
	Implicature	[Human] is able to decide the difference between [Entity1] and [Entity2]
21	Pattern	[Human1 = *Schoolchild*] **tell** {tale} [on | against [Human2 = *Schoolchild*]]
	Implicature	[Human1 = Schoolchild] reports to [Human 3 = {Teacher | Authority] some [Action] done by [Human2 = Schoolchild] that is against a [Rule], and by doing so breaches a code of honour among schoolchildren.
	Gloss	One child tells tales on another child.

There is a strong case to be made for regarding the patterns recorded in PDEV as compatible with the notion of constructions, in the sense that each word pattern is uniquely associated with a meaning or implicature. Pattern 21 in Table 4.1 is a particularly good example of a construction, as its meaning is non-compositional, that is, not predictable from the form alone. The other patterns are more predictable and less striking, but can also be interpreted as constructions without difficulty.

Hanks' notion of exploitations can also usefully be applied to constructions, even though Hanks takes the word as central and asks 'what unusual uses of this word occur?', whereas researchers such as Goldberg start from the construction and ask 'what unusual words occur in this construction?'. Both might conclude, however, that examples such as 'he urged the ship onwards' or 'she smiled herself an upgrade' are examples of exploitation of a linguistic norm.

However, CPA presents a challenge to the description of constructions described in this book, raising the question of whether constructions should be annotated in terms of the semantics of their contributing elements. Because the preference here is to annotate the 'output' function rather than the 'input' category, labels of this kind have not been used. However, some information about lexical sets has been included as part of construction descriptions. Here are some examples:

- Pattern: **V n -ing**. Cx 10: the 'spend time doing something' construction. Description: A person spends time doing something. The NP following the verb indicates the period of time. Example: *We spent the day exploring*. (BNC)
- Pattern: **V *on* n**. Cx 23: the 'build on' construction. Description: A person or entity uses another person or entity as a basis for increase or improvement. Example: *The proposed draft protocol builds on existing pollution controls*. (BNC)
- Pattern: **V n *about* n**. Cx 6: the 'know a lot about something' construction. Description: A person knows or learns about something. The NP following the verb indicates an amount. Example: *She knew a lot about birds*. (BNC).

We now turn to the schemas that code the output of patterns, starting with SFG (Halliday and Matthiessen 2014).

4.3 Participant Roles in Systemic Functional Grammar

It will be explained in Chapter 5 that SFG separates three roles that the clause plays: it constitutes an exchange or interaction between speaker and hearer (the interpersonal metafunction); it is the carrier of a message, comprising ordered pieces of information (the textual metafunction); and it construes a situation or set of events (the experiential metafunction). Within each metafunction, the speaker has a range of alternate resources available to them, such as interacting with interrogative or declarative mood, or beginning the clause in a marked or unmarked way. Of most relevance here is the experiential metafunction, which interprets clauses in terms of how they represent the social and physical world. The main distinctions made are between process types, and part of the way that process types are recognised is by the participant roles they occur with. For example, a clause built around a mental process verb phrase will have a Senser and a Phenomenon, whereas a clause with a verbal process verb phrase will have a Sayer and a Message. The main process types proposed by Halliday (1970) are material, mental, and relational. These reflect the three major ways of construing the world: as a set of events and happenings (material processes); as a set of perceptions and thoughts (mental processes); and as a representation of connections between things, including connections between reified events and happenings (relational processes). The other process types are verbal, behavioural, and existential.

The identification of process types and their associated participant roles constitutes a large part of what make this kind of grammar 'functional'. Halliday and Matthiessen explain that traditional labels such as 'Subject' and 'Object' in fact conflate different kinds of information (Halliday and Matthiessen 2014: 79–82). They go into considerable detail in examining the varying relationships that can exist between the verb element in a clause and the Subject and Object elements. Examples taken from Halliday and Matthiessen (2014: 226–307), are given here:

- The lion caught the tourist: Actor-Process-Goal (p226)
- They played a game of tennis: Actor-Process-Scope (p238)
- I gave my love a ring: Actor-Process-Recipient-Goal (p239)
- They washed the plates clean: Actor-Process-Goal-Attribute (p238)
- Mary liked the gift: Senser-Process-Phenomenon (p248)
- The gift pleased Mary: Phenomenon-Process-Senser (p248)
- Mice are timid creatures: Carrier-Process-Attribute (p267)
- Mr Garrick played Hamlet: Identified-Process-Identifier (p277)
- He told me the truth: Sayer-Process-Receiver-Verbiage (p306)
- He praised my teaching ability: Sayer-Process-Target (p307)

One aim of SFG is to account for all combinations of Process and Participant in a language. Of necessity, this means that the labels used are somewhat general and relate to overall distinctions of use rather than to context-specific distinctions. One response to this is to propose sets of labels that are functional in a different way (Hunston and Sinclair 1999: 79), linking the labelling of elements of clauses to the rhetorical function of the clause. The term 'Local Grammar', taken from Gross (1993), is used to describe this approach, described in the next section.

4.4 Local Grammar

The difference between the participant roles used in SFG and the element labels in LG might be illustrated with an invented example based on one used by Sinclair (personal communication): 'A dog is a beloved companion'. The indeterminacy of the meaning is captured in the possibility of two codings in SFG: this is either Carrier-Process-Attribute, meaning that a dog has the characteristics of being lovable and companiable, or it is Identified-Process-Identifier, meaning that the identifying description of a dog is as a loved companion. Sinclair essentially rephrases this distinction in terms of the function of the clause: it is either an evaluation of a dog or a definition of a dog. In one, the constituent elements might be coded 'Target + Evaluation'; in the other, it might be 'Definiendum + Definiens'. For a reader to know which coding is correct, they have to use common sense to decide whether 'a beloved companion' evaluates or defines 'a dog'.

When a LG is devised, therefore, it proposes semantic role labels that are specific to a given rhetorical function. The labels are relevant only to clauses that perform that function. Local Grammars are useful in determining what roles are relevant to a given function, how those roles are expressed and what options are available for doing so, and in making it possible to quantify the occurrence of the various options in a corpus. Although each LG study is comprehensive in scope, inevitably only a handful of language functions have received attention of this kind, so that Gross's (1993) initial ambition of extending the description to the whole of a language is currently not within reach.

Barnbrook's work on the LG of definitions (Barnbrook 2002, see also Barnbrook and Sinclair 1995, 2001) is the most extensive and comprehensive study of this kind. The aim was to identify and quantify the different formats of definition used in the *Collins* COBUILD *Student's Dictionary* (Sinclair 1990). Barnbrook (2002: 135–136) identifies 17 types of definition, divided into four groups. The types range in frequency (in the CCSD) from over 10,000 instances to just 14. A finite set of terms is used to label the elements, such as 'Definiendum' (that which is defined), 'Definiens' (the defining element), 'Superordinate' (part of the defining element, that assigns the defined thing to a class), 'Discriminator' (that which separates the defined thing from others in the class), and 'Hinge' (which joins parts of the definition to each other).

Barnbrook's general approach has been adapted by other researchers and applied to other functions: evaluation (Hunston and Sinclair 1999; Hunston and Su 2019); disclaiming (Cheng and Ching 2018); apologising (Su and Wei 2018; Su 2020); thanking (Su 2018); data commentary (Zhang et al. 2024); defining (Zhang and Su 2023); and exemplifying (Su et al. 2022). Much of this work is relatively small scale, but a paper by Yu et al. (2024) applies a larger-scale approach using Large Language Models. Their paper illustrates the difficulty in quantifying types of rhetorical patterns. In Barnbrook's case, the definitions were all located in a dictionary and are identified as definitions in the dictionary database; in the case of naturally occurring apologies, the apologies have to be found first, and only then can they be parsed. Inevitably it is only the more explicit apologies that are identified and analysed.

Table 4.2 gives some examples of LG coding.

Table 4.2 *Examples of Local Grammars*

Definitions (Barnbrook 2002)				
Hinge	Co-text	Definiendum	Match	Definiens
When	a student	graduates	he or she	has successfully completed a degree course . . .
Data Commentary (Zhang et al. 2024)				
Data	Hinge	Graphic	Act	Interpretation
Our correlations	in	table 7	show	that bettergoverned countries have . . .
Exemplification (Su et al. 2022)				
Exemplified	Exemplification – supporting research	Indicator	Supporting statement	
This negotiation process actually involves complex mechanics.	Schiffrin (1987: 24–28)	for example	proposes a five-plane model which involves . . .	

4.5 FrameNet

FrameNet is one of the most detailed and influential approaches to the description of form and meaning in language. A clear account of its principles, outputs, and working methods can be found in publications such as Fillmore et al. (2003) and Fillmore (2014), and the data and other resources can be found at framenet.icsi.berkeley.edu. FrameNet is based on Frame Semantics (Fillmore 1976), which proposes that the meaning of a word is dependent on the real-world situation or concept in which that word occurs:

> The central idea of Frame Semantics is that word meanings must be described in relation to *semantic frames* – schematic representations of the conceptual structures and patterns of beliefs, practices, institutions, images etc. that provide a foundation for meaningful interaction in a given speech community. (Fillmore et al. 2003: 235).

There are a number of important concepts in FrameNet:

The frame. There are hundreds of frames listed on the FrameNet website (framenet.icsi.berkeley.edu/frameIndex). Some indicate objects (e.g. Containers, Clothing). Some relate to recognisable events (e.g. Commercial_transaction, Cooking_creation). Some are more abstract (e.g. Causation, Conduct). While many relate to physical actions, many relate to speech (e.g. Citing, Chatting) or to emotions or attitude (e.g. Candidness, Coming_to_believe). Some frames are clearly more specific versions of other frames. For example, there are 34 listed frames that specify a type of cause, such as Cause_benefit_or_detriment, Cause_to continue, and Cause_to_land, or Cause_to_perceive. Relations between frames are formalised using a variety of concepts, of which the most transparent are 'inherits from', 'is inherited by', and 'uses' or 'is used by'. For example, the Coming_to_believe Frame inherits aspects of the Event Frame and is inherited by the See_through Frame. It uses the Mental_activity Frame and is used by the Falling_for and the Turning_out Frames.

The lexical unit. Every word analysed in the FrameNet project is said to evoke one or more frames, on which its meaning depends. A word and its associated sense comprise a lexical unit (LU). For example, the verb *buy* belongs to two LUs, one evoking the Commerce_buy Frame (which inherits from the Getting Frame), and one evoking the Fall_for Frame (which uses the Coming_to_believe Frame). An example of the first would be 'I bought a new coat', while an example of the second would be 'I don't buy that idea'. The FrameNet website offers information about each LU. This comprises the valency patterns that the LU is found in, and examples that are coded for Frame Elements. For example, the LU *buy*, in the Commerce_buy Frame, is shown to occur in about 30 valency patterns (an approximate number because as of March 2024, the entry is listed as not yet complete). Using the pattern grammar conventions, these include, for example: **V n *at* n** ('buy an item at a price'); **V n *from* n** ('buy an item from someone'); **V n** ('buy something'); **V n *for* n** ('buy something for someone'; 'buy something for an amount of money').

Frame Element. A crucial aspect of the FrameNet project, and the one most relevant to this chapter, is the identification of Frame Elements (FEs). Frame Elements are the semantic roles identified for each frame, and are divided into Core and Peripheral Elements. All the examples listed under each LU are coded for the Elements they exemplify. The Commercial_transaction Frame has four core Elements: BUYER, GOODS, MONEY, and SELLER. It has three peripheral Elements: MEANS, RATE, and UNIT. In instances where Core Elements do not occur, they are implied. For example, the Revenge Frame has five core Elements: AVENGER, INJURED_PARTY, INJURY, OFFENDER, and PUNISHMENT. This means that every description of an act of revenge evokes a scenario with these elements. However, many examples of this frame leave implicit one or more of these Elements. For example, *I'll get even with you for this* (from the FrameNet website entry for GET EVEN) includes the Elements AVENGER (*I*), OFFENDER (*you*), and INJURY (*this*), but the INJURED_PARTY and the PUNISHMENT are left implicit.

Both Construction Grammar and FrameNet were pioneered by Fillmore, and have shared origins (Fillmore et al. 2012). Fillmore (2014) explicitly explores the connections between them. As shown in Chapter 2, others have sought to use the notion of frames in building a network of constructions: a constructicon. Perek

(2025) comments that 'frame semantics is often considered the semantic component of construction grammar', adding that both see a 'continuity between lexical and constructional meaning'. Taking this argument further, Perek finds it logical to 'represent constructional meaning using the same theoretical apparatus as lexical meaning i.e. semantic frames'. Perek and Patten (2019) and Perek (2025) describe a Constructicon of English which draws on the Pattern Grammar resources (Francis et al. 1996) to derive constructions that are presented and annotated with FEs taken from FrameNet. Perek and Patten (2019) give an example of the 'Communication "V that" construction', which uses the form of the **V that** pattern and has FEs belonging to the Communication Frame. A further 14 more specific frames are identified that directly inherit from or use the Communication Frame and which occur with verbs identified as occurring with **V that** in Francis et al. (1996). Examples are: Communication_response; Request; Reasoning; and Reporting. One such frame, Statement, itself has a further seven frames that directly inherit or use it, including Telling, Reveal_secret, and Predicting.

Consideration was given in the study described in this book to following a similar procedure and to apply FE annotations to the identified constructions. This proved impossible to do consistently, mainly because the constructions had been identified without reference to the FrameNet framework. As a consequence, in many cases, a construction as proposed in this project might evoke several frames. For example, one of the constructions proposed for the pattern **V *of* n** is the 'complain of' construction, exemplified by ... *both sides complained of ceasefire violations* (BNC). The verbs listed as occurring in this construction are: BOAST, COMPLAIN, SPEAK, TALK, TELL, and WARN. In FrameNet, each of these is regarded as evoking a different frame. This makes sense, as 'boasting of something' and 'complaining of something', for example, clearly relate to different real-world situations. Table 4.3 shows six verbs that occur with the **V *of* n** pattern and

Table 4.3 *Frames evoked by verbs in the 'complain of' construction (from framenet.icsi.berkeley.edu)*

Verb	Frame	Example	Frame Elements
BOAST	Bragging	'She has boasted of her tendency ... '	SPEAKER; TOPIC
COMPLAIN	Complaining	'Schools have complained of interference'.	COMPLAINER; COMPLAINT
SPEAK	Chatting	'Let us speak of the present'.	INTERLOCUTORS; TOPIC
TALK	Statement	'He talks often of events at home'.	SPEAKER; TOPIC
TELL	Telling	'One woman tells of being forced to give up her baby'.	SPEAKER; MESSAGE
WARN	Warning	'Activists warn of political repercussions'.	SPEAKER; TOPIC

the frames that these LUs evoke. In each case the table shows and example and lists the FEs appearing in the example.

A conclusion that might be drawn from Table 4.3 is that the Elements SPEAKER, MESSAGE, and TOPIC might be found in several frames, with a note that the specific role of the speaker ('BOASTER', 'COMPLAINER', 'WARN-ER', etc.) and the nature of the message ('BOAST', 'COMPLAINT', and 'WARNING') depends on the frame. Further attempts to use FrameNet as the source for semantic labelling of construction elements made it apparent that applying this consistently would indeed require taking frames as the starting point for the study, as Perek and Patten (2019) do. Frame Elements cannot reliably be mapped on to the constructions that have been identified in this project. However, it can be argued that the current constructions are available for revision by other researchers who may wish to increase the compatibility of patterns, constructions, and frames.

4.6 Semantic Fields and Participant Roles in This Study

It is clear from these descriptions of approaches to form and meaning that the annotation of unit elements is an inspiring, if ambitious, goal. Several annotation schemes are available, in most cases linked to specific reference resources, such as FrameNet or the PDEV. The schemes are dependent on the aim of the project and also on its starting point. The PDEV, for example, starts from the analyses of thousands of verbs in English and has built up an ontology of semantic roles that are necessary to annotate the distinctive elements of each pattern. FrameNet, by contrast, starts with the concept of the Frame and allocates labels that are specific to each Frame. The current study starts with neither the verb nor the Frame but with the pattern. The constructions that are derived from the patterns are not single-verb specific and it would therefore be unfeasible to apply Hanks' (2013) ontology reliably. Similarly, the constructions do not necessarily map uniquely on to Frames, so applying the FrameNet semantic labels is similarly unfeasible.

The project has adopted from FrameNet, however, the principle that semantic labels have to relate to a semantic field, so that a comprehensive labelling would entail having an extensive and finite set of such fields. That is also outside the scope of this study, but as a trial, nine semantic fields have been selected for annotation. The fields are inspired by, though not entirely based on, SFG and the distinction between process types. This enabled the identification of fairly broad semantic areas. A finite set of participant or argument roles were assigned to the elements in the constructions related to those fields. Because there are only nine fields, by no means all the constructions identified in the study are coded in this way. The semantic fields chosen can be divided into the following SFG process types: material, relational, mental, and verbal. The list of semantic fields is:

- Related to material processes
  - Causation
  - Change
  - Creation
  - Location change
  - Possession transfer
- Related to relational processes
  - Equivalence
  - Logical relations
- Related to mental and verbal processes
  - Cognition
  - Communication

The relationship between semantic fields and constructions is the basis of Chapters 6–8. In this chapter, the participant roles assigned to each field are listed and briefly explained. The terminology used for the participant roles is again in part inspired by that used in SFG but there is no strict adherence to that schema and the labels are atheoretical. In particular, in SFG (e.g. Halliday and Matthiessen 2014), fine distinctions of meaning are made between related participant roles, but the role labels used here are less finely distinguished. The principle is to have as few roles as is feasible, to avoid errors in coding. Many of the participant role labels are used across a large number of constructions, such as ‘Sayer’ or ‘Cognizer’. Some are used in more than one semantic field, such as ‘Cause’ or ‘Source’. A few are more restricted in their use, however. One example is the role ‘Time’, which is used when an element in a construction expresses a time period. It is used in the Cognition and Equivalence fields, in examples such as (5) and (6).

(5) The following day saw a remarkable change in the weather . . . (BNC)

(6) Dangerfield had started the day tired . . . (BNC)

In example (5) *the following day* is construed metaphorically as something that perceives. In example (6), *the day* is an additional element in the equivalence clause ‘Dangerfield was tired’.

One point that needs to be stressed is that the coding procedure allows for multiple labelling. That is, it is considered that a single construction, and a single example, can exemplify more than one semantic field. In other words, the semantic fields are not mutually exclusive. For example, the ‘call someone something’ construction, from the pattern **V n n**, is assigned to both the Communication field and the Equivalence field. In an example such as *She called him a coward*, there is a representation of an action of communication ('she communicated a message'), with the participant roles 'Sayer' and 'Message', and also a statement of equivalence ('he is a coward'), with the participant roles Carrier and Attribute.

A further point to be made is that, unlike in the FrameNet model, only the verb arguments as identified by the construction are analysed. Other parts of the clause are not coded, even though they may be an integral part of the situation or Frame. This is illustrated in example (7).

(7) He pushed it [the door] open with his foot. (BNC)

The relevant FrameNet entry (for the LU *push* evoking the 'Cause_motion' frame) suggests that the FEs are: Agent (*he*); Theme (*the door*); Instrument (*his foot*). However, the pattern identified here is **V n adj** (not 'V n adj *with* n') and the construction specifies 'A person or entity moves something so that it is open or closed'. Because what is analysed here is the construction rather than the frame, the prepositional phrase *with his foot* is not part of the pattern or construction and is therefore not allocated a participant role.

The allocation of participant roles in relation to each set of semantic fields will now be discussed.

Fields Related to Material Processes

Table 4.4 summarises the Participant Roles in the fields associated with material processes. The fields are: Causation, Change, Creation, Location Change, and Possession Transfer. Although no distinction is made between 'core' and 'peripheral' roles, intuitively one might say that some roles are more basic to the processes than others. In the case of Change, Creation, and Location Change there are two basic or core roles:

- Change: Agent + Affected e.g. *He lowered the volume*;
- Creation: Creator + Outcome e.g. *They published a book*;
- Location Change: Cause-move + Mover e.g. *She shifted the furniture*.

In the case of Causation and Possession Transfer there are, arguably, three basic roles:

- Causation: Cause + Affected + Result e.g. *The party elected a businessman as its leader*;
- Possession Transfer: Donor + Possession + Recipient e.g. *John borrowed money from Jim*.

Table 4.4 *Participant roles in the fields associated with material processes*

Role	Explanation	Examples
Causation		
Cause	The person or entity that makes something happen.	**The party** elected a businessman as its leader.
Affected	A person or entity that is affected by a cause.	The party elected **a businessman** as its leader. The news surprised **her**.
Result	The outcome of a caused event.	The party elected a businessman as **its leader**. The play left **a lasting impression**.
Change		
Affected	The entity that undergoes change.	Losing her hair has affected **her** deeply. . . . the iron deposits changed **Corby** into a red brick town.
Outcome	The consequence of the change.	. . . the iron deposits changed Corby into **a red brick town**.
Agent	The entity that makes the change happen.	**Losing her hair** has affected her deeply. . . . **the iron deposits** changed Corby into a red brick town.
Parameter	The parameter along which the change occurs.	He lowered the volume by **5 decibels**. The rice increased in **volume**.
Means	The entity that is added to something to make a change.	He sweetened his coffee with **sugar**.
Creation		
Creator	The person who creates something.	**They** published a book.
Outcome	The entity that is created.	They published **a book**.
Beneficiary	A person for whom something is created.	He built **her** a castle.
Location	The place where something is created. The location is changed by the creation.	She carved the words in **the tree bark**.
Constituent	The material from which something is created.	They make the Gollum out of **clay**.
Location change		
Mover-physical	A physical entity that moves from one place to another.	The servants brought **ladders**.
Mover-abstract	An abstract entity in a construction that construes abstract change as movement from one place to another.	He was gathering **information about the incident**. . . . introducing **environmental safeguards** into its structural adjustment.

Table 4.4 (*cont.*)

Role	Explanation	Examples
Location	The place where someone or something moves to or from.	Her mother had dragged her into **her room**.
Cause-move	The person or entity that makes something or someone move.	**The servants** brought ladders.
Possession transfer		
Donor	The person who originally has the item. The donor may voluntarily give the item or may have it taken from them.	**They** fed the troops. He robbed **the family next door**. John borrowed from **Jim**.
Recipient	The person to whom possession is transferred. The person may be given the item or may take it.	The fed **the troops**. **He** robbed the family next door. **John** borrowed from Jim.
Possession	The item, physical or abstract, that is transferred.	They provided **money**. He took **the television**. John deprived Jim of **his birthright**.

Other roles are identified where they occur as parts of a construction, which in turn means they occur as elements in a pattern. An obvious example is the Beneficiary role that occurs when the pattern **V n n** expresses the Creation field (e.g. *He built her a castle*). Less obviously perhaps, the pattern **V n *in* n** contributes to a construction in the Change field and the noun phrase following *in* is coded as Parameter (e.g. *The rice increased in volume*). The same pattern contributes to a construction in the Creation field, where the noun phrase in the same position is coded as Location (e.g. *She carved the words in the tree bark*).

One of the features of the Location Change semantic field is that abstract entities may be construed as moving, as well as physical ones. For example, the verb INTRODUCE, used in the pattern **V n *into* n**, may be used to construe a physical movement, as in example (8), or an abstract one, as in example (9).

(8) [They] do not recommend introducing pigs into existing woodland . . . (BNC)

(9) . . . to introduce adversarial elements into the criminal process. (BNC)

In example (8), *pigs* is coded 'Mover-physical', meaning 'a physical entity that changes location'. Example (9) is considered to express metaphorical movement and *adversarial elements* is coded 'Mover-abstract'. Both *existing woodland* and *the criminal process* are coded Location, although these could be distinguished as 'physical' and 'abstract' also.

Fields Related to Relational Processes

In SFG, relational processes express connections between two entities or actions, most usually processes of 'being' or of 'having'. In this project, the concept of 'relation' is interpreted more widely. Two separate fields are proposed, though one of them is in fact a portmanteau for a range of relation types. Table 4.5 shows the two fields and the participant roles associated with them. The first field is Equivalence. The prototype for this field might be example (10).

(10) Until his death in 1768, the Duke was the most powerful man in England. (BNC)

In this example, there is an equation or equivalence between *the Duke* and *the most powerful man in England*. Following Halliday (Halliday and Matthiessen 2014: 267)), in this example *the Duke* is coded Carrier and *the most powerful man in England* is coded Attribute. The category of Attribute raises the possibility of a more fine-grained analysis; the Attribute can be a quality ('She is clever'), or an identity ('She is a Swiss national'), or a role ('She is the President'). Moving beyond the simple 'a = b' Equivalence, the Attribute can relate to a state (' … translate a book into German'), the composition of the Carrier ('The images are composed of pixels'), the purpose of the Carrier (' … designate an area for mistakes'), or an addition to the Carrier ('I decorated my bicycle with flags'). These subdivisions add a useful degree of specificity, but in the end are difficult to apply consistently. For this reason, the superordinate term 'Attribute' only is used in the coding.

As previously noted, double coding is used in this project and the semantic field of Equivalence is coded when the construction belongs to other fields also. Examples (11) and (12) illustrate both Equivalence and Cognition, example (13) illustrates both Equivalence and Communication, while example (14) belongs to both Equivalence and Causation. As shown in these examples, the participant roles of Cognizer, Source, Sayer, and Causer are included even in the Equivalence semantic field coding.

(11)

	John	likes	his coffee	hot. (BNC)
Equivalence	Cognizer		Carrier	Attribute
Cognition	Cognizer		Phenomenon	....

(12)

	His designs	revealed	him	as highly competent. (BNC)
Equivalence	Source		Carrier	Attribute
Cognition	Source		Phenomenon	....

(13)

	John	professes	himself	amazed. (BNC)
Equivalence	Sayer		Carrier	Attribute
Communication	Sayer		Message	....

(14)

	The party	elected	a businessman	as its leader. (BNC)
Equivalence	Causer		Carrier	Attribute
Causation	Causer		Affected	Outcome

Table 4.5 shows two other participant roles used with the Equivalence semantic field. 'Actor' is used to code a participant that acts upon a Carrier without causing the Attribute (as in *The attacker captured him alive*). 'Time' is used in the construction illustrated by *Stocks started the day higher.*

The second field related to relational processes is given the name 'Logical relations'. Prototypically, this is intended to provide a coding for constructions that express a relationship between two entities or events that is other than simple equivalence. The following relations are identified and the roles shown in Table 4.5:

- Influence. One entity or process influences another. The influence may be as strong as 'causation', but it may also be that one thing enables or facilitates another. The roles involved are Influencer and Influenced. An example is: *The durability of the coins* [=Influencer] *has ensured the survival of these images* [=Influenced].
- Condition. One event is conditional upon another. The roles are Conditional and Conditioner. An example is: *The opening of the service* [=Conditional] *necessitated Blackpool buying trams* [=Conditioner]. In this example, the service is able to open only because Blackpool buys trams.
- Sequence. Two or more events happen in sequence. There is only one role, Sequential, but the constructions each contain more than one of these elements, with the order of events shown by numbers. An example is: *The presentation* [=Sequential 1] *was followed by a reception* [=Sequential 2]. In some cases, a person is construed as placing two events in a sequence. The role Sequencer is used to indicate this. An example is: *Martin* [=Sequencer] *prefaces his lesson* [=Sequential 2] *with a statement that* . . . [=Sequential 1].
- Correspondence. Two entities or actions are similar to or different from each other, or are connected through coexistence. There is one role – Correspondence – but a construction will contain more than one. Unlike in the Sequence relation, there is no ordering. An example is: *The arrows* [=Correspondence] *correspond to the decision path* [=Correspondence]. In some cases, a person construes the correspondence. This role assigned is Correspondence-Causer. An example is: *They* [=Correspondence-Causer] *couched their teaching*[=Correspondence] *in story form* [=Correspondence]. This logical relation is very close to the Equivalence semantic field.
- Evidential. One entity, situation or event provides evidence for another. The roles are Evidencer and Evidenced. An example is: *Further drilling* [=Evidencer] *proved the presence of a Permo-Triassic basin* [=Evidenced].

Table 4.5 *Participant roles in the fields associated with relational processes*

Role	Explanation	Examples
Equivalence		
Carrier	Something that is assigned a quality, identity, or role.	**John** appears to be the wealthiest man in the world. John likes **his coffee** hot.
Carriers 1 and 2	Numbers used to show the sequence of occupiers of a role or two Carriers that are connected.	**Moynihan** [Carrier2] had replaced **Spencer** [Carrier1] as Professor of Painting. . . . the structure of **your own language** differs from that of **the new language**.
Attribute	The quality, form, identity, or role assigned to the Carrier. This includes attributions of quantity, purpose, and compositions, and denotes items added to the Carrier.	John is **the wealthiest man in the world**. John professes himself **amazed**. The dollar peaked at **£0.86.** . . . plunging the passageway into **semi-darkness**. His weight had compressed the carbon atoms into **diamond crystals**. The party elected a businessman as **its leader**. . . . to designate an area for **mistakes**. I decorated my bicycle with **flags**.
Cognizer	A person who believes or wishes that a Carrier has an Attribute.	**John** likes his coffee hot.
Sayer	A person who communicates that a Carrier has an Attribute.	**John** professes himself amazed.
Causer	A person or entity that causes a Carrier to possess an Attribute.	**John** pushed the door open.
Actor	A person or entity that acts upon a Carrier with an Attribute but does not cause it.	**The attacker** captured him alive.
Time	A time period or event during or at which a Carrier has an Attribute.	Stocks started **the day** higher.
Source	An entity that provides evidence for a Carrier having an Attribute.	**His designs** revealed him as highly competent.
Logical relations		
Influencer	An entity, action, event, or situation which influences another entity, action, event, or situation. The influence may be cause, enablement, or a lesser degree of influence.	**Quinn's background** dictated that he could take care of himself. **The durability of the coins** has ensured the survival of these images . . .

Table 4.5 (*cont.*)

Role	Explanation	Examples
Influenced	An entity, action, event, or situation which is influenced by an influencer.	Quinn's background dictated **that he could take care of himself**. The durability of the coins has ensured **the survival of these images** . . .
Conditional	An action or event whose occurrence is conditional upon another. The condition may be causative or only a necessary condition.	**The opening of the service** necessitated Blackpool buying trams . . .
Conditioner	An action or event which is a condition for a Conditional.	The opening of the service necessitated **Blackpool buying trams**.
Sequential	An action or event which occurs in a time sequence with another.	**The presentation** [Sequential1] was followed by a **reception** [Sequential2]. Martin prefaces **his lesson** [Sequential2] with **a statement that** . . . [Sequential1]
Sequencer	A person who does two or more things in a sequence.	**Martin** prefaces his lesson with a statement that . . .
Correspondence	An action or entity which is connected to another in a relation of similarity, contrast, or necessary co-existence.	**The arrows** correspond to **the decision path**. They based **their ideas** on **ancient writings**.
Correspondence-Cause	A person who construes a correspondence between two entities.	**They** couched their teaching in story form.
Evidencer	An entity which provides evidence for a situation.	**Further drilling** proved the presence of a Permo-Triassic basin.
Evidenced	A situation for which evidence is provided.	Further drilling proved **the presence of a Permo-Triassic basin**.

Fields Related to Mental and Verbal Processes

The semantic fields related to mental and verbal processes are Cognition and Communication. Prototypical examples of each would be:

Cognition ('thinking'): *We thought she was really stupid!* (BNC)
Communication ('saying'): *My brother said that I would make a good banker.* (BNC)

Halliday specifies formal criteria that distinguish process types including mental and verbal (Halliday and Matthiessen 2014: 249); they are not simply 'clauses that indicate someone is speaking or thinking'. For the identification of semantic fields rather than process types, however, a much broader definition is adopted. This means that whereas some constructions are similar to the 'thought that' and 'said that' examples, others are very different, such as those in examples (15) and (16).

(15) The images . . . stuck in his mind. (BNC)

(16) Louise chuckled at the recollection. (BNC)

Including examples such as these in the Cognition and Communication fields allows us to capture more data and give a broader sense of the resources available to express them. Similarly, while some terminology from SFG is used to provide participant role labels, the role labels used here are not limited to those used in SFG. Here, I explain the process towards the various decisions taken in specifying participant roles in these semantic fields. The full range of roles can be seen in Tables 4.6 and 4.7.

Table 4.6 *Participant roles associated with the Cognition semantic field*

Role	Explanation	Examples
'Thinker' roles		
Cognizer	An actor in a cognitive process. It may be a person or a part of a person.	**I** remember the teacher telling us . . . The images stuck in **his mind**. **Those** who believe in theory . . . The thought hit **me** that she was lying.
Desirer	An actor in a desiderative process.	**He**'s never hankered after the travelling life. **Joe** wanted to see the results. **He** still shrank from returning to England.
Perceiver	An actor in a perceptive process.	**She** watched him cross the road.
Emoter	An actor in an emotive process.	**She** likes her coffee strong. **I** envy her her confidence. Guilt gnawed at **him**. It is easy to delude **oneself** that the results do not matter.
Emoter-Actor	An actor who brings about a mental state in themselves.	**He** deluded himself that . . .

Table 4.6 (*cont.*)

Role	Explanation	Examples
Source	Something represented as doing something which leads to an inference.	**Similar tests** showed it to have a well-defined field of view.
Inferer	A person who draws an inference from a source.	The discovery proved to **us** that our theory was correct.
Time	A time period expressed as a perceiver.	**The third week** saw him finish the task.
'Thought-about' roles		
Phenomenon	A representation of what someone thinks or perceives.	He wondered **what she wanted**. I saw **some people I recognised** . . . She thought **him a fool**. She saw **him leave**.
Phenomenon-topic	A representation of the entity a person thinks or has an emotion about.	Both sides worried about **the ceasefire**.
Phenomenon-thought	An idea or emotion or expression conceptualised as an active participant in an act of cognition.	**The thought** hit me that she was lying. **Guilt** gnawed at him. He was seething with **anger**.
Inference	The information that is derived from a source.	The discovery proved **that our theory was correct**.
Other roles		
Cognition-cause	An entity that causes someone to think or feel something.	**Their actions** decided him against pushing on . . . . . . **an investigation** that shakes her out of her complacency. Migrants gain happiness from **moving to another country**.
Amount	An element that indicates that a lot or a little is shown.	. . . the study fails to reveal **much** about ordinary ideology . . .
Proxy	A person on whose behalf someone experiences an emotion.	I felt for **those players who played**.
Anticipatory	'It' or 'what' in a cleft or pseudo-cleft sentence that anticipates later content.	**What** I like about you is your innocence.

The first roles that might be identified are the 'speaker' or 'thinker' roles e.g. *we* and *my brother* in the previous Cognition and Communication examples. Within the Cognition field, Halliday's distinction between thinking, perceiving

Table 4.7 *Participant roles associated with the Communication semantic field*

Role	Explanation	Examples
'Speaker' roles		
Sayer	The speaker, writer, or signer in the representation of an act of communication. It may be a person, part of a person, or an institution.	**Debbie** asked them to pay her directly. Jeremy listened to **the soothing voice** until he fell asleep.
Source	An entity represented as the source of communication.	**The results** told us that the rocks dated from before the Ice Age.
Behaver	A person who communicates through voice or gesture.	**He** shot her an angry glance. **He** motioned to them. **He** chuckled at the memory.
'Hearer' roles		
Receiver	The person to whom speech, writing, signing, or paralinguistic communication is directed. Also a person who hears, reads or sees a communication.	He apologised to **the audience**. **She** listened intently to the broadcast. He shot **her** an angry glance. . . . beckoning **the others** to be quiet.
Inferer	A person who draws an inference from a source.	The results told **us** that the rocks dated from before the Ice Age.
'Speech content' roles		
Message	A representation of the content of communication.	Piaget argued **that children** . . . **lack the ability to explain** . . . The Council commanded the warden **to cease these unlawful practices**. He asked her **how old she was**. All the witnesses described **him leaving the bank**. . . . beckoning the others **to be quiet**.
Topic	A representation of the topic of communication but not the content itself.	Greenpeace has criticised **ICI's plans**. He told us **where the treasure was buried**. . . . both sides complained of **ceasefire violations**.
Inference	The information that is derived from a source.	The results told us **that the rocks dated from before the Ice Age**.
Other roles		
Scope	An element that is not acted on by the verb but that with the verb constitutes an act of communication.	She told us **a story**. He shot her **an angry glance**.
Amount	An element that indicates that a lot or a little is said.	He told us **a lot** about her.
Stimulus	Something that causes a behavioural reaction.	He chuckled at **the memory**.
Situation	An element used only with 'talk your way' to indicate a situation that is or is not the case as the result of communication.	. . . lie your way out of **a situation**.

and feeling is maintained (Halliday and Matthiessen 2014: 258), and the following roles are proposed:

- Cognizer: an actor in a cognitive mental process. E.g. *I remember the teacher telling us . . .*
- Desirer: an actor in a desiderative mental process. E.g. *Joe wanted to see the results.*
- Perceiver: an actor in a perceptive mental process. E.g. *She watched him cross the road.*
- Emoter: an actor in an emotive mental process. E.g. *I envy her her confidence.*

In the Communication field there is one equivalent role:

- Sayer: the speaker, writer or signer in the representation of an act of communication. E.g. *Debbie asked them to pay her directly.*

However, in both the Cognitive and Communication fields, an inanimate entity may be the source of information, as in examples (17) and (18):

(17) Similar tests showed it to have a well-defined field of view. (BNC)

(18) The results told us that the rocks dated from before the Ice Age. (BNC)

As argued in Hunston (2013), these examples are instances of interpersonal grammatical metaphor (Halliday and Matthiessen 2014: 659–731; Thompson 2014: 246–251). In both cases, the situation is construed as if the information arose unproblematically from inanimate entities: 'tests' and 'results'. Plausible paraphrases, however, would be 'Our reading of the tests/results led us to the conclusion that it had a well-defined field . . . / that the rocks dated . . . '. Both examples, therefore, could be said to belong to the semantic field of Cognition. In addition, in example (Example 18), an inanimate entity is represented as speaking (*told us*), as if it was animate. This example, then, belongs also to the Communication field. In both the Cognitive and Communication fields, the role of 'Source' is identified to account for instances such as these:

- Source (in Cognition): Something represented as doing something which leads to an inference. E.g. *Similar tests . . . showed it to have a well-defined field of view.* (BNC)
- Source (in Communication): An entity represented as the source of communication. E.g. *The results told us that the rocks dated from before the Ice Age.*

The complementary role to Sayer in the Communication field is 'Receiver'. This includes people who are aware of a communication, whether or not it is directed to them. Where the person receiving the message infers the message from a Source rather than from a Sayer, they are termed the Inferer. Unlike Receiver, the role of Inferer can be found in both the Communication and the Cognition fields:

- Receiver: The person to whom speech, writing, or signing is directed. Also, a person who listens to, hears, reads, or sees a communication. E.g. *I . . . apologised to the audience*. (BNC)
- Inferer: A person who draws an inference from a source. E.g. *The results told us that the rocks dated from before the Ice Age.*

The other main part of an act of thought or communication is what is variously called the Message (that which is said/written/signed) or the Phenomenon (that which is thought). The problem for coding is that Messages/Phenomena can be expressed in various forms, which can be combined or separated for coding. A common distinction (see, e.g. the previous discussion of FrameNet) is between a Message, which presents a form of words, or from which a form of words can be deduced, and a Topic, which does not. In the example *The Council commanded the warden to cease these unlawful practices*, it is a reasonable inference that the Council (is supposed to have) said something like 'You must cease these practices which are against the law'. However, in the example *They argued about the height of buildings* it is not possible to infer actual words, and *the height of buildings* might be more reasonably coded as a Topic than as a Message.

It is possible to propose finer distinctions in the Message or Phenomenon category. For instance, in an example such as *She called / thought him a fool*, it could be argued that the wording 'he is a fool' can be deduced and that this Message or Phenomenon represents a non-dynamic Situation. In contrast, the Message or Phenomenon elements of examples such as *She saw him leave* could be seen to represent a dynamic Situation ('he left') and those of examples such as *He asked / wanted to see the results* could be seen to represent an Action that took place as a result of a desire or communication ('he saw the results'). The difficulty with this level of granularity is that it is difficult to tell where to stop with making fine distinctions and with more closely related categories there is a greater danger of inconsistency. An alternative and simpler solution is to identify two roles in each of Communication and Cognition:

- Message: A representation of the content of communication. E.g. *He asked what she wanted; Piaget argued that children . . . lack the ability to explain . . . ; She called him a fool.*
- Topic: A representation of the topic of communication, but not the content itself. E.g. *Both sides complained of the ceasefire; Greenpeace has criticised ICI's plans.*
- Phenomenon: A representation of what someone thinks or perceives. E.g. *He wondered what she wanted; I saw some people I recognised; She saw him leave.*

- Phenomenon-Topic: A representation of the physical or abstract entity a person thinks or has an emotion about. E.g. *Both sides worried about the ceasefire.*

While these roles account for the most central instances of the Communication and Cognition fields, accounting for the many constructions in these fields necessitates the proposal of many other roles, some of which have a very restricted use. For example, the role Proxy is used only with constructions such as ‘sympathise with someone’ or ‘feel for someone’ and the role Emoter-Actor is used only in constructions with a reflexive pronoun (e.g. *He deluded himself that* . . .). Tables 4.6 and 4.7 give a full account of the roles used.

Special mention should be made of constructions which sit on the periphery of the Communication or Cognition semantic fields and which are therefore annotated with roles that are less predictable in the context of Communication or Cognition than those previously discussed. Mostly these are connected with metaphoric representations of cognitive acts. In Cognition (Table 4.6) an example would be the role Time, which is used when a period of time is represented metaphorically as though it were a participant in an act of perception. Another example is the role Phenomenon-thought, where an idea or emotion is expressed as an active participant, with the Cognizer or Emoter having a more passive role. In the following example, the verb *hit* is a material process, though the construction as a whole construes an act of thinking.

- Time: A time period expressed as a perceiver. E.g. *The third week saw him finish the task.*
- Phenomenon-thought: An idea or emotion or expression conceptualised as an active participant in an act of cognition. E.g. *The thought hit me that she was lying.*

Specialised roles in Communication (Table 4.7) include ‘Scope’. This is a term used by Halliday (e.g. Halliday and Matthiessen 2014: 496); it is used here to denote an element that is not acted upon by the verb; instead verb and noun together express an action e.g. ‘sing a song’ or ‘tell a story’. Another example is Behaver, which indicates someone who communicates paralinguistically, through a vocalisation such as laughter, a facial expression or a gesture. In SFG, these constructions would belong to the Behavioural process type rather than Verbal (Halliday and Matthiessen 2014: 301–302), whereas in this book they are treated as part of the Communication semantic field. Where the Behaver responds to something, that is termed the Stimulus.

- Scope: An element that is not acted on by the verb but that with the verb constitutes an act of communication. E.g. *She told us a story.*

- Behaver: A person who communicates through voice or gesture but without words. E.g. *He shot her an angry glance.*
- Stimulus: Something that causes a behavioural reaction. E.g. *He chuckled at the memory.*

Recording the Semantic Roles

The constructions that are interpretable in terms of one or more of these nine semantic fields have been annotated on the Transitivity-Net website. Table 4.8 gives an example. The pattern illustrated in that table is **V n that** (verb + noun phrase + that-clause) and the construction is the 'persuade someone that something is the case' construction. The description of this construction is: 'A person causes someone to change their cognition'. This description distinguishes the construction from similar ones such as 'inform someone that something is the case', where a change in cognition may well take place but it is not entailed by the construction. The 'persuade' construction is recorded as using only two verbs: PERSUADE and CONVINCE. Example (19) illustrates this construction.

(19) Gould succeeded in persuading Darwin that his were the right decisions. (BNC)

The annotation schema treats the construction as having three relevant components: NP1 (*Gould* in example (19)); NP2 (*Darwin*); that-clause (*that his were the right decisions*). It is worth noting that it is the construction rather than the example that is being coded. If the example were in the passive ('Darwin was persuaded that Gould was right'), *Darwin* would still have to be interpreted as NP2.

This construction belongs to both the Communication and the Causation semantic fields, so has a double coding: Sayer, Receiver, and Message; and Cause, Affected, and Result. Table 4.8 shows how this appears on the website.

Table 4.8 *A database entry showing participant role annotation*

Pattern	V n that
Construction name	the persuade someone that something is the case construction
Construction number	4
Construction description	A person causes someone to change their cognition.
Verbs	convince, persuade
Example	Gould succeeded in persuading Darwin that his were the right decisions.
Semantic field and roles	Communication. NP1: Sayer; NP2: Receiver; that-clause: Message Causation. NP1: Cause; NP2: Affected; that-clause: Result

4.7 Conclusion

This chapter has explained the choices, and in some cases the dilemmas, involved in mapping semantic roles onto the formal elements of constructions. This has been discussed in the context of other approaches to the same issue, from SFG, CPA, LG, and FrameNet. The point has been made that the selection of semantic role labels is dependent on the starting point of the research project and its purpose. In this project, the annotation has been carried out in relation to nine semantic fields only. For each field, a finite set of labels is used to annotate all the constructions identified as belonging to that field. The labels are not drawn from any one approach, but they are inspired mostly by the participant roles in SFG. This marks a shift in the focus of this book from an emphasis on constructions to an emphasis on SFG. Chapter 5 provides background on SFG.

5 Background to Systemic Functional Grammar

5.1 Introduction: Systemic Functional Linguistics

Founded on the work of Michael Halliday, Systemic Functional Linguistics (SFL) commands a huge following and proposes an all-encompassing theory of language (Matthiessen 2023). In Halliday's approach, language is primarily a social, as opposed to mental, phenomenon. Systemic Functional Linguistics is also a theory of meaning, being concerned with what meanings a society makes and how (Halliday 2013: 194; Webster 2019: 36). Rather than representing language as a series of rules, SFL regards language as a set of resources; these are represented as paradigmatic systems that express the options available to the language user.

In producing an instance of language, a speaker has a range of options available that can be used to construe the social or physical or internal world in a specific way. The role of the linguist is to identify what resources are available and how they might be modelled. The connection between 'what people say', 'what they might have said', and 'how we see the world' has made SFL the theory most used in Critical Discourse Analysis and other approaches concerned with the social impact of language (O'Grady 2019).

As a comprehensive theory of language, SFL offers ways of modelling aspects such as context (Taverniers 2021), genre (Hasan 1996/1984), evaluative language (Martin and White 2005), and multimodal communication (Kress and van Leeuwen 2006). Detailed accounts of Systemic Function Linguistics can be found in Bartlett and O'Grady (2017) and Thompson et al. (2019). At the heart of SFL, however, is the lexicogrammar: the resources of lexis and grammar that are used in the production of individual utterances. The hybrid term 'lexicogrammar' indicates that for Halliday, lexis and grammar comprise a single system for making meaning. The following section will explain Systemic Functional Grammar (SFG) in more detail, and this is followed by a section discussing approaches to the place of lexis in the model. The final section explains the use made of SFG in this book.

5.2 A Brief Introduction to Systemic Functional Grammar

The fullest account of SFG is found in Halliday and Matthiessen (2014), and a more accessible account is found in Thompson (2014).

The clause is the central unit of lexicogrammar, and a key innovation in Halliday's model is that any clause performs three functions and is analysed in three ways: as a construal of experience (the experiential metafunction); as an enactment of social relations (the interpersonal metafunction); and as a means of creating discourse (the textual metafunction) (Webster 2019: 36). Figure 5.1 (adapted from Thompson 2014: 34, figure 3.8) shows three analyses applied to a single clause: 'Did you take her calculator just now?' The experiential, or ideational analysis identifies the Process element, the Participants that accompany it (Actor and Goal), and a Circumstance. In other words, the experiential analysis tells us about the situation construed by the clause: who did what kind of action to what and when. The interpersonal analysis deals with the fact that the clause is a question: one person is seeking information from another. This is expressed by the splitting of the Finite element of the verb phrase from the Predicator, and the insertion of the Subject between them. The textual analysis is concerned with the order of the information given. In Figure 5.1, the clause begins with the Finite and Subject elements – these constitute the Theme or initial part of the clause. The rest of the clause constitutes the Rheme.

The clause illustrated in Figure 5.1 makes use of particular options in the experiential, interpersonal, and textual metafunctions. Alternative versions of the clause would construe different meanings. Examples (1)–(4) illustrate this.

(1) Did you take her calculator just now?

(2) You took her calculator just now.

(3) Her calculator was taken by you just now.

(4) The theft of the calculator was wrong.

Example (1) is the original clause from Thompson (2014: 34). Example (2) makes changes that affect the interpersonal metafunction: the clause is now a statement not a question. Example (3) is in the passive and this change affects

Type of structure	Did	you	take	her calculator	just now?
experiential		Actor	Process	Goal	Circumstance
interpersonal	Finite	Subject	Predicator	Complement	Adjunct
textual	Theme		Rheme		

Figure 5.1 Analysis of a clause showing three metafunctions (from Thompson 2014: 34)

the textual metafunction: the starting point or Theme of the clause is 'her calculator' instead of 'you'. Example (4) makes a change to the experiential metafunction: the process is one of being, expressed by the verb 'was', instead of one of doing, expressed by 'take'. The action of taking is construed by the noun 'theft' – it is a 'thing' rather than an 'action'.

Later versions of SFG include a fourth metafunction: the logical metafunction (Thompson 2014: 38), which relates to connections between clauses. In this book, we are concerned with the experiential or ideational metafunction only. From the perspective of this metafunction, a clause 'construes a quantum of change in the flow of events as a figure, or configuration of a process, participants involved in it and any attendant circumstances' (Halliday and Matthiessen 2014: 212). Thompson (2014: 92) puts this more prosaically:

> From the experiential perspective, language comprises a set of resources for referring to entities in the world and the ways in which those entities act on or relate to each other.

Those resources are modelled as networks of transitivity, one of which is the classification of process types. The process types identified by Halliday are: Material, Mental, Relational, Verbal, Behavioural, and Existential (Thompson 2014: 95–111). The first three of these are the most basic in that they construe three different types of situation: a dynamic one where events take place (Material); a static one where relationships exist between entities or events (Relational); and one where the situation exists in the 'inner world' of someone's mind (Mental). The other process types account for clauses that do not fit the first three types. The division into process types is to some extent a semantic classification. For example, the process 'take' in example (1) means that a physical action took place, whereas the process 'was' in example (4) expresses the relationship between the act of theft and the evaluation of it as wrong. The process type in example (1) is Material, while the process type in example (4) is Relational.

However, the identification of process types is not left to a subjective judgement of meaning. Instead, process types are identified by grammatical behaviour and participant type. For example, Material process verbs are unremarkably found in the progressive ('he is running'), while Mental process verbs are more likely to be found in simple aspect ('she thinks'). Verbal process verbs are typically complemented by a that-clause ('she said that . . . '). In terms of participants, Material processes have Actor and Goal as participants, while Mental processes have Senser (person who thinks) and Phenomenon (what they think). Process, participant and circumstance together constitute transitivity (Webster 2019: 38). The semantic fields identified in this book (see Chapter 4) are inspired by, but are not reliant on, these process types. Similarly, the participant roles are inspired by those in Halliday's framework.

As previously noted, Halliday sees meaning as paradigmatic and contrastive: the meaning of a language feature depends on what other features are available in that context. The paradigm is expressed as a system network. Matthiessen (2023: 7) notes that system networks 'model [language] theoretically as a resource rather than as a system of rules'. Webster (2019: 43) describes system networks as 'a way to represent meaning potential not simply syntagmatically as an inventory of sequentially ordered items, but instead primarily as paradigmatically organized sets of options', though as Thompson (2014: 35) points out, describing a node in a network as a 'choice' does not mean that the speaker consciously chooses between options. Neither, as Matthiessen (2023: 206) notes, should the network be read as a taxonomy. Rather, the network represents the full set of meaning resources available to the speaker (Matthiessen 2023: 7). The network arrangement shows the dependency of one choice upon another. Moving from left to right along the network, the items become more specific: in Halliday's terminology, there is an increase in 'delicacy' (Thompson 2014: 36). System networks have been devised for all areas of language (Matthiessen 2023). Figure 5.2 shows a simple network for Mood choices in English. The information and layout come from Thompson (2014: 41), but the figure uses the type of diagram used in this book, rather than the conventional SFG format. Reading from left to right, this figure summarises the following information:

- An independent clause in English may be indicative or imperative. If it is indicative, it may be interrogative or declarative.

The network might also be read right to left, though this is the less conventional approach. In this case, the figure summarises this information:

- Clauses in English may be interrogative, declarative, or imperative. Interrogative and declarative clauses are like each other in that both are indicative, whereas imperative clauses are not. All the clause types are subcategories of independent clause.

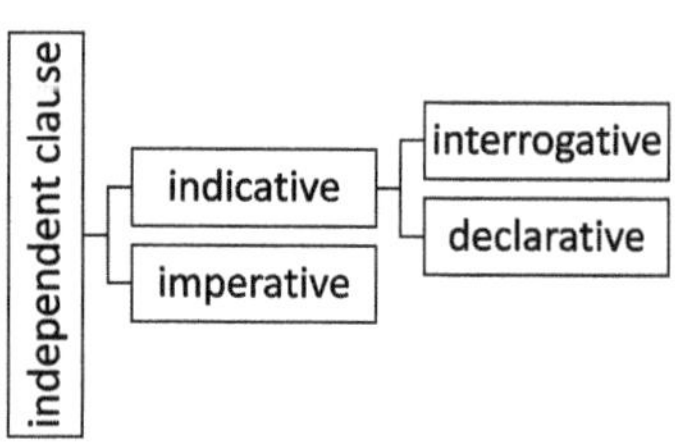

Figure 5.2 Mood choices in English (adapted from Thompson 2014: 41)

In drawing system networks, square brackets are used to show mutually exclusive alternatives. Curly brackets are used to show simultaneous, or independent, choices. An example is shown in Figure 5.3, which is a simplified version of part only of the network of mental processes shown in Halliday and Matthiessen (2014: 258), but using the layout used in this book. It shows that there is a choice between types of sensing (whether the process is one of thinking, wanting, seeing, etc.), but also a choice between directions of sensing: whether the event is construed as the Senser acting on the thing, as in 'Peter liked the film', or as the thing acting on the Senser, as in 'The film pleased Peter'. Finally, there is a choice between whether the phenomenon is specified in the clause or not. Thus, an example such as (5)

(5) I liked the poem about Grantchester. (BNC2014)

is the consequence of three independent or simultaneous choices: it is the emotive type of sensing, it is the emanating direction, and the phenomenon ('the poem') is specified in the clause. It therefore contrasts with three different alternative clauses, shown here as examples (6)–(8):

(6) I considered the poem about Grantchester. (cognitive, not emotive)

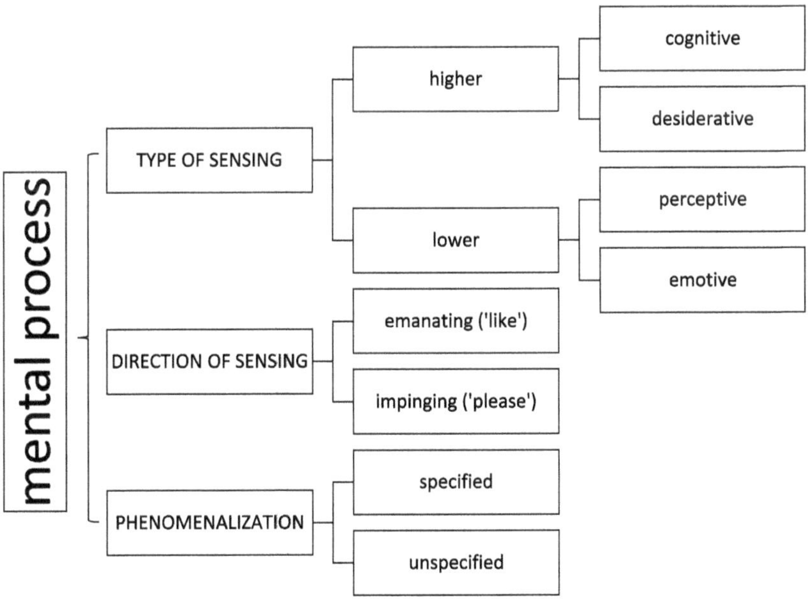

Figure 5.3 A simplified network for mental processes (adapted from Halliday and Matthiessen 2014: 258)

(7) The poem about Grantchester pleased me. (impinging, not emanating)

(8) I rejoiced (when I read the poem). (phenomenon unspecified in the clause)

Although SFG involves a qualitative assignment of category labels, it has embraced the opportunities for quantitative research offered by Corpus Linguistics (Halliday 1993: 1; Matthiessen 1999, 2006). Halliday and James (1993) found that, in an 18 million word corpus, clauses with positive or negative polarity occurred in a ratio of approximately 9:1, while clauses with present or past tense occurred in the ratio 5:5. This accorded with Halliday's view that system options would tend to be 'skew' (like polarity) or 'equi' (like tense) (Halliday and James 1993: 35). Where two options have equal probability, there is no marked or unmarked form, whereas where the probability is skew, the less probable form is marked. Halliday and James (1993) raise the question of whether genre/register would greatly change these figures, a question answered from work in a different tradition (Biber et al. 1999). Biber et al. (1999: 456) demonstrate, for example, that present and past tense are roughly equal in news discourse, but that present tense predominates in conversation and academic discourse, while past tense is more frequent in fiction. Matthiessen (2006) measures the frequency of process types: material and relational processes occur with approximately equal frequency, then mental and verbal, and finally behavioural and existential processes. These frequencies are to some extent dependent on register: material, relational, and verbal processes are proportionally more frequent in written than spoken registers, whereas mental and behavioural processes are proportionally more frequent in spoken registers. He also shows in detail how the frequency of various language features such as process type and mood vary against each other; in other words, the probability of one choice within a system depends on choices within other systems. For example, whereas all process types are most likely to take the 'declarative' mood choice, the process types of relational and existential are very unlikely to take the 'imperative' choice and verbal process clauses are less likely to be yes/no interrogatives than the other process types are (Matthiessen 2006: 129). Detailed quantitative work of this nature is essential in the exploration of the uniqueness of single texts or collections of texts – what makes them representative of or markedly different from others from a similar context. The outcome might be explained in terms of 'style' or of 'ideological bias', or similar.

As the remainder of this book makes considerable use of networks, it is necessary to mention an important caveat. Of necessity, networks represent 'either/or' choices: a clause is either active or passive; a process is either mental or material, and so on. However, many categories are 'fuzzy' and blend into one another, meaning that a network representation is somewhat idealised, to the point where it may be inaccurate. Thompson (2014: 77) follows Martin and White (2005) in using a slanting line in a network to show that choices are placed on a cline rather than in opposition to each other. This is in a network of choices in modality: the type of modality is either modalization or modulation, but the level of commitment, ranging from high to low, is a continuum rather than an either/or. More radically, typologies that are represented as system networks can instead be represented as 'topologies' (Halliday and Matthiessen 2014: 217–220). This is particularly relevant to process types, which instead of being shown in a network (either material or mental or relational etc.), can be shown as a continuous circle: relational blending into verbal, which blends into mental, which blends into behavioural and so on. This is the representation of process types chosen for the cover of Halliday (1994). Although the current book prioritises the typological over the topological, it is worth remembering that both representations exist.

5.3 Perspectives on Systemic Functional Grammar and Lexis

There is agreement that some features of language are 'grammar-like' and some are 'lexis-like'. In English, inverting the order of Subject and Verb changes a declarative clause to an interrogative one: this is a 'grammar' observation. The use of the word *cast* in *cast your mind back to …* is a 'lexis' observation. There are (at least) three ways of looking at this distinction. One view is that grammar and lexis are entities of different kinds that are described using different frameworks and stored in different parts of the brain. Information about them is found in different books – dictionaries and grammars. An alternate view is that grammar and lexis are not distinct: 'pieces of language' consist of both closed-class grammar features and open-class lexical features, but the relationship between the 'grammar-like' and the 'lexis-like' is not systematic. What lies between the extremes of 'grammar-like' and 'lexis-like' could be represented as a cloud rather than as a taxonomy (Herbst 2024).

The third view, from SFG, is that lexis and grammar form a continuum. According to Matthiessen (2023: 80): 'The stratum of lexicogrammar is extended systemically (i.e. along the paradigmatic axis) in delicacy from the grammatical zone to the lexical zone.' Interestingly, in light of the approach taken in this book, Matthiessen' (2023: 81) proposes 'constructions' as lying between grammar and lexis. He argues that:

> Lexical distinctions will be located within systems whose points of origin are grammatical; they do not suddenly appear mid-delicacy unrelated to any grammatical systems. Paradigmatically, the move along the cline of delicacy from grammar is a move from closed systems to open sets; and syntagmatically, it is a move from grammatical structures to lexical collocations. (Matthiessen 2023: 82)

Matthiessen exemplifies this principle in relation to all the metafunctions. Under the heading of 'experiential', he proposes a movement from the system of process type, to the closed systems of 'grammaticalized lexical verbs' (DO, HAPPEN), to 'high-frequency verbs' that have features of both closed systems and open sets (DO, MAKE, TAKE; SAY, THINK; BE, HAVE), to open sets of verbs.

In principle, then, it should be possible to move along the continuum from the most general choices, such as between process types, to the most specific, or most delicate, such as between verb types (Neale 2006: 143; Matthiessen 2014: 143; Davidse 2017). In practice, determining how to integrate observations about lexis and those about grammar has proved far from straightforward, and a number of different proposals have been put forward. This section focuses on four studies: Hasan's seminal paper on 'the grammarian's dream' (Hasan 1996/1987); Matthiessen's (2014) reinterpretation of Levin's (1993) work on alternations; the 'Cardiff Grammar' as discussed in the work of Fawcett (2017), Neale (2002, 2006) and Chrispin (2021); and Fontaine's (2017, 2025) alternative view.

Hasan: The Grammarian's Dream

The proposal to extend the representation of grammar as paradigmatic system into lexis has been referred to as 'the grammarian's dream' (Halliday 1961: 267; Hasan 1996/1987: 73; Matthiessen 2023: 80). Neale (2006: 143) points out that this could be achieved by going from the grammar to the lexis, or vice versa. Hasan (1996/1987) adopts the second of these options, with lexis as the starting point. She discusses groups of verbs drawn from the same semantic field, such as GATHER, COLLECT, ACCUMULATE, SCATTER, DIVIDE, DISTRIBUTE, STREW, SPILL, and SHARE (Hasan 1996/1987: 99). These are instances of material process, specifically 'action' processes. She then devises networks to account for the differences between them. The class of 'action' is divided into types such as 'disposal', 'transformation', and 'locomotion' (and others that are not specified in the paper). The verbs GATHER, COLLECT etc. all belong to the 'disposal' type. Distinguishing between them requires the application of several criteria rather than a simple grouping into types. To put this another way, a system network specifying a number of simultaneous feature paradigms is needed. Taking 'disposal' as the entry point, there are two major simultaneous paradigms: 'access' and 'character'. Under 'access', the choice is between 'acquisition' (e.g. GATHER) and 'deprivation' (e.g. DISTRIBUTE). Under 'character', the choice is between 'iterative' (e.g. ACCUMULATE) and 'non-iterative', which is not discussed in the paper. Simultaneously with all of these is another set of choices, with 'action' as the entry point, under the heading of 'benefaction'. The options are 'beneficile' (e.g. *gather Mary some flowers*) and non-beneficile (e.g. the impossibility of **scatter Mary some flowers*). Within each of these options there are further choices, many dependent on choices at other points in the network, leading to a complex system network.

One way of looking at the network is that it acts as a heuristic in identifying the features that are of significance in distinguishing between verbs. It answers the question 'What makes GATHER different from ACCUMULATE and DISTRIBUTE different from SCATTER?' For example, the verb GATHER is an example of 'acquisition', not 'deprivation'; it is used with plural nouns that construe discrete items, such as *flowers*, but not uncount nouns such as *water*; it construes an 'iterative' action; it can be used with a benefitting party that can be indicated in an object or in a prepositional phrase ('gather someone some flowers'/'gather flowers for someone'). The networks are also used to describe the options taken up in specific instances of verb use. One of the examples quoted by Hasan is shown here as example (9):

(9) She divided the apple between John and Jenny. (Hasan 1996/1987: 93)

Here the verb *divided* realises the following options: 'deprivation' (not 'acquisition'); 'iterative'; 'inherent benefactor'; 'planned' (not 'random'); 'constrained' (the benefactors must be in a prepositional phrase).

Hasan's paper on 'the grammarian's dream' is referred to in all subsequent work on lexis within the SFG framework. It is important in many ways. For one thing, it demonstrated that the concept of treating lexis in the same way as grammar is a valid one. That is, it is possible to itemise the resources available and to model each instance of usage as the outcome of choices within those resources. The idea of binary choice, and of simultaneous choice, can be applied to the fine distinctions between verbs as it can to the more abstract concepts of transitivity. Secondly, it showed that modelling the distinction between verbs requires that attention be paid to features of meaning; that is, a verb has to be considered as a bundle of meaning features, rather than as an item with a simple meaning. Finally, discussion of examples such as (9) shows that, when the feature choices are instantiated, they are instantiated as a verb in context (in this case 'divide entity between people'), or, it might be said, as a construction, rather than as a verb alone.

Although Hasan's work is much admired, the amount of manual work involved made it unfeasible to extend it across all semantic fields (Matthiessen 2014: 147). Subsequent work on the grammar and lexis continuum, of the kind discussed next, has involved two major departures. Firstly, information from other approaches to lexis has been incorporated into the research. This includes references to Levin (Matthiessen 2014), Construction Grammar, FrameNet, Pattern Grammar (Neale 2002; Matthiessen 2014), and Corpus Pattern Analysis – CPA (Chrispin 2021). Secondly, the emphasis has shifted from identifying the distinguishing features of groups of verbs to allocating verbs to process types and sub-types, thus testing and expanding the process type framework. It might be said that a final legacy of Hasan's work is to inspire further research exploiting the synergies between SFG and other traditions, in particular corpus-based research.

Matthiessen: Process Type and Levinian Verb Classes

Matthiessen (2014: 141) credits both Halliday and Fillmore with developing grammars of transitivity but distinguishes between Halliday's focus on the paradigmatic and Fillmore's concern with the syntagmatic. He sees more similarity between Halliday's work and that of Levin (1993), arguing that: 'they are concerned with paradigmatic contrasts (or as Levin calls it, with 'diathesis alternations' (argument alternations)), they see grammar and lexis as continuous, and they are based on the insight that grammar is semantically natural . . .' (Matthiessen 2014: 143).

Matthiessen (2014: 144) seeks to extend the delicacy of process types, moving from the 'most general' distinctions between six process types (material, relational, mental, etc.) towards the 'least general' distinctions between lexis. He argues that to occupy this area of 'mid-range delicacy' successfully, it is necessary to draw on the work of large-scale classification projects, such as FrameNet (Ruppenhofer et al. 2016), or the COBUILD project (Francis et al. 1996), or Levin's verb classes project (Levin 1993).

Levin (1993) reports the output of a large project to classify verbs in English based on the combination of behaviours (or alternations) they allow. In a simple example (Levin 1993: 6–7), she shows that four transitive verbs (TOUCH, HIT, CUT, and BREAK) each permit a different combination of behaviours. This may be summarised thus (terminology is a simplified version of that used by Levin):

- The 'two argument' behaviour e.g. 'Margaret cut the bread' is allowed by all the verbs.
- The 'middle' behaviour e.g. 'Crystal vases break easily' is allowed by CUT and BREAK only.
- The 'conative' behaviour e.g. 'Carla hit at the door' is allowed by HIT and CUT only.
- The 'body part' behaviour e.g. 'Terry touched Bill on the shoulder' is allowed by TOUCH, HIT, and CUT only.

Thus, each of these four verbs has a unique combination of behaviours. However, if other verbs are subjected to the same behaviour tests, it is found that there is a group that shares all behaviours with BREAK (e.g. CRACK, RIP, SHATTER, SNAP), a group that behaves like CUT (e.g. HACK, SAW, SCRATCH, SLASH), a group that behaves like TOUCH (e.g. PAT, STROKE, TICKLE), and a group that behaves like HIT (e.g. BASH, KICK, POUND,

TAP). It is entirely feasible, in other words, to classify verbs into groups based on alternations such as these. Overall, Levin classifies 3,100 verbs divided into 48 primary classes, 150 secondary classes, and 29 tertiary classes. Matthiessen (2014: 152) illustrates the notion of 'primary', 'secondary', and 'tertiary' with the example of 'verbs of motion'. 'Verbs of motion' constitute the primary class (e.g. MOVE). One of the secondary classes is 'Verbs of motion using a vehicle' (e.g. RIDE). One of the tertiary classes is: 'Verbs of motion using a vehicle that are vehicle names' (e.g. HELICOPTER).

Matthiessen (2014: 144) reinterprets Levin's work in SFG terms. He argues that 'verb classes and alternations' can be seen as 'transitivity configurations', with processes, participants, and circumstances, and proposes to 'interpret her verb classes as clause nuclei'. He specifically locates these clause nuclei as occupying a space between the least delicate 'Grammar' and the most delicate 'Lexis', describing them as 'more delicate process types'.

Matthiessen then classifies Levin's verb classes into the SFG process types. He finds that all the primary classes can be allocated to a process type, but that some of the secondary classes from the same primary one have to be allocated to different types. An interesting example is illustrated by the verb PEER in the example *she peered at the dog*. Levin classes this as a 'perception' verb, but Matthiessen classifies it as 'behavioural' (not 'mental – perception'). This is because *at the dog* is analysed in SFG as a circumstance not a participant (Matthiessen 2014: 160). In the Pattern Grammar work, this distinction between participant and circumstance is elided, and the example treated as though 'peer at' is the verb and 'the dog' the Object.

The result of Matthiessen's work is on the one hand a validation of the SFL process types (mostly) and on the other hand a taxonomy of more delicate process types that successfully progresses the process type networks towards greater delicacy of description. He does, however, insist on a distinction between taxonomy and system, arguing that:

> . . . while Levin's (1993) scheme is a strict taxonomy, a systemic description represented in a system network is not; there are often simultaneous systems in a system network, such as the systems of PROCESS TYPE and AGENCY, and interactions between simultaneous systems . . . must be taken into account when the systemic description of motion or of any other experiential field is extended in delicacy. The result is likely to be a multi-dimensional description of a field such as motion of the kind that can be accommodated in a system network . . . rather than a one-dimensional one of the kind that can be accommodated in a strict taxonomy. (Matthiessen 2014: 158)

In the subsequent chapters of this book I shall propose that to account for the verbs and patterns involved in expressing a semantic field, two kinds of network are needed. In Matthiessen's terms, the one-dimensional taxonomies are what I shall call 'Meaning Networks', and the multidimensional system networks are what I shall call 'Systemic Networks'.

Matthiessen (2014: 168) concludes that:

> the fact that it proved possible to classify all her [Levin's] verb classes in terms of the six process types and their more delicate subtypes can be seen as powerful evidence for current views that grammar and lexis form a continuum.

This comment holds true provided that 'grammar' is defined to include the distinction between process types.

The Cardiff Grammar

Although all researchers in SFL follow the same principles, there are inevitably differences of perspective and methodology. A team of researchers based at Cardiff University have developed a model of lexicogrammar which differs in some key respects from the 'classical' SFL model based on Halliday's work. The Cardiff Model (or Cardiff Grammar) is based on the work of Fawcett (summarised in Fawcett 2017), though of most relevance to the current book is the work of Tucker (1998), Neale (2002, 2006), and Chrispin (2021).

One of the features of the Cardiff Grammar is that it places emphasis on the findings of Corpus Linguistics, particularly the focus on phraseology and on the idiosyncratic behaviour of individual words. An early and highly influential attempt to build system networks to account for lexical items is Tucker's (1998) work on adjectives. Tucker works with 200 adjective senses and builds networks that essentially explore the grammatical roles of adjectives and the range of meanings they express. The broadest categories of meaning are (Tucker 1998: 125):

- Relative quality i.e. similarity, familiarity, normality
- Situation-oriented quality i.e. usuality, likelihood, and event
- Thing-oriented quality, divided into epithetic and classifying
  - Epithetic quality i.e. evaluative, effect, dimension, and physical, **typically human**, age, colour
  - Classifying quality i.e. substance, identity, human, and domain

Further system networks give further detail of each of these categories. To take an example, the 'typically human' type of adjective, shown in bold, is divided into physical state, behaviour, emotion, and social status (Tucker 1998:133). One interesting feature of Tucker's work is its similarity to and difference from Martin and White's (2005) Appraisal framework. The quality 'normality' is one of the subcategories of Judgement in Martin and White's framework, for example. To take another instance, Tucker's 'evaluative' meaning network identifies as separate qualities 'function', 'moral judgement', 'fact', 'value', 'aesthetic', and 'emotive'. Function and Moral Judgement might be said to align with Martin and White's category of Judgement, while Value, Aesthetic quality and Emotive (e.g. *fantastic*) align with Appreciation. In general, Tucker (1998) and Martin and White (2005) observe similar categories but arrange the networks accounting for them differently. This is because their starting point is different: Tucker explores the behaviour of adjectives; Martin and White explore the semantic area of evaluation.

According to Fawcett's (2017) account, the Cardiff Model differs from the Sydney (Halliday's) Model in several key respects. One is the insistence that a model of language should be testable and verifiable. The second is the inclusion of a cognitive dimension to the model – what is specified in the Cardiff Model is how a speaker produces an utterance, using resources that are similar to, though not identical to, the systemic networks developed by Halliday and others. The process of production requires the concept not only of language resources but also of realisation rules that take the speaker from the available options to the actual words said or written. Fawcett (2017: 71) notes that:

> Unlike the SM [Sydney Model], the CM's [Cardiff Model's] cognitive-interactive architecture introduces several different types of component, each with a processor or structure appropriate for its function (e.g. decision trees for the microplanners, and taxonomies for the belief system).

The validity of this model is tested by using it to program computers to produce utterances, following the proposed realisation rules. These realisation rules incorporate what might be called the higher level, or more grammar-like systems (Mood, Theme, etc.), but also incorporate the grammatical behaviour of specific lexical items.

Of most relevance to this book, however, is the set of process types proposed by the Cardiff Model, which is somewhat different from those found in the Sydney Model and in the work of Matthiessen, Thompson, and Hasan, discussed earlier. The 'Cardiff' process types are: 'Action'; 'Relational'; 'Mental'; 'Influential'; 'Event-relating'; 'Environmental'. Neale (2017) itemises each process type and lists the sub-types that have different configurations of participant roles. She also details the tests used to determine each sub-type. For illustration, the following are the process types, each with two examples of the many sub-types identified, taken from Neale (2017):

- Action. Examples of sub-types:
    - Agent only e.g. *We all used to cheat in exams*. 'we all' = Agent; 'cheat' = Process.
    - Agent + Range e.g. *Have you read that article*? 'you' = Agent; 'read' = Process; 'that article' = Range.

- Relational. Examples of sub-types:
  - Simple Carrier + Attribute e.g. *He doesn't resemble the robber.* 'he' = Carrier; 'resemble' = Process; 'the robber' = Attribute.
  - Affected Carrier + Location e.g. *Soviet Territory borders on Poland.* 'Soviet Territory' = Affected Carrier; 'borders' = Process; 'Poland' = Location.

- Mental. Examples of sub-types:
  - Emoter + Phemenon, Emoter-oriented e.g. *She is in love with him.* 'she' = Emoter; 'is in love with' = Process; 'him' = Phenomenon
  - Affected-perceiver + Phenomenon + Agent e.g. *Francis concealed the machine from us.* 'Francis' = Agent; 'concealed' = Process; 'the machine' = Phenomenon; 'us' = Affected-perceiver.

- Influential. Examples of sub-types:
  - Agent + Created Participant, causative e.g. *The state must ensure law-abiding people are protected.* 'the state' = Agent; 'ensure' = Process; 'law-abiding people are protected' = Created Participant.
  - Affected + Range, stage of process e.g. *The girder kept on bending.* 'the girder' = Affected; 'kept on' = Process; 'bending' = Range.

- 'Event-relating'. Examples of sub-types:
  - Cause + Range, cause-to-effect e.g. *A degree in English could lead to a carer in journalism.* 'a degree in English' = Cause; 'lead to' = Process; 'a career in journalism' = Range.
  - Cause + Range, premise-to-inference e.g. *The merger will mean the closure of the company's Sydney office.* 'the merger' = Cause; 'mean' = Process; 'the closure of the company's Sydney office' = Range.

- 'Environmental'
  - As process e.g. *It rained.* 'rained' = Process.
  - As attribute e.g. *It is sunny.* 'is' = Process; 'sunny' = Attribute.

One point of note here is the willingness to treat verb + prepositions, such as *lead to* or *kept on*, or even phrases such as *is in love with* as single Processes.

Further work in the Cardiff tradition has used methods and output from Corpus Linguistics studies to identify groups of verbs and assess their alignment with the Cardiff process types. The hypothesis is that if verbs that have been observed to have similar behaviour (the same alternations, in Levin's (1993) terms), they form a class that should be accountable for within the process type taxonomy. If a class of verbs needs to be split across process types, this suggests that the taxonomy needs to be adjusted. Two examples of such work is briefly summarised here: Neale (2002) and Chrispin (2021). Neale (2002) uses West's (1953) *A General Service List of English Words* as well as the verb descriptions in the Collins COBUILD English Dictionary (Sinclair 1995) and in Francis et al. (1996) as the source of information on the behaviour of verbs. Chrispin (2021) undertakes a CPA (Hanks 2004) of selected intransitive verbs in order to classify them.

The outcome of Neale's (2002) research is a Process Type Database of 5,400 verb senses in English, based on the most frequent verbs in English as identified by Francis et al. (1996). Each sense is annotated for its process type and its configuration of participant roles. The basis for her analysis is the Cardiff Grammar process types and a set of 27 participant roles, also based on the Cardiff Grammar (Neale 2002: 220). In simple terms, verb senses are annotated with whether each participant is always, sometimes, or never found. Neale (2002: 235) claims three important innovations: she includes realisation rules in keeping with the Cardiff Grammar; she includes multi-word verbs whereas most similar endeavours exclude them; she includes estimates of probabilities of each item in the system network, i.e. the relative frequencies. The verbs are grouped in terms of meaning, using various resources such as Levin (1993), Francis et al. (1996), and Roget's *Thesaurus*. The end point of the research is a series of system networks that extend in delicacy from the process type to a set of verbs. Neale (2002) exemplifies this with three examples:

1 Action process type, one role, affected only;
2 Action process type, two roles, agent plus affected;
3 Relational process type, three roles, directional.

To give a sense of the networks proposed, we will follow a series of choices starting with the first kind of Action process, where there is only one participant, who is affected by the process. There are four sub-types: stopping being, change of state, involuntary behaviour, and emission. Of these, 'change of state' is estimated to account for 60 per cent of the total verbs. This is further divided into 'change of state as such' and 'change of state specified'. The latter accounts for 80 per cent of the total. In turn, this group is divided into several subgroups, one of which is 'change by moving', which accounts for 40 per cent of the 'change of state specified' group (Neale 2002: 240). 'Change by moving' has five subcategories, one of which is 'moving relative to upright state'. A further system divides this into specific meanings: capsizing, overturning, toppling, and overbalancing (Neale 2002: 246).

This brief illustration shows the progression in delicacy from Process Type to group of verbs. Figure 5.4 is derived from several figures from Neale (2002), omitting all information except the route through from 'change of state' to the specified verbs.

Following Neale's pioneering work, Chrispin (2021) also uses corpus data, and some secondary corpus data, to challenge and support SFL claims. Her focus is 'pure' intransitive verbs, that is, verbs that are used only intransitively

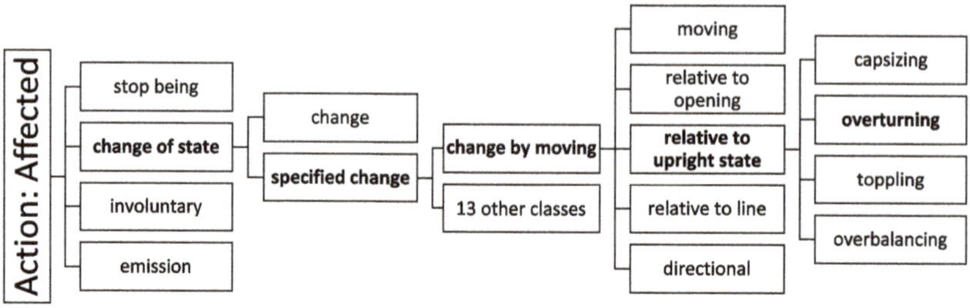

Figure 5.4 Progression in delicacy from 'Action: Affected participant' to 'overturning'. (Based on Neale 2002)

and not also transitively or ergatively. In terms of grammar patterns, the intransitive includes verbs used in the pattern **V** (a pattern not considered at all in this book) and also those used in patterns where the verb is complemented by a prepositional phrase, such as **V *at* n** etc. A major question raised and answered is whether intransitive verbs should be included in the Behaviour process type or the Action process type, and if they are divided between those types, what the criteria are for assigning a verb to one type or the other. Chrispin (2021) uses a variety of methods to annotate and classify the verbs studied; she finds Hanks' (2004) CPA particularly useful for establishing patterns that specify not only formal features, such as prepositional phrases, but also semantic categories, such as animate Subjects.

Overall, Chrispin (2021: 237) finds that verbs that have been categorized as belonging to the Behaviour process type do share characteristics, such as being unlikely to occur with a that-clause complement (the pattern **V that**), occurring with an animate subject and occurring in a perfective aspect (e.g. *she sneezed* rather than *she was sneezing*). On the other hand, it is not only Behaviour verbs that share these characteristics. Chrispin (2021: 239) then determines what distinguishes Behaviour verbs from Action verbs that are intransitive, finding that lexical aspect and animacy are the key distinguishing features. (Lexical aspect is a verb categorisation that reflects the relationship of the verb to time. For example, KNOW is static while RUN is dynamic; the action of POST (*a letter*) relates to a single point in time while the action READ (*a letter*) relates to an extended period of time; FALL indicates an action that is completed, or telic, while PLAY indicates an ongoing or atelic action.) Taking all the evidence into account, she proposes that intransitive verbs with animate subjects be classed as Behaviour whereas those with inanimate subjects be classed as Action. This means that verbs such as RUN, SWIM, and SING, which tend to cause difficulty in categorisation, are considered members of the Behaviour process type (Chrispin 2021: 239).

Chrispin (2021) goes on to discuss, essentially, what the intransitive 'means'. This is where complementation pattern becomes important. For example, whereas intransitive verbs are typically atelic, indicating an activity without a defined end-point, when the verb is complemented by a prepositional phrase it may become telic, e.g. *she ran* versus *she ran to the shop*. Similarly, an intransitive verb may take on a 'transitive-like' meaning in certain patterns e.g. *she listened* versus *she listened to the lecture*. This observation is reminiscent of the analysis of verb patterns in Francis et al. (1996), where the element 'to the lecture' is analysed as a 'Prepositional Object' (i.e. 'like an Object but with a preposition') rather than as an Adjunct. For Chrispin, the classification of the verb depends on its most frequent usage. For example, perception verbs such as *look* and *listen* are usually found with prepositional phrases and are therefore transitive-like Action verbs, whereas a verb such as *laugh*, which can also occur with the preposition *at*, is classified as Behaviour, because it is much more frequently found in the pattern 'animate-Subject + verb' (Chrispin 2021: 243).

Fontaine: Lexis as Most Local Context

Both Neale (2002) and Chrispin (2021) offer ways of demonstrating that grammar and lexis form an unbroken continuum, or cline of delicacy, by linking individual verbs – instances of lexis – with process type categories – instances of grammar. An alternative view is proposed by Fontaine (2017, 2025), who raises questions about the nature of the lexicogrammar, noting that:

> Perhaps because it mediates between semantics and expression, the lexicogrammar has somewhat of an identity crisis; sometimes seen as meaning, sometimes as form'. (Fontaine 2025: 2)

She concludes that 'It is difficult to see how a lexeme could be represented as a choice in the system networks' (Fontaine 2017: 8).

The main thrust of Fontaine's argument is that the organising principles that might model the grammar and the lexis are different: the 'grammar end' of the lexicogrammar consists of systems with small numbers of components, such as that shown in Figure 5.2; the 'lexis end' consists of a large number of sets of items. Citing Hunston and Francis (2000) that lexis and grammar are mutually dependent, she goes on to conclude that 'it is difficult to imagine a continuum as the best metaphor for this relationship' (Fontaine 2025: 8). As an alternative she suggests the concept of meaning-potential, a notion taken from Hanks (2013). She proposes a distinction between the 'lexeme', which might be glossed informally as 'a word having a variety of meanings depending on the specifics of each instance of use', and a 'lexical item', which might be glossed as 'a word or phrase as used in a specific instance'. The lexeme has a meaning potential, which is instantiated by the lexical item (Fontaine 2017: 13).

Fontaine's proposal for how to account for lexis within the Systemic Functional approach is by analogy with Halliday's (1991) view of both context and language. This view posits systems that are instantiated by each instance of language use. The system makes possible the instance and each instance contributes to the system. In terms of context, culture is a system while a situation type is an instance. For example, the socialisation of children via formal education might be an aspect of culture, while the situation type 'lesson' is an instance of that culture. Formal education enables lessons to take place and the format of lessons constitutes what formal education is. In the same way, while 'language' is a system, the language that is found in an individual text is an instance of that system. By analogy, Fontaine (2017: 13) proposes that the lexeme can be described in terms of system but the lexical item must be described in terms of its individual instance, or rather instances, of use. Corpus Linguistics, by focusing on multiple instances of use, can give information about instances, leading to the construction of a system.

The work of Tucker, Neale, and Chrispin responds to Fontaine's call for further work on lexis in the context of SFL but drawing on work in Corpus Linguistics and lexicology. However, the optimum way of modelling lexis in SFL remains an open question. Seeing the lexeme as a unit with meaning potential and the lexical item as an instance of that potential is an interesting possibility. The consequences of Fontaine's work, and the other work discussed in this chapter, will be considered in Section 5.4.

5.4 Conclusion

Systemic Functional Linguistics is a framework for the description of language that encompasses everything from social context to phonology, with lexicogrammar at its heart. Although there are differences of opinion within SFL, notably the distinction between 'Sydney Grammar' and 'Cardiff Grammar', it does for the most part constitute a coherent view of language and the principles behind describing it. In some ways, the very coherence of the framework makes it difficult to use unless one is wholly embedded in its community. It is true that the concepts of process type and of grammatical metaphor are used extensively in Critical Discourse Analysis, and the Appraisal framework (Martin and White 2005) is used particularly in the analysis of academic discourse, but otherwise, the ideas behind SFL are to be adopted wholesale or not at all. It will be obvious that the study described in this book is not located within the framework of SFG, and its primary function is not to contribute to debates in the SFL community. Neither does it seek to reframe SFG, in the way that the Cardiff Model has done, for example. The study very much sits outside SFL.

However, SFG has been a very large influence upon the study. This influence is apparent (though not always explicitly acknowledged) in the Pattern Grammar publications, especially Francis et al. (1996). The meaning groups for the pattern **V n**, for example, owe much to the process types proposed by Halliday. One very significant departure from the principles of SFG, however, is the treatment of complementation patterns as integral to verb behaviour. As previously noted, prepositional phrases which in SFG would be analysed as Adjuncts, in Francis et al. (1996) are labelled as prepositional Objects.

This study also has made use of many of the concepts in SFG. In the first place, the SFG notion of network as a way of representing layered options is adopted, as shown in Chapter 3, as a way of representing the meanings associated with each verb complementation pattern. The networks essentially organise the constructions that have been identified into hierarchies of meaning. It will be noted too that many of the distinctions that determine how the networks are configured draw on SFG concepts, such as 'process type'. Secondly, the semantic fields that were presumed as the basis for annotating semantic roles, as shown in Chapter 4, are inspired by the process type distinctions described in Halliday and Matthiessen (2014). The same semantic fields are the basis of the descriptions in Chapters 6–8. Those descriptions also use networks to represent the resources available to construe each semantic field. Finally, the concept of system network, as distinct from a taxonomic network, is used to highlight the salient meaning choices that are in play in each semantic field (see Chapters 6–8).

Having acknowledged this debt to SFG, the question remains as to whether this study is able to contribute to discussions within SFG, and in particular the discussions of the place of lexis in SFG outlined in Section 5.3. It must be said that for the most part the answer is 'no', because the purpose of this study was not to test the distinctions between process types, as Neale (2002) and Chrispin (2021) have done, or to propose a novel set of process types, as the Cardiff Model (Neale 2017) has done.

On the other hand, there are two ways in which the study presented in this book, and the database that sits behind it, could be of use to SFG researchers. One is that the Meaning Networks and Systemic Networks presented in Chapters 6–8 could be scrutinised to discover the extent to which they support or challenge proposed process types. This issue will be discussed further in Chapter 9.

Secondly, it will be noted that this study diverges markedly from the approach to lexis taken by Hasan, Matthiessen, Neale, and Chrispin, discussed in Section 5.3. In all of those studies, as in Levin's study, the unit of investigation is the verb. Typically, the combination of behaviours of a verb is used to classify that verb; verbs with the same set of behaviours, sometimes taking into account frequency, are said to belong to the same class. In this study, the unit of investigation is the verb and its complementation pattern: what is termed in this book the 'verb argument construction'. For this study, then, instances such as 'smile to think that', 'smile at the idea', and 'smile with happiness' are three different entities, and it is not presupposed that what we are dealing with here is a unit constituted by the verb SMILE. This may be something akin to what Fontaine (2017) means by the distinction between 'lexeme' (e.g. 'smile') and 'lexical item' (e.g. 'smile at something'). Consideration of this alternative view might be of use to future researchers in the place of lexis in SFG.

This brings us, of course, to the question of what 'lies between' the grammar end and the lexical end of the lexicogrammar, and whether it can be modelled as a series of ever-expanding networks (lexis as the most delicate grammar) or whether a different representation is needed. This discussion is taken up again in Chapter 9. For the moment, what might be said is that, as always, the answer to the question depends to a large extent on what the starting point is. In this study, form is the initial starting point (see the networks shown in Chapter 4, each one developed from a single verb complementation pattern), but then the meaning is taken as another starting point (see the networks in Chapters 6–8). The two sets of networks do not connect up, and neither provides a route from transitivity to verb. Rather, they perhaps challenge the notion that there is a single answer to the question.

The next three chapters in this book take the constructions discussed in Chapters 3 and 4 as given, and use them to build networks around semantic fields. As noted, they draw heavily on the notion of network and owe a great deal to work in SFG.

6 Constructions in Meaning Networks: Causation

6.1 Introduction

Chapter 3 described how Verb Argument Constructions were derived from the verb complementation patterns recorded in Francis et al. (1996). The concept of network was used to model the relationship between constructions. Chapter 4 showed how further information was added to some of those constructions, based on the notion of semantic fields and their associated participant roles. In those sections, the main concern was to reconcile Pattern Grammar and Construction Grammar and to demonstrate how the outcome from large-scale corpus research can be used to inform a cognitively based linguistic theory.

This chapter turns attention to the intersection between constructions and Systemic Functional Grammar – SFG (introduced in Chapter 5). It seeks to model the language resources available for making meaning in a given semantic field using systemic networks. The aim is to explore how a corpus-informed taxonomy of Verb Argument Constructions might be useful in populating networks in SFG. A complementary aim is to demonstrate how the concept of network, as used in SFG, might contribute to constructicon building.

The method followed to derive networks is first to identify the constructions belonging to a given semantic field, then to arrange those constructions in Meaning Networks, and finally to propose the Systemic Networks. To explain how these networks are presented in this book, I use here an imaginary and very trivial example: the choices involved in making a hypothetical journey from Birmingham to London.

Example: Birmingham to London

As a potential traveller, there are a number of ways I could organise my journey, such as travel by train in the afternoon on a return ticket; travel in the morning on a single ticket, either on the bus or the train; take the bus in the morning on a return ticket; and buy a ticket for a single bus journey and use it in the evening. These options can be organised in a bullet-point list or taxonomy, as follows:

- I can choose to travel by train or by bus.
  - If I travel by train, I can go in the morning or in the afternoon.
    - If I go in the morning, I can purchase:
      - A single ticket: the 'TMS' option ('train, morning, single')
      - A return ticket: the 'TMR' option
    - If I go in the afternoon, I can purchase:
      - A single ticket: the 'TAS' option
      - A return ticket: the 'TAR' option
  - If I travel by bus, I can go in the morning or the evening.
    - If I go in the morning, I can purchase:
      - A single ticket: the 'BMS' option
      - A return ticket: the 'BMR' option
    - If I go in the evening, I can purchase:
      - A single ticket: the 'BES' option
      - A return ticket: the 'BER' option

This gives a total of eight options. This 'prose' version of the taxonomy can be translated into a network that is the equivalent of the Meaning Networks used in this book. Figure 6.1 shows this network.

It is obvious that although Figure 6.1 shows how the options ('TMS', 'BER', etc.) relate to one another, it is somewhat repetitious. The travel 'features' that go into the make-up of each option can be extrapolated. There are three key features:

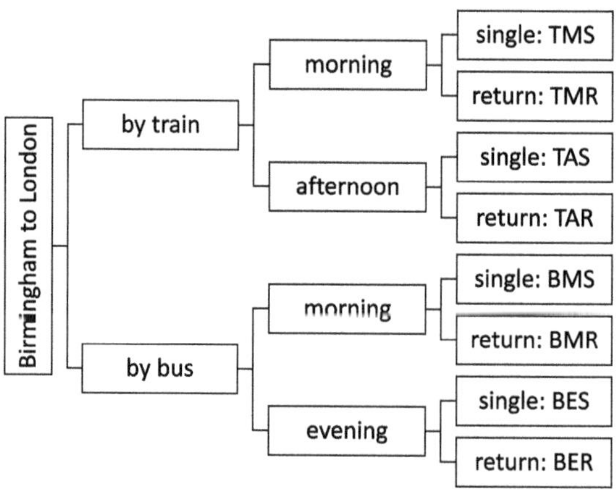

Figure 6.1 The imaginary Birmingham to London journey: taxonomy of options

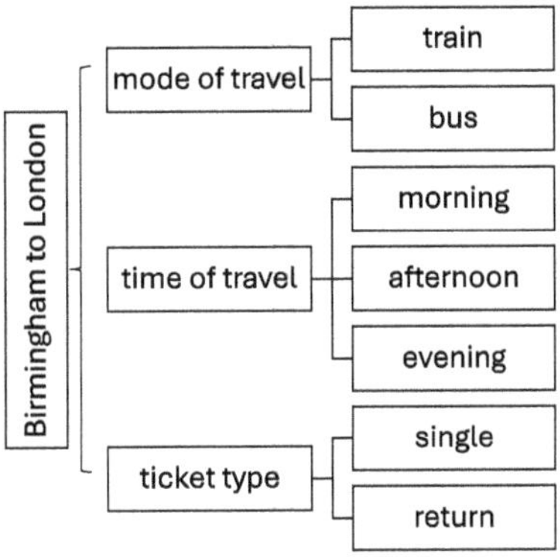

Figure 6.2 Systemic Network of travel options

mode of travel, time of travel, and type of ticket. These can be expressed as a Systemic Network, as shown in Figure 6.2. Each of the options is a combination of choices from each of the features. Taken together, Figures 6.1 and 6.2 show what features the traveller takes into account in deciding how to travel, and what options are the consequence of what choices. They are the equivalent of the Meaning Networks (the taxonomies, showing how the constructions relate to one another, like Figure 6.1) and the Systemic Networks (showing what language features contribute to the constructions, like Figure 6.2).

The remainder of this chapter repeats this exercise, but with a genuine semantic field: Causation.

6.2 Causation

The concept of causation is a contested one in Philosophy (see, e.g. Mumford and Anjum 2013). In linguistic studies, causation is considered to be expressed (a) using specific lexical verbs such as KILL (= 'cause to be dead'), BREAK (= 'cause to be broken'), or DROP (= 'cause to fall') (Katamba 1993: 213); (b) analytically or periphrastically, with verbs such as CAUSE, HAVE, MAKE, and GET in constructions such as 'make someone do something' (Gilquin 2010); and (c) adverbially, with clauses beginning with *because*, etc. or noun phrases beginning *due to*, etc. (Khachatryan 2009). Specific verbs expressing causation are exemplified by Biber et al.'s (1999: 363) list of single-word verbs of facilitation or causation: ALLOW, CAUSE, ENABLE, FORCE, HELP, LET, REQUIRE, and PERMIT.

Gilquin (2010) provides an extensive, corpus-based, and quantitative account of periphrastic causative constructions, in which she refers to three models taken from the literature (Gilquin 2010: 153). These are: the Iconic Sequencing model, the Billiard-ball model, and the Direct manipulation model (Gilquin 2010: 154). Examples (1)–(3), taken from Gilquin (2010: 151–155) illustrate these.

(1) **I** make them clean theirs thoroughly. (BNC) [Iconic Sequencing]

(2) **The tree** falling on it made the lorry lose its loading. [Billiard-ball]

(3) **I** got John to repaint the wall. [Direct manipulation]

In each, there is a Causer (shown in bold) and a Causee (underlined). In example (2) there is also a Patient ('its loading'), which is affected by the action, and in example (3) there is also an Effect ('repainting the wall') brought about by the action.

The meaning of causation tends to become fuzzy around the edges, with no sharp demarcation between what is caused and what is not. It might be argued that this occurs when the causation is expressed lexically, and where one or more of the participants is assumed to be present in the situation without being expressed in the clause. Gilquin (2010: 67), for example, talks about ' . . . the controversial question of the relation between periphrastic causatives and lexical causatives'. It is generally accepted that the verb KILL can be paraphrased as 'cause to die'; it is less apparent that TEACH necessarily means 'cause to learn'. Even more controversial is a verb such as BREAK. In an example such as (4), a reasonable interpretation is that the assistant caused the bottle to break, meaning that *broke* is a lexical causative. In an example such as (5), however, no Causer is present in the clause and it must be taken on trust that 'middle' clauses of this type entail a causative action by an unnamed force.

(4) . . . after an assistant had broken a bottle of salad cream . . . (BNC)

(5) . . . but most unfortunately the bottle broke in the post . . . (BNC)

As well as causative constructions, the literature contains discussions of resultative constructions (Goldberg and Jackendoff 2004). Some resultatives, such as example (6), imply but do not express a cause, while others, such as example (7), include a cause element. Examples (6) and (7) are taken from Goldberg and Jackendoff (2004).

(6) The pond froze solid.

(7) Bill rolled the ball down the hill.

In this book, the term 'Causation' refers to those constructions that indicate that some person or entity brings about a state, thought, or action. The constructions that are subsumed under this meaning can be divided into three main types, as follows:

Periphrastic Causatives

These are the classic causative constructions, such as those investigated by Gilquin (2010). In their canonical form, they include an element that is a non-finite clause that indicates the caused action. Examples (8)–(12) are (invented) examples of these.

(8) Rose made Max cross the road.

(9) Rose forced Max to cross the road.

(10) Rose sent the stone spinning across the lake.

(11) The barrier prevented Rose from entering.

(12) Rose talked Max into/out of leaving.

An extension of this type is when the process in the non-finite clause is nominalisation, that is, expressed as a noun. Examples (13) and (14) illustrate this (again the examples are invented):

(13) Rose incited Max to violence.

(14) Rose pressured Max into crime.

Lexical Causatives

Most of the lexical causatives included here involve causing a change to someone's mind or emotions. Examples (15) and (16), which are invented, illustrate this.

(15) The argument convinced Sam.

(16) This argument decided Sam on /against leaving.

There is no doubt that this study under-represents lexical causation, for a number of reasons. One is that other semantic fields, such as Change or Location_transfer, could be included under the heading of 'causation'. Another is that many instances of lexical causation utilise the **V n** pattern which, as noted in Chapter 3, is not dealt with fully in Francis et al. (1996). A final reason is that many lexical causatives can also be classified under 'resultatives', which is the next category.

Resultatives

In resultatives, a cause performs an action that leads to a state. The action and state may be expressed explicitly or implicitly. In most cases the constructions are transitive, with the cause being expressed by the subject of the active clause and the affected entity by the object. Examples (17) and (18) illustrate this. In other cases, the construction is not transitive, though the arrangement of cause and affected entity are the same (example (19)). In some constructions, the affected entity is the subject and the cause is expressed by a prepositional phrase (examples (20) and (21)).

(17) Sam pushed the door open.

(18) They elected Sam president of the association.

(19) The publicity led to Sam's failure.

(20) Sam died of a broken heart.

(21) Sam benefitted from the publicity.

Congruent versus Metaphoric Constructions

Chapter 5 introduced the notion of grammatical metaphor (Halliday and Matthiessen 2014; Thompson 2014). The concept is borrowed here to describe constructions where either cause or effect must be deduced from the construction rather than being expressed explicitly. These are considered to be non-congruent, or metaphoric, expressions of the semantic field. In each case, at least one element of the cause-effect chain is left implicit. In examples (22)–(25), the outcome of the Causer's actions is expressed indirectly. In (22), we must assume that Sam is now in a state of having no insecurities. In (23), Sam is now in a state of suffering harm. In (24), the concert is in a state of being more lively than it was before. In (25), the tree is presumably now in a state of have ribbons on it.

(22) Rose rid Sam of his insecurities.

(23) The publicity caused Sam harm.

(24) The comedian's appearance breathed new life into the concert.

(25) Rose decorated the trees with ribbons

Example (26) is a little different, in that Rose's actions are the indirect cause of the car leaving. Presumably, Rose did something that caused someone else to cause the car to leave. A potential paraphrase – 'Rose caused the car to leave at 10am' – changes the example from metaphoric to congruent, but also changes the meaning. Example (27) is different again, in that the action of the car is expressed in a noun phrase rather than as a verb.

(26) Rose arranged that the car should leave at 10am.

(27) Rose's actions ensured the car's prompt departure.

6.3 The Causation Meaning Network

In this study, a total of 105 Verb Argument Constructions have been identified that express the semantic field of Causation, drawing on 26 verb complementation patterns. It should be remembered that each construction is used with several verbs, not just the one that appears in the construction name. These Verb Argument Constructions are the starting point for identifying features of difference in the expression of causation. Inevitably this means that the view of causation is somewhat different from more theoretical studies. For example, the primary distinction identified involves the nature of what is caused: an action, a state, or a thought or emotion. Examples (28)–(30), illustrate each of these:

(28) Rose made Max cross the road. (action)

(29) Sam pushed the door open. (state)

(30) The argument convinced Sam against leaving. (thought)

The task in building the Causation Meaning Network, then, is to arrange the 105 identified constructions in a way that makes sense, using the SFG concept of choice between language features. Because it is impractical to show the whole network in a single legible diagram, parts of the network are shown separately. Figure 6.3 shows the left-most, most general set of distinctions, with 'Causation' as the entry point to the network. All the constructions are then organised into three sets: causing a state, causing a thought or emotion, and causing an action or event. Each of the options in that network is developed in more detail in further figures. Figure 6.4 has 'Cause thought/emotion' as the entry point; Figure 6.5 has 'Cause action/event' as the entry point; and Figure 6.6 has 'Cause state' as the entry point.

Two versions of Figure 6.4 are given, to illustrate the kind of decision-making that goes into making the networks. Figure 6.4 shows an initial version of the network. It makes a distinction between thought and emotion, and then

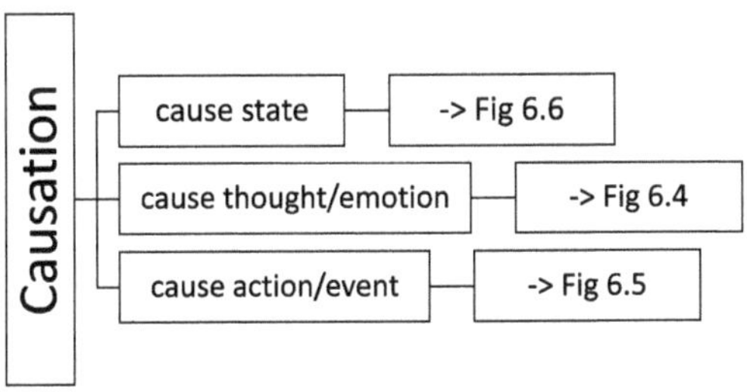

Figure 6.3 Causation Meaning Network

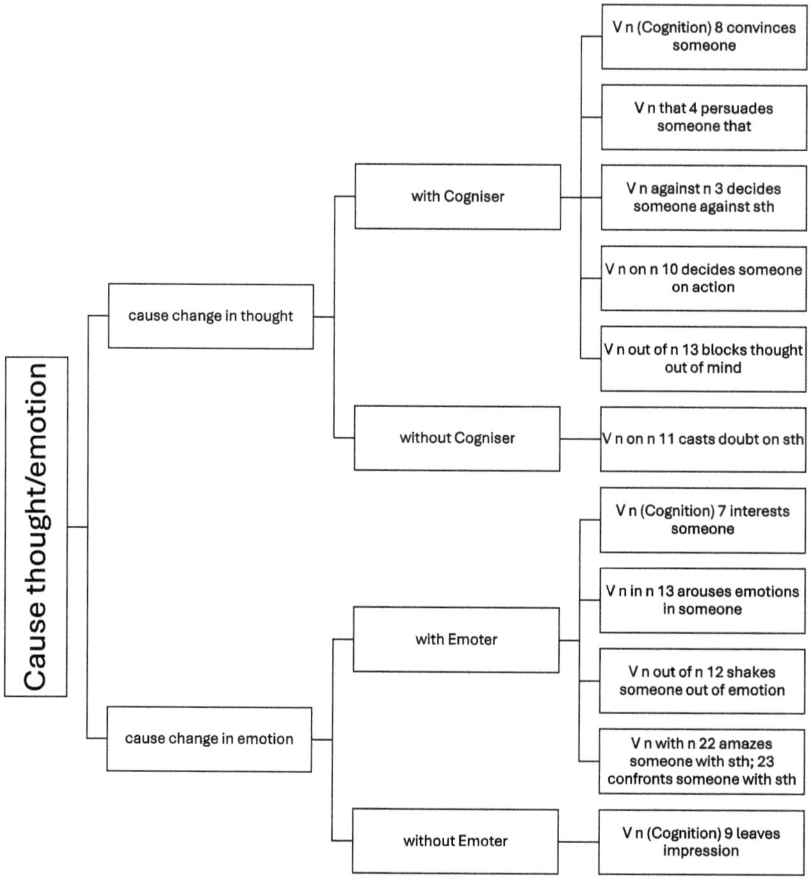

Figure 6.4a Cause thought/emotion Meaning Network: initial version

a distinction between with/without Cogniser/Emoter. The only other distinctions shown are between the patterns. It is apparent, though, that further points of sameness and difference can be identified. Figures 6.4b and 6.4c show the final version of the network. This divides the patterns/constructions into those where the Cogniser/Emoter is the clause object (e.g. 'persuade Cogniser that') and those where that role appears in the prepositional phrase (e.g. 'arouse emotion in Emoter'). Where relevant, it also shows a distinction between constructions that include the content of the change in thought/emotion (e.g. 'amaze Emoter with Content') and those that do not (e.g. 'convince Cogniser'). This illustrates the hypothetical nature of the networks. Each one represents a possible but not definitive modelling of the available resources.

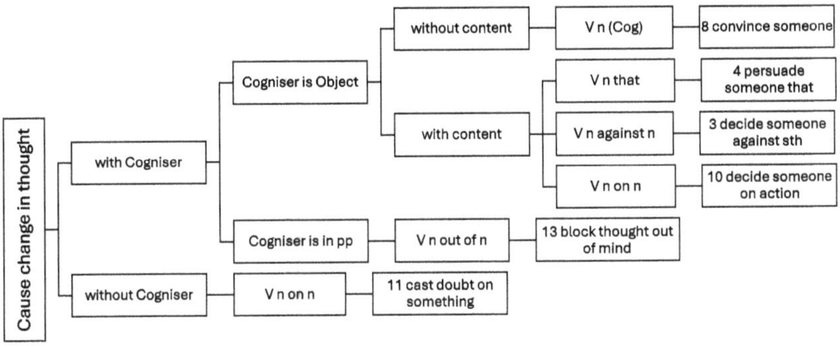

Figure 6.4b Cause change in thought network: final version

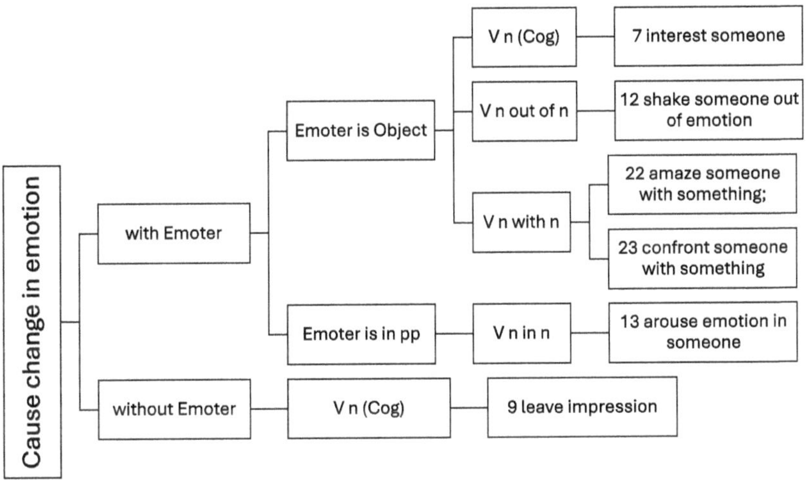

Figure 6.4c Cause change in emotion network: final version

Figure 6.5, showing the 'Cause action/event' network, is divided into four figures (6.5a–d) for improved legibility. Starting from Figure 6.5, there is a primary division between 'congruent' and 'metaphoric' (as previously explained). The 'metaphoric' branch of the network is expanded in Figure 6.5d. The 'congruent' branch is divided into patterns including a clause element and those including a prepositional phrase. The clausal element branch is expanded in Figure 6.5b and the prepositional phrase branch is expanded in Figure 6.5c. Figure 6.6a–f similarly shows a series of networks comprising a single network with 'Cause state' as the entry point.

The next sections show a prose account of each of the networks shown in Figures 6.4–6.6. In each case there is a short introductory paragraph, then

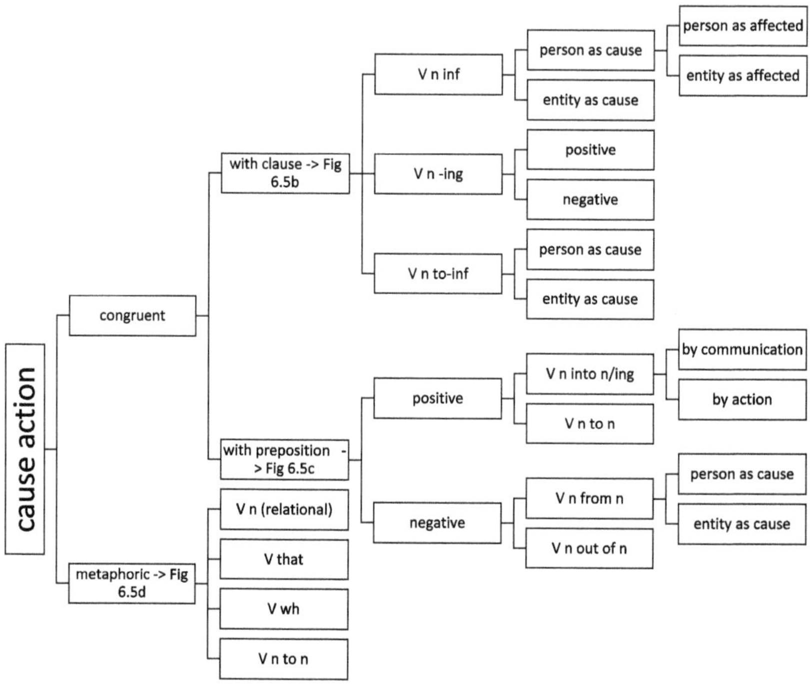

Figure 6.5a Cause action/event Meaning Network

a bullet-pointed list that explains with examples the alternatives that are expressed in the accompanying figure. The list uses the abbreviation 'cx' for 'construction', and each construction is numbered in line with the Transitivity-Net website. In this discussion as in the explanation mentioned earlier, to ensure short and easily compared examples, all examples are invented.

The 'Cause Thought/Emotion' Meaning Network

A simple distinction is made here between causing a change in thought (e.g. 'The argument convinced Sam') and causing a change in emotion (e.g. 'The letter shook Sam out of her apathy'). The next distinction is between constructions that include a Cognizer or Emoter (e.g. 'Sam persuaded Clint that the sky was green'; 'The new evidence interested Sam') and those that do not (e.g. 'The new evidence cast doubt on the verdict'; 'Sam's singing left a deep impression'). Where there is a Cogniser or Emoter, this may be found in the clause object or in the prepositional phrase. This distinguishes between 'The argument convinced Sam' and 'The thought blocked the idea of Sam out of Clint's mind'.

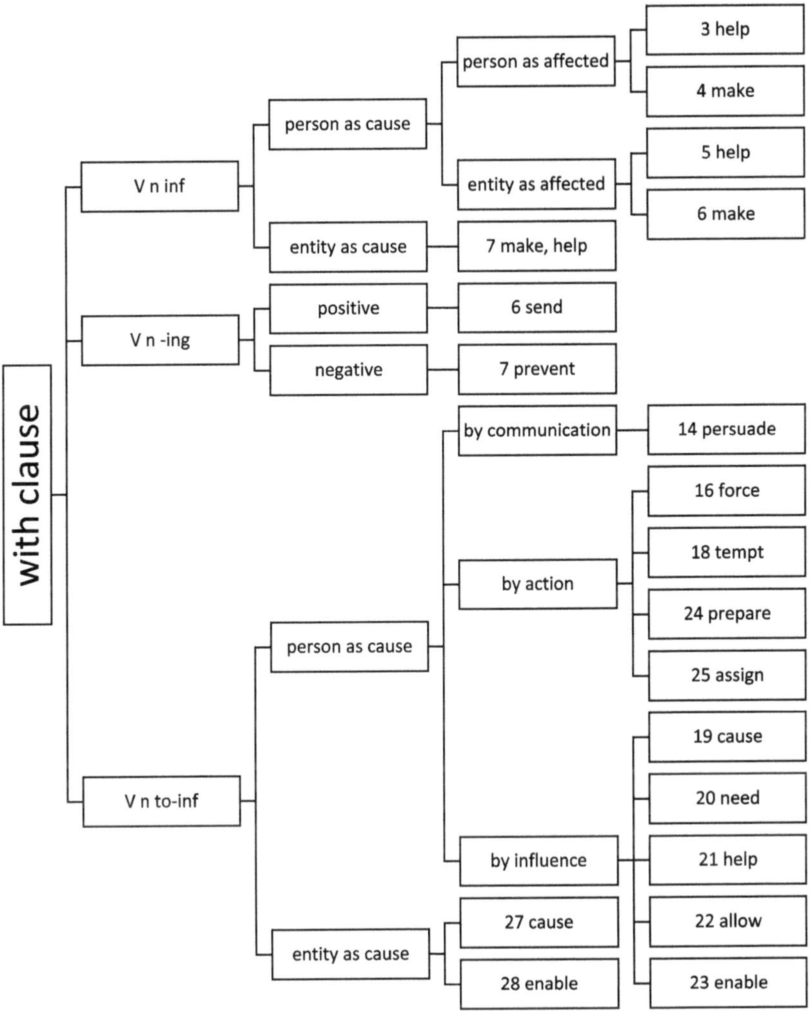

Figure 6.5b Cause action/event: congruent, the with clause network

In cases where the Cogniser is the object, a further distinction is made between the **V n** pattern, where no content is expressed (e.g. 'The argument convinced Sam') and the other constructions, where there is a reference to the content (e.g. 'Sam persuaded Clint that the sky was green'). The remaining distinctions are between patterns. In most cases, only one construction per pattern expresses this meaning. Here is the full account of the choices within this meaning. This

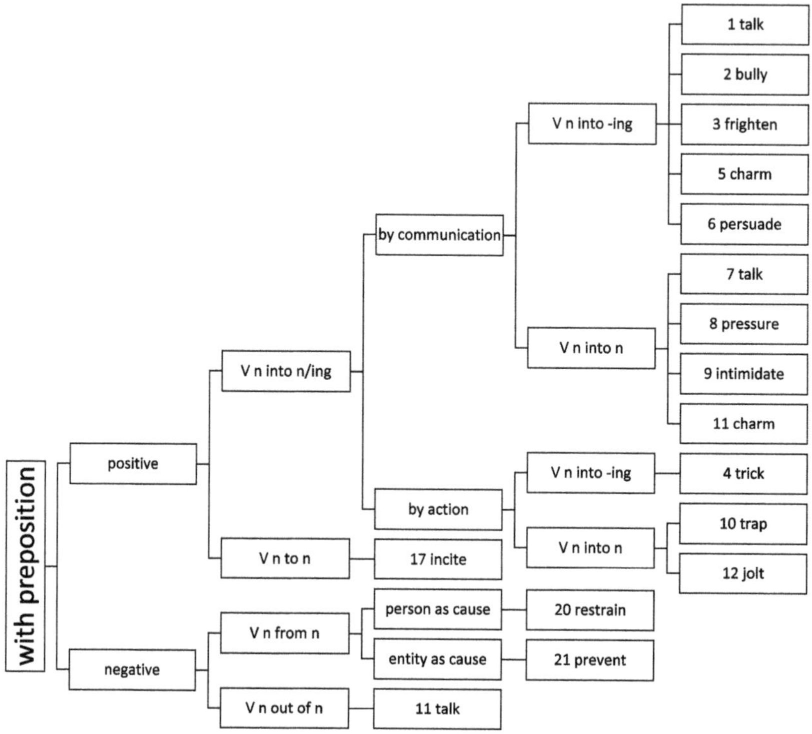

Figure 6.5c Cause action/event: congruent, the with prepositional phrase network

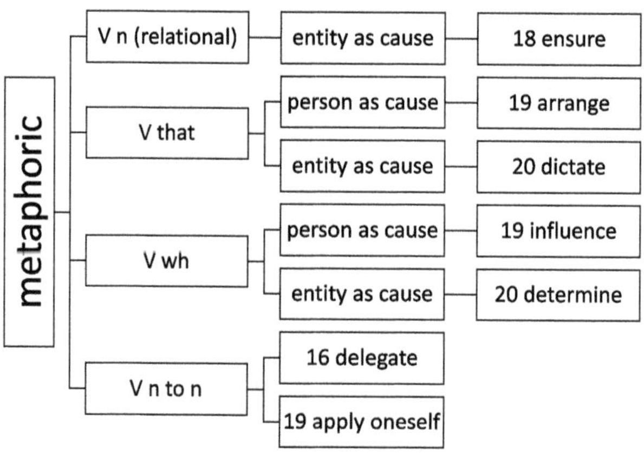

Figure 6.5d Cause action/event: the metaphoric network

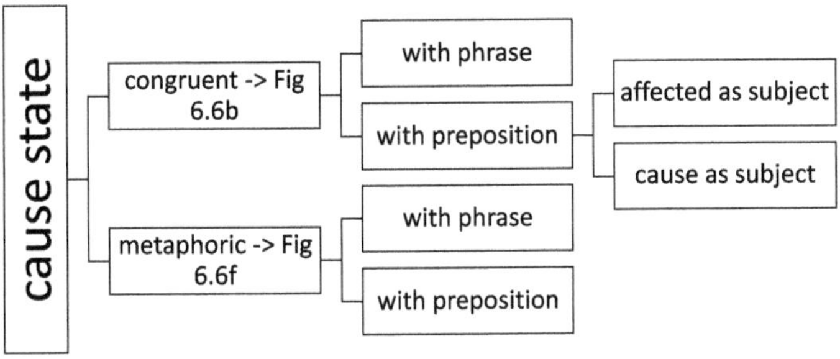

Figure 6.6a Cause state Meaning Network

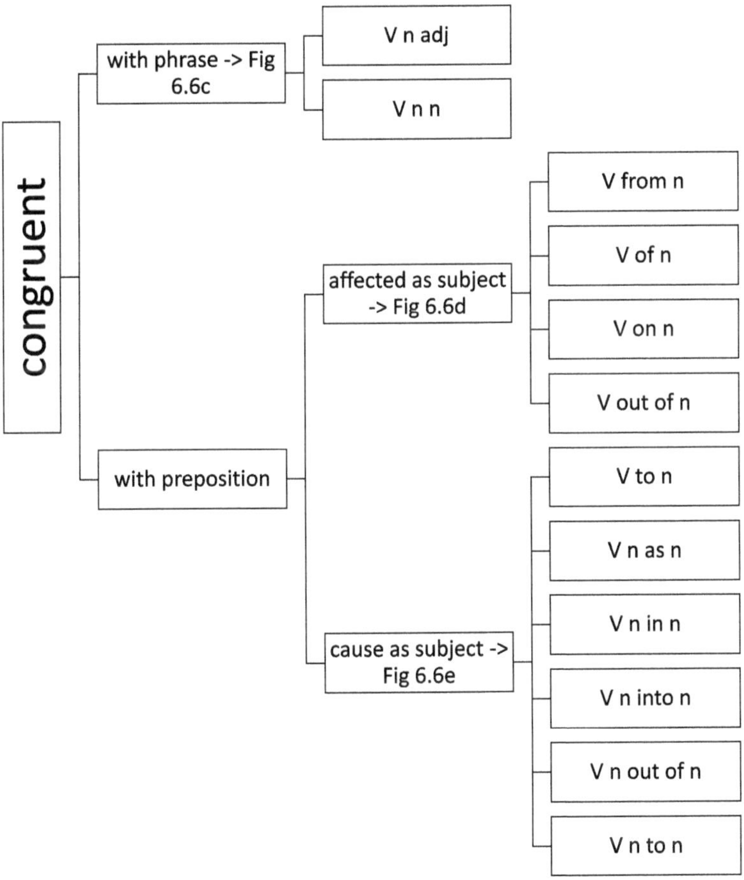

Figure 6.6b Cause state: the congruent network

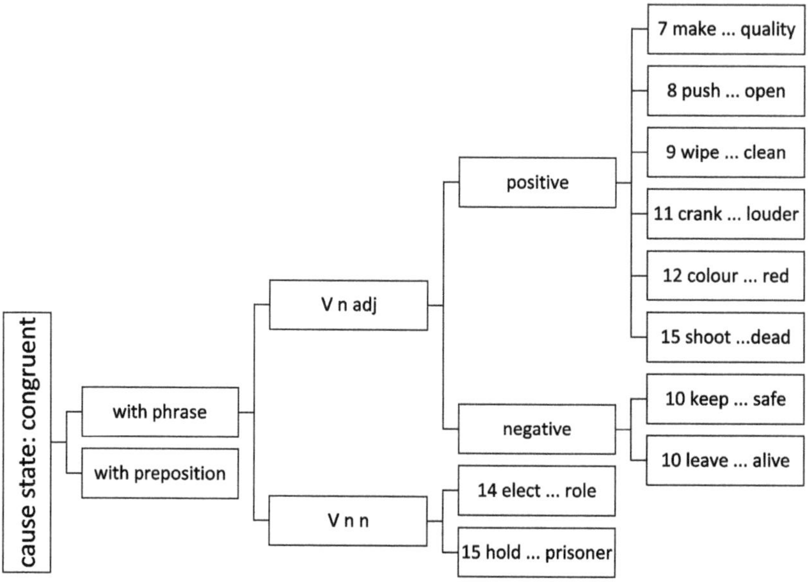

Figure 6.6c Cause state: congruent, the with phrase network

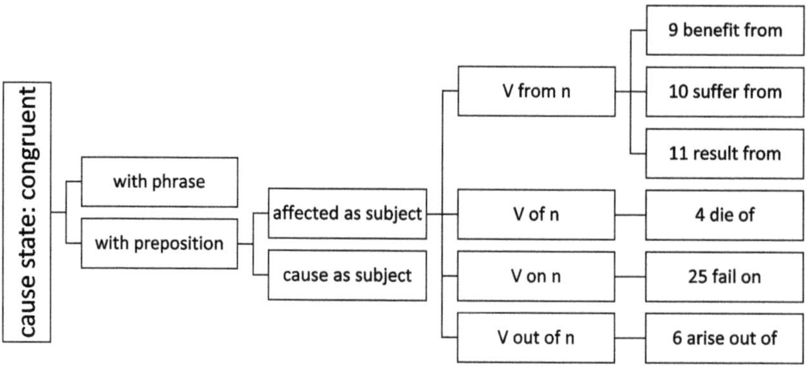

Figure 6.6d Cause state: congruent, the with prepositional phrase network, showing affected as subject choices

account explains the 'cause thought/emotion' network that appears in Figure 6.4b.

The 'Cause Thought/Emotion' Meaning Network: Choices and Examples

- Cause a change in thought (see Figure 6.4b)
  - Construction includes a Cogniser

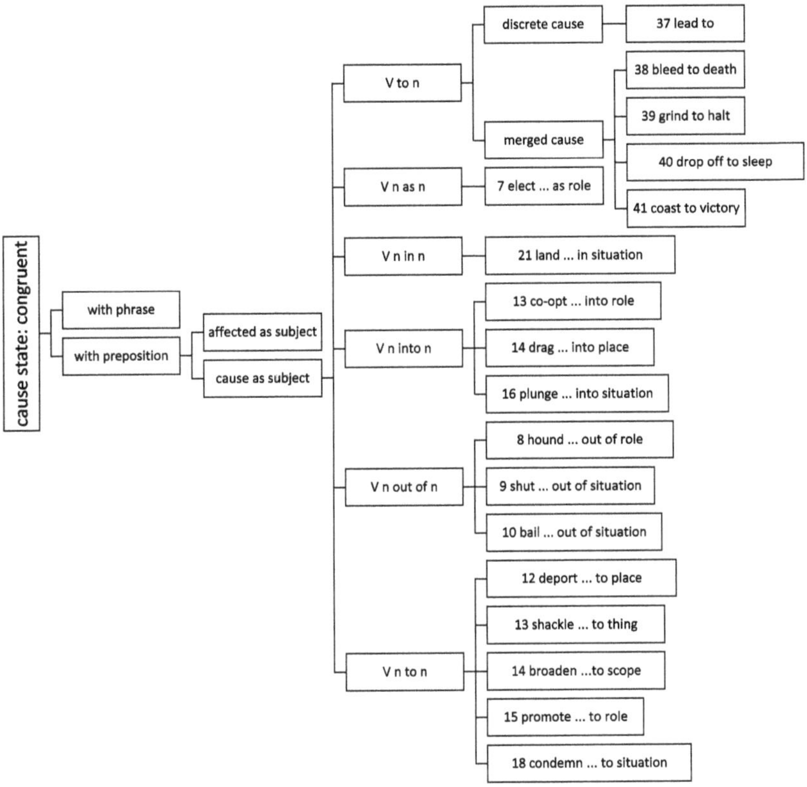

Figure 6.6e Cause state: congruent, the with prepositional phrase network, showing cause as subject choices

- The Cogniser is the clause object
  - There is no expressed thought content
    - V n (Cognition). Cx8 e.g. 'The argument convinced Sam'.
  - The context of the thought is expressed
    - V n that. Cx4 e.g. 'Sam persuaded Clint that the sky was green'.
    - V n against n. Cx3 e.g. 'Sam's argument decided Clint against demonstrating'.
    - V n on n. Cx10 e.g. 'Sam's argument decided Clint on leaving'.
- The Cogniser is the object of the prepositional phrase
  - V n out of n. Cx13 e.g. 'The thought of Mary blocked the idea of Sam out of Clint's mind'.

◦ Construction does not include a Cogniser
- V n on n. Cx11 e.g. 'The new evidence cast doubt on the verdict'.

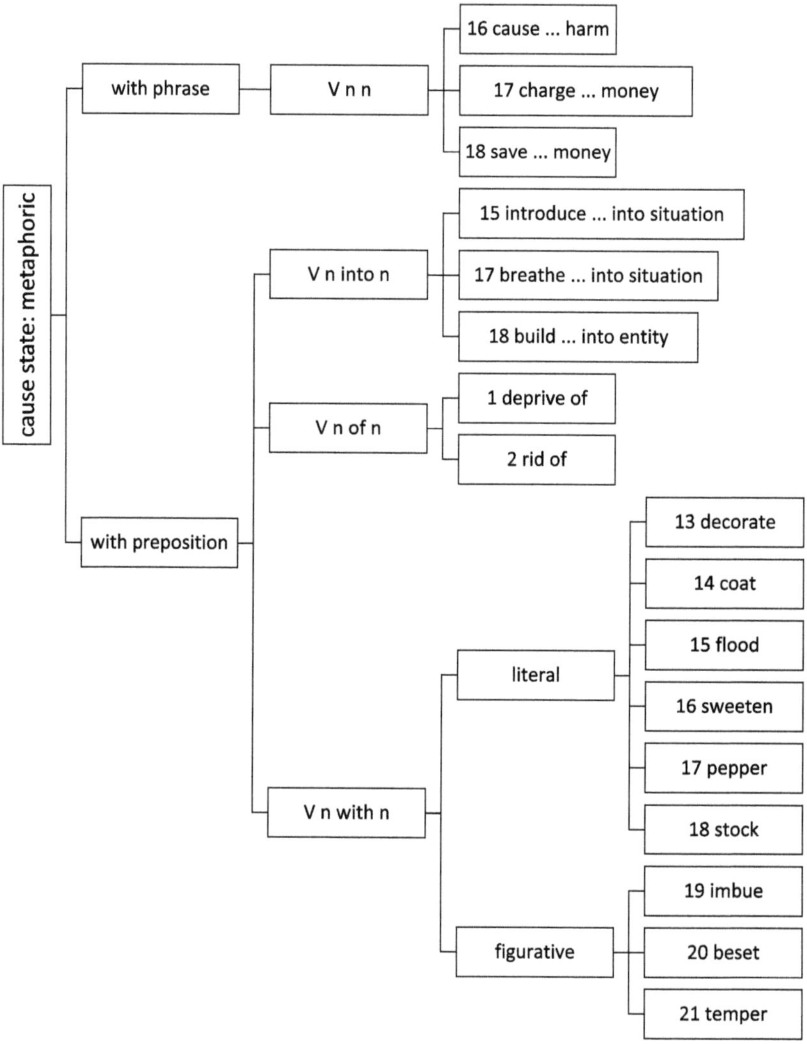

Figure 6.6f Cause state: the metaphoric network

- Cause a change in emotion (See Figure 6.4c)
  - Construction includes an Emoter
    - The Emoter is the clause object
      - V n (Cognition). Cx7 e.g. 'The new evidence interested Sam.'
      - V n out of n. Cx12 e.g. 'The letter shook Sam out of her apathy.'

- V n with n. Cx22 e.g. 'Sam amazed the audience with her singing.' and Cx23 e.g. 'Clint confronted Sam with the evidence.'
  - The Emoter is the Object of the prepositional phrase
    - V n in n. Cx13 e.g. 'The film aroused strong feelings in Clint.'
- Construction does not include an Emoter
  - V n (Cognition). Cx9 e.g. 'Sam's singing left a deep impression.'

The 'Cause Action/Event' Meaning Network.

This network is more complex, involving more patterns and more constructions than are involved in the 'cause thought/emotion' network. The patterns themselves can be grouped, based on two distinctions. Firstly, in most patterns, the verb is followed by a noun phrase that indicates the person or thing affected by the act of causing, as in 'Raj talked Lucy into leaving' or 'Max forced Rose to leave'. In a few cases, such as the pattern **V n** and the example 'Additional investment ensured the continuation of manufacture', the entity that is affected, presumably a business enterprise, is left implicit. To make sense of this a distinction is proposed between constructions with an explicit affected entity as a separate pattern element, and those without. As noted earlier, Halliday's (Halliday and Matthiessen 2014) distinction between 'congruent' and 'metaphoric' representation is borrowed to describe these alternatives. Secondly, some patterns include a preposition, while others are composed of phrases and clauses. For example, **V n *into* n** (e.g. 'Raj talked Lucy into leaving') includes a preposition whereas **V n to-inf** (e.g. 'Max forced Rose to leave') includes a clause but no preposition. Within each of the congruent/metaphoric categories, then, a distinction is made between patterns with and without prepositions. Further distinctions are proposed where appropriate. These are: the subject (Causer) is a person or an entity (e.g. 'Max forced Rose to leave the room' versus 'Additional investment ensured continuation of manufacture'); the affected thing is a person or an entity (e.g. 'Rose made Max cross the road' versus 'Max helped the situation calm down'); the act of causing is explicitly communication (e.g. 'Raj talked Lucy into leaving') or is not (e.g. 'Lucy tricked Raj into stealing the money'); and what is caused is action (e.g. 'Raj talked Lucy into leaving') or the absence of action (e.g. 'Raj prevented Lucy from leaving'). The full account of the choices within this meaning is given in the following.

The 'Cause Action/Event' Meaning Network: Choices and Examples

- Congruent: the affected entity is explicit
  - Patterns with a clause (See Figure 6.5b)
    - V n inf
      - Cause is a person

      - Affected thing is a person. Cx3 e.g. ‘Rose helped Max cross the road.’ and Cx4 e.g. ‘Rose made Max cross the road’.
      - Affected thing is an entity. Cx5 e.g. ‘Max helped the situation calm down.’ and Cx6 e.g. ‘Max made the results appear logical’.
        - Cause is an entity. Cx7 e.g. ‘The price reductions helped/made customers buy more’.
  - V n -ing
    - Positive: an action/event is caused. Cx6 e.g. ‘Rose sent the stone spinning across the lake’.
    - Negative: an action/event is prevented. Cx7 e.g. ‘Max stopped the rocket leaving the launchpad’.
  - V n to-inf
    - Cause is a person
      - Action is caused by communication. Cx14 e.g. ‘Rose persuaded Max to leave the room’.
      - Action is caused by a specific action
        - Cx16 e.g. ‘Max forced Rose to leave the room’.
        - Cx18 e.g. ‘Rose tempted Max to break the rules’.
        - Cx24 e.g. ‘Rose prepared Max to run the marathon’.
        - Cx25 e.g. ‘Max assigned Rose to run the marathon’.
      - Action is caused by a non-specific action or influence
        - Cx19 e.g. ‘Rose caused Max to join the army’.
        - Cx20 e.g. ‘Max needed Rose to help him’.
        - Cx21 e.g. ‘Rose helped Max to join the army’.
        - Cx22 e.g. ‘Max allowed Rose to help him’.
        - Cx23 e.g. ‘Max enabled Rose to join the army’.
    - Cause is an entity. Cx27 e.g. ‘The rise in prices caused Max to go broke.’ and Cx28 e.g. ‘The fall in prices enable Rose to save money’.
- Patterns with a preposition (See Figure 6.5c)
  - Positive: an action/event is caused
    - V n into n/-ing
      - Action is caused by communication
        - V n into -ing
          - Cx1 e.g. ‘Raj talked Lucy into leaving’.
          - Cx2 e.g. ‘Lucy bullied Raj into leaving’.
          - Cx3 e.g. ‘Raj frightened Lucy into leaving’.
          - Cx5 e.g. ‘Lucy charmed Raj into helping her’.
          - Cx6 e.g. ‘Lucy persuaded Raj into helping her’.
        - V n into n
          - Cx7 e.g. ‘Raj talked Lucy into crime’.
          - Cx8 e.g. ‘Lucy pressured Raj into crime’.
          - Cx9 e.g. ‘Raj intimidated Lucy into betrayal’.

        - Cx11 e.g. 'Raj charmed Lucy into an unwise course of action'.
      - Action is caused by action
        - V n into -ing. Cx4 e.g. 'Lucy tricked Raj into stealing the money'.
        - V n into n. Cx10 e.g. 'Raj trapped Lucy into a life of crime.' and Cx12 e.g. 'Lucy's words jolted Raj into action'.
    - V n to n. Cx17 e.g. 'Debs incited Lucy to violence'.
  - Negative: an action/event is prevented
    - V n from n
      - Cause is a person. Cx20 e.g. 'Lucy restrained Debs from violence'.
      - Cause is an entity. Cx21 e.g. 'The barrier prevented Lucy from entering'.
    - V n out of n. Cx11 e.g. 'Lucy talked Debs out of leaving'.

- Metaphoric: the affected entity is implicit (See Figure 6.5d)
  - V n (Relational). Cx18 e.g. 'Additional investment ensured the continuation of manufacture'.
  - V that
    - Cause is a person. Cx19 e.g. 'Debs arranged that the band would play at 10'.
    - Cause is an entity. Cx20 e.g. 'Circumstances dictated that the party end early'.
  - V wh
    - Cause is a person. Cx19 e.g. 'Raj influenced what happened to the leader'.
    - Cause is an entity. Cx20 e.g. 'Circumstances determined what happened to the leader'.
  - V n to n. Cx16 e.g. 'Debs delegated the most difficult task to Raj.' and Cx19 e.g. 'Lucy applied herself to finishing the painting'.

The 'Cause State' Meaning Network

The largest number of 'Causation' constructions express this meaning. As with the 'cause action/event' meaning, a distinction is made between explicit and implicit representation, but in this case it is the caused state that may be explicit or implicit rather than the affected entity. For example, in 'They elected him President', the resulting state ('he is President') is explicit, expressed by the two noun phrases following the verb. The same is true of 'The changes led to Brian's success', where the resulting state ('Brian is successful') is expressed by the noun phrase following the preposition. In the case of 'Joan died of a broken heart', the resulting state ('Joan is dead') is expressed by the verb. The term Congruent is again used to refer to constructions such as these. In other constructions, the caused state is implied but not stated. For example, in 'The decision saved Brian £200', the caused state ('Brian is richer by £200') must be inferred. The same is true of 'The committee built breaks into the timetable'), where the caused state is 'The timetable included breaks', and 'Joan rid Brian of his fear of flying', where the caused state is 'Brian is unafraid'. The term Metaphoric is used to refer to these constructions.

Within both congruent and metaphoric options there are distinctions of pattern, primarily between patterns with and without prepositions. Patterns with phrases but no prepositions include **V n adj** (e.g. 'They made the fence stronger') and **V n n** ('The publicity caused Brian harm'). Each pattern involved is listed as a separate option within these major divisions. Further choices occur within specific patterns. For example, the **V n adj** pattern is used with constructions that indicate that a change is made, such as 'Joan pushed the door open', and those that indicate that a change is not made, such as 'Joan left her partner alive'. The patterns with a preposition are divided into those with the affected entity as subject (e.g. 'Brian's success arose out of the changes') and those with the cause as subject (e.g. 'The changes led to Brian's success'). In the pattern **V n *with* n** there is a specific distinction between making a change to a physical object, as in 'Joan coated the cake with icing' and making a change to an abstract entity, as in 'Brian imbued the situation with menace'. Special mention needs to be made of the pattern **V *to* n**, where the cause may be indicated by the subject alone, as in 'The changes led to Brian's success' or by the subject along with the verb, as in 'Joan dropped off to sleep', where the caused state is 'Joan is asleep' and the cause is 'Joan dropped off'. The terms 'Discrete cause' and 'Merged cause' are used to express this distinction. This construction is at the verge of exclusion from the causation semantic field because there is no distinct Cause element.

What follows is the full account of the choices within this meaning. This account explains the 'cause state' networks that appear at Figure 6.6.

The 'Cause State' Meaning Network: Choices and Examples

- Congruent: the cause and effect are explicit (See Figure 6.6b)
  - Patterns with a phrase (See Figure 6.6c)
    - V n adj
      - Positive: a change is made
        - Cx7 e.g. 'They made the fence stronger'.
        - Cx8 e.g. 'Joan pushed the door open'.
        - Cx9 e.g. 'Brian wiped the surface clean'.
        - Cx11 e.g. 'Joan cranked the volume louder'.
        - Cx12 e.g. 'Brian coloured the sky blue'.
        - Cx15 e.g. 'Joan shot her partner dead'.
      - Negative: a change is not made
        - Cx10 e.g. 'Brian kept his partner safe'.

        - Cx10 e.g. 'Joan left her partner alive'.
      - V n n. Cx14 e.g. 'They elected him President.' and Cx15 e.g. 'They held him prisoner'.
  - Patterns with a preposition
    - Affected as Subject (See Figure 6.6d)
      - V from n
        - Cx9 e.g. 'Brian benefitted from the change'.
        - Cx10 e.g. 'Joan suffered from the change'.
        - Cx11 e.g. 'Brian's success resulted from the change'.
      - V of n. Cx4 e.g. 'Joan died of a broken heart'.
      - V on n. Cx25 e.g. 'The car failed on three counts'.
      - V out of n. Cx6 e.g. 'Brian's success arose out of the changes'.
    - Cause as Subject (See Figure 6.6e)
      - V to n
        - Discrete cause
          - Cx37 e.g. 'The changes led to Brian's success'.
        - Merged cause
          - Cx38 e.g. 'The victim bled to death'.
          - Cx39 e.g. 'The train ground to a halt'.
          - Cx40 e.g. 'Joan dropped off to sleep'.
          - Cx41 e.g. 'Brian coasted to victory'.
      - V n as n. Cx7 e.g. 'The committee elected Joan as chair'.
      - V n in n. Cx21 e.g. 'The publicity landed Brian in trouble'.
      - V n into n
        - Cx13 e.g. 'The committee co-opted Brian into the role'.
        - Cx14 e.g. 'The team dragged the car into place'.
        - Cx16 e.g. 'The publicity plunged Joan into trouble'.
      - V n out of n
        - Cx8 e.g. 'The press hounded Joan out of office'.
        - Cx9 e.g. 'The committee shut Brian out of the discussion'.
        - Cx10 e.g. 'Joan bailed Brian out of jail'.
      - V n to n
        - Cx12 e.g. 'The court deported Brian to Canada'.
        - Cx13 e.g. 'Joan shackled the lock to the door'.
        - Cx14 e.g. 'Brian broadened the discussion to the issue of racism'.
        - Cx15 e.g. 'Brian promoted Joan to vice-president'.
        - Cx18 e.g. 'Joan condemned Brian to a boring job'.
- Metaphoric: the cause and effect are implied (See Figure 6.6f)
  - Patterns with a phrase
    - V n n
      - Cx16 e.g. 'The publicity caused Brian harm'.
      - Cx17 e.g. 'The company charged Joan £200'.

        - Cx18 e.g. 'The decision saved Brian £200'.
  - Patterns with a preposition
    - V n into n
      - Cx15 e.g. 'Brian introduced another factor into the situation'.
      - Cx17 e.g. 'Joan's enthusiasm breathed life into the situation'.
      - Cx18 e.g. 'The committee built breaks into the timetable'.
    - V n of n. Cx1 e.g. 'Joan deprived Brian of his freedom.' and Cx2 e.g. 'Joan rid Brian of his fear of flying'.
    - V n with n
      - Literal: change to a physical object
        - Cx13 e.g. 'Brian decorated the tree with baubles'.
        - Cx14 e.g. 'Joan coated the cake with icing'.
        - Cx15 e.g. 'The children flooded the area with water'.
        - Cx16 e.g. 'Brian sweetened the punch with honey'.
        - Cx17 e.g. 'Joan peppered the dish with cloves'.
        - Cx18 e.g. 'Brian stocked the larder with tins'.
      - Figurative: change to an abstract entity
        - Cx19 e.g. 'Brian imbued the situation with menace'.
        - Cx20 e.g. 'The situation beset Brian with problems'.
        - Cx21 e.g. 'Joan tempered her criticism with humour'.

6.4 The Causation Systemic Network

The Meaning Network for Causation, though extensive, is simple in that at any point in the network a distinction is made between forms or meanings that are relevant at that point. The disadvantages are partly practical, in that the result is a massive network that contains a substantial amount of repetition. For example, the distinction between 'Cause as subject' and 'Affected as subject' appears more than once, as does the distinction between a 'positive' cause, making something happen, and a 'negative' cause, preventing something from happening. The disadvantages are also conceptual, in that the broader picture cannot be seen in the mass of detail. To use terms from SFG, it is not clear what language resources are 'at risk' in making the meaning of Causation. To fill this gap a complementary network is proposed: the Causation Systemic Network. This network appears as Figure 6.7. It shows mainly independent or simultaneous choices and provides a summary of the distinctions that appear in the Meaning Networks.

At the left-most, most general, side of the network a distinction is made between 'meaning' and 'form', though the distinction is admittedly a little arbitrary. It indicates that talking about causation entails making choices related to meaning, such as what type of outcome there is, and choices related to form, such as what pattern to use. Within 'meaning' the following choices are represented:

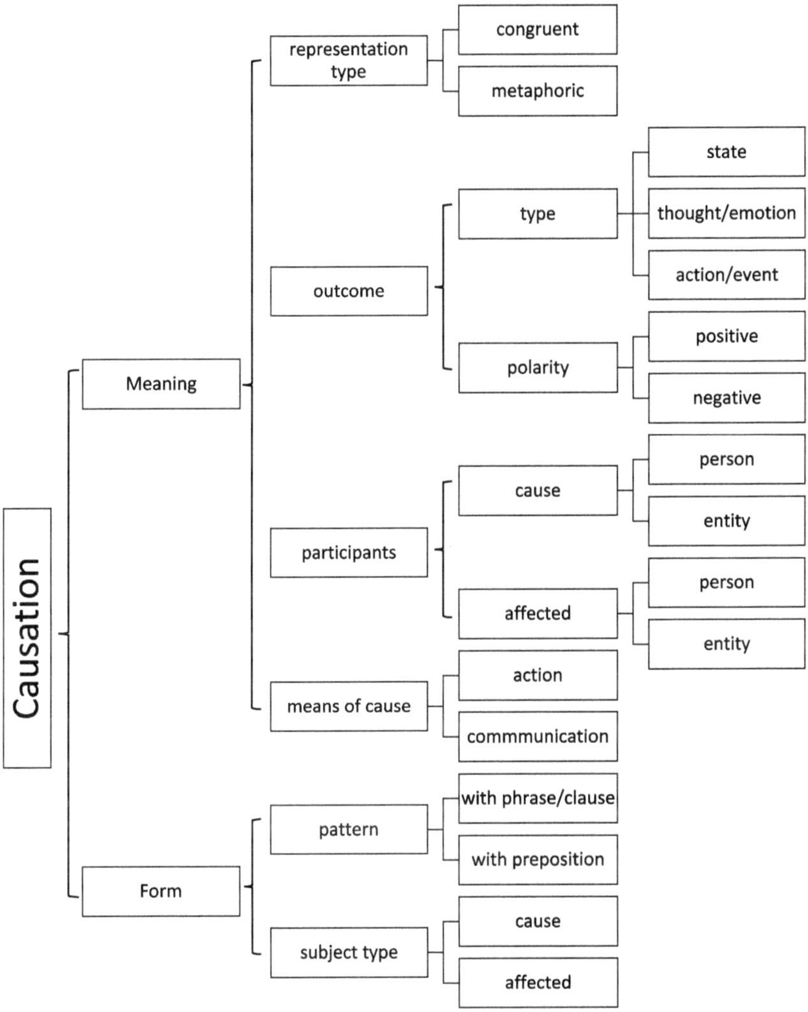

Figure 6.7 Causation Systemic Network

- Representation type: this is congruent or metaphoric, as explained in Section 6.2. Metaphoric representation leaves part of the cause-effect process inexplicit. This accounts for the difference between 'The meal made Brian ill' (the effect – 'Brian is ill' – is explicit) and 'The meal caused Brian harm' ('Brian is ill' is implicit).
- The nature of the outcome of the act of causation. A distinction can be made regarding the type of outcome – state, thought or emotion, and action or

event – and regarding what is termed here the 'polarity', meaning that something is caused to happen or caused not to happen. The polarity distinguishes between 'shoot someone dead' and 'keep someone safe'.

- The nature of the participants involved. Both the cause participant and the affected participant may be a person or an entity. This distinguishes 'Journalists hounded him out of office' from 'The events aroused jealousy'.
- How the cause is brought about (the 'means of cause'). This may be construed as an action or as a means of communication. This distinguishes between 'Journalists hounded him out of office' and 'The minister talked him into leaving'.

The following choices of 'form' are represented in Figure 6.7:

- The pattern used. This may specify phrases and clauses only or may specify a preposition.
- The arrangement of the participants in the clause. Specifically, the subject may indicate the cause or the affected participant. This accounts for the difference between 'Gerald co-opted Brian on to the committee' and 'Brian's place on the committee resulted from Gerald's support'.

No attempt is made here to match up the Systemic Network with the Meaning Network. This would involve specifying which combination of feature choices from the Systemic Network resulted in each construction. Examples of this are easy to produce. For example, the combination of features listed here:

- Representation type: **congruent** + Outcome type: **action/event** + Outcome polarity: **positive** + Participant_cause: **person** + Participant_affected: **person** + Means: communication + Pattern: **with preposition** + Subject type: **cause**

leads to two patterns: **V n *into* -ing** and **V n *into* n** (Figure 6.5b). These in turn are divided into nine constructions:

(a) the 'talk someone into doing something' construction;
(b) the 'bully someone into doing something' construction;
(c) the 'frighten someone into doing something' construction;
(d) the 'charm someone into doing something' construction;
(e) the 'persuade someone into doing something' construction;
(f) the 'talk someone into an action' construction;
(g) the 'pressure someone into an action' construction;
(h) the 'intimidate someone into an action' construction; and
(i) the 'charm someone into an action' construction.

This is consistent with Hasan's (1996/1987) modelling of semantic and formal features that have individual verbs as outcomes, though here the construction, both more and less specific than an individual verb, is proposed as the end point.

Although it is straightforward to illustrate in this way how choices from the Systemic Network can lead into constructions on the Meaning Network, showing all the potential choices combinations in a single network would lead to excessive complexity. It is for this reason that the alternative – Meaning Networks and Systemic Networks shown separately – is used in this book.

6.5 Conclusion

This chapter has described how Verb Argument Constructions can be organised as networks. The networks represent the resources available via verbs in English for expressing a given meaning and show those resources as a series of alternatives. Specifically, the resources referred to in this section are Verb Argument Constructions, and such constructions constitute the most delicate, right-most end of the Meaning Networks. The example given in this chapter is the semantic field of Causation. It has been proposed that it is best to employ two kinds of network to show how the constructions are related to one another. The Meaning Network is a vast and repetitive network showing no simultaneous or independent choices and no cross-over lines. Reading from left to right, the network indicates 'A speaker making this kind of meaning can use one of these alternatives'. For example, a speaker representing a situation in which someone or something causes a change in thought can do so using a verb complementation pattern that includes an indication of the Cogniser, or one that does not (Figure 6.4b). Reading from right to left, the same network indicates 'The constructions expressing this semantic field represent these dimensions of similarity and contrast'. For example, the construction 'shake someone out of an emotion' is similar to 'amaze someone with something' (Emoter is the clause Object). It is different from 'arouse an emotion in someone' (Emoter is in the prepositional phrase) and more different still from 'leave an impression' (no Emoter). The Systemic Network summarises the dimensions of choice, or the language features involved in these choices, and provides a summary of 'what matters' when Causation is expressed in English.

This book is about Verb Argument Constructions, that is, one kind of construction only. Language is, of course, about much more than constructions of this kind. The resources modelled in this chapter are not the only ones available for expressing Causation in English. Causation can be expressed using:

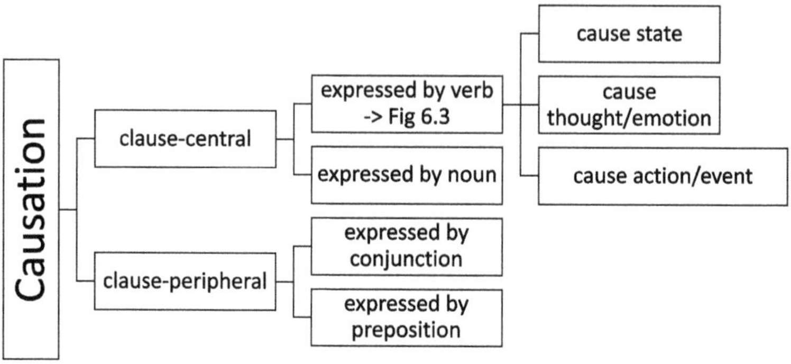

Figure 6.8 Superordinate Causation Network

- A verb e.g. . . . *the decline in apprenticeships has led to a reduced demand for part-time craft courses*. (BNC)
- A noun e.g. . . . *told me that the dent was the result of an accident with a bicycle*. (BNC)
- A conjunction e.g. *Local authorities had missed residents because they had failed to use up-to-date maps*. (BNC)
- A preposition e.g. . . . *a strong post-Carboniferous coalification took place due to a thick cover of . . . sediments*. (BNC)

Clearly, Verb Argument Constructions comprise only one of these four alternatives. The examples above, and the constructions they exemplify, can be further grouped into those that involve central elements of a clause (Subject, Verb, Object or Complement) and those that express peripheral elements such as adverbials, including subordinate clauses. This means that to fully account for the semantic field of Causation it is necessary to propose another network, more general than that shown in Figure 6.3, expressing these options. Figure 6.8 illustrates this.

This chapter has explained the process of deriving networks for the semantic field of Causation in some detail. The following chapters will address the other semantic fields in turn.

7 Semantic Fields: Cognition and Communication

7.1 Introduction

Chapter 6 explained the process of arranging the constructions that express a given semantic field into two kinds of network: the taxonomic network referred to in this book as the Meaning Network and the network that makes explicit the relevant features in the semantic field, referred to as the Systemic Network. The example used in Chapter 6 was the semantic field of Causation.

This chapter repeats the process of deriving networks in relation to two further semantic fields: Cognition and Communication. As explained in Chapter 5, the focus on these fields is inspired by the process types identified by Halliday (e.g. Halliday and Matthiessen 2014) as Mental and Verbal, though the semantic field includes constructions that would not be classified as belonging to those process types. Cognition might be defined as 'the representation of what someone thinks, feels, or perceives', while Communication is 'the representation of communication through speech, sign, writing, gesture, or expression'. What these fields have in common is that they represent a situation as mediated through a thinker, perceiver, or communicator. Grammatically, the situation may be expressed in a that-clause, occurring with a verb of thought, perception, or communication, as illustrated in the invented examples (1)–(3).

(1) Zak thought that the bus was late.

(2) Zak saw that the bus was late.

(3) Zak told Zinnia that the bus was late.

There are, however, numerous other ways in which cognition and communication may be represented. The alternative lexicogrammatical options for expressing cognition and communication have been extensively researched, in part because there are considered to be significant ideological implications to choosing between ways of representing speech and thought (e.g. Thompson 1994: 150–187). This is often discussed in relation to the choice of reporting verb, such as ADMIT, which implies that the speaker acknowledges a wrongdoing, or CLAIM, which implies that the reporter does not agree with the speaker (Hunston 1995). Semino and Short (2004: 141) give an interesting example in the context of the presentation of thoughts in news reports. They make the point that when thoughts are reported this must be the consequence of an inference: the journalist cannot possibly know what someone else thinks. They argue that when journalists describe politicians, for example, as 'believing' something, they do so to protect themselves from challenge.

This chapter gives a brief, selective overview of some of the research in this area (7.2), then summarises the approach taken in this study (7.3), before describing the Systemic Network and Meaning Networks for Cognition (7.4) and Communication (7.5). The chapter ends with a conclusion.

7.2 The Semantic Fields of Cognition and Communication: Selected Concepts

This section begins with a brief overview of the account of Mental and Verbal clauses given in Halliday and Matthiessen (2014), because it is these categories of clause-type that has inspired the identification of Cognition and Communication as semantic fields in this study. As noted earlier, however, the different purposes of the two enterprises will inevitably lead to differences in the outcome. The purpose of defining Mental and Verbal clauses in Systemic Function Grammar (SFG) is to enable consistent analysis of texts. The purpose of identifying a semantic field in this study is to model the constructions that comprise that field. Halliday and Matthiessen (2014) treat Mental clauses as one of the three main types of clause, alongside Material and Relational clauses. They differentiate between Material and Mental clauses thus: 'While "material" clauses are concerned with our experience of the material world, "mental" clauses are concerned with our experience of the world of our own consciousness' (Halliday and Matthiessen 2014: 245). They identify four types: perceptive, cognitive, desiderative, and emotive, roughly equating to 'seeing', 'thinking', 'wanting', and 'feeling' (Halliday and Matthiessen 2014: 256).

Mental clauses contain a Senser who is a conscious being or a being endowed with consciousness. This observation might be reversed, in that entities that are the subjects of Mental process clauses are construed as having consciousness and thus being Sensers. This includes examples such as (4).

(4) My computer doesn't want to load a CD (enTenTen21)

They also contain a Phenomenon, which 'may be not only a thing but also an act or a fact' (Halliday and Matthiessen 2014: 251). Halliday and Matthiessen (2014: 251–252) exemplify this with examples repeated here as (5) and (6).

(5) He saw the sand dredger heading for the cruiser. (Phenomenon is an act)

(6) I regret . . . that I was away from home. (Phenomenon is a fact)

Two key grammatical properties distinguish Mental from Material clauses (Halliday and Matthiessen 2014: 249). One is that Mental process verbs permit projection, that is, complementation by a that-clause. The other is that the unmarked form of the verb is simple rather than progressive aspect: 'I like' rather than 'I'm liking'.

Verbal clauses are defined as 'clauses of saying' (Halliday and Matthiessen 2014: 302). They are treated as one of the 'other' process types, along with Behavioural and Existential. This is perhaps because, unlike Mental processes, they do not construe a separate type of experience – Verbal clauses, like Material clauses, are concerned with the material world, albeit one of sounds or symbols. They are also less clearly identified through grammatical features: they '[exhibit] certain characteristics of other process types' (Halliday and Matthiessen 2014: 306). The participants in a Verbal clause are: a Sayer, which is often a person but can be anything conveying a message (Halliday and Matthiessen 2014: 304), a Receiver (or hearer), a Target, and Verbiage, which may be the content of what is said or the 'name of the saying', such as 'She told a story' or 'He asked a question' (Halliday and Matthiessen 2014: 306).

Halliday and Matthiessen prioritise grammatical characteristics, including participant type, in distinguishing clause types, and as a result, they treat Mental and Verbal processes as very different from one another. Other approaches take what might be called a more semantic approach and divide the phenomena very differently. One of the most influential and comprehensive studies of the language of cognition and communication is by Semino and Short (2004). Working within the field of stylistics, they give a quantitative and qualitative account of the presentation of speech, writing, and thought in a corpus of British English comprising prose fiction, news reports, and (auto) biography (Semino and Short 2004: 19). It is significant that they focus on speech, writing, and thought only: they do not seek to distinguish mental and verbal processes from other clause types, as Halliday and Matthiessen do. On the other hand, they are concerned with choice and the social effects of that choice, as SFG is. Semino and Short propose categories of speech, writing, and thought presentation that are distinguished by the degree of 'involvement' or 'control' exercised by the writer (the 'reporter') (Semino and Short 2004: 10). If a direct quote is used, for example, the speaker of the quotation might be said to have control of the words. If a speech act is summarised, as in 'He asked if he might leave', a greater degree of control remains with the reporter. A writer of fiction, news or (auto)biography selects (even if unconsciously) from the options to achieve a particular effect.

An essential point made by Semino and Short is that the phenomenon they are investigating is 'presentation' rather than 'representation' or 'reporting'. This is because in a novel there is no actual communicative act to report – the world and its events are fictional – and even in news reporting or autobiography, where there is an anterior communicative event, there is no guarantee that apparent reports reflect actual prior words used. Furthermore, as they point out, thought is not a communicative act and there is no prior or anterior situation to be reported (Semino and Short 2004: 50). They therefore prefer the term 'presentation', which might be regarded as similar to Halliday's use of 'construal': the language used makes, or construes, or presents, situations in the world, rather than reflecting or reporting them.

The categories of speech, writing, and thought are placed on a scale of authorial control, revised by Semino and Short (2004: 49) from an earlier version proposed by Leech and Short (1981). Each category has a 'speech', 'writing', and 'thought' version. They are:

- Narrative report of voice, writing or internal voice
- Narrative report of speech/writing/thought act
- Indirect speech/writing/thought
- Free indirect speech/writing/thought
- Direct speech/writing/thought

Examples of each of the 'speech' categories, taken from Semino and Short (2004) are given in examples (7)–(11).

(7) She talked on. (Narrator's Report of Voice. There is no indication of speech act or content.)

(8) He . . . told her about his imminent return. (Narrative Report of Speech Act. There is an indication of the speech act of 'telling', and a general topic, but no representation of what was said.)

(9) He . . . told her that he would return the following day. (Indirect Speech. There is a representation of what was said in a that-clause.)

(10) He looked at her. He would come back tomorrow. (Free Indirect Speech. This blends aspects of Indirect and Direct Speech.)

(11) He . . . said 'I'll come back tomorrow'. (Direct Speech. There is a quotation.)

There is a wealth of quantitative information given in Semino and Short's book, based on painstaking annotation of the corpus to allow comparisons of frequency. Overall, the proportions of speech, writing, and thought presentation in the sub-corpora are as might be expected. Presentation of speech is the most frequent of the three overall and is particularly frequent in the news corpus; the biography corpus has the highest proportion of writing presentation; and thought is most frequently presented in the fiction corpus. Within the speech presentation, Direct Speech is most frequently found in fiction, while Indirect Speech and Narrative Report of Speech Acts occur most frequently in news reports (Semino and Short 2004: 150). There are also interesting examples of qualitative interpretation of specific instances. In a case study of a biography of a medium who claims to be in contact with the spirits of people who have died, for instance, Semino and Short (2004: 206–210) demonstrate that Direct Speech is used when the medium is presenting communication with the people who have died where Narrative Report of Speech Act is used to present communication with their relatives on earth. They argue that this is an act of validation of the medium's claims – the communication with the departed is more immediate and 'real' than that with the living relatives. Thus, the series of choices in a presentation made by the biography authors influence the reader's interpretation of events.

As pointed out by Halliday and Matthiessen (2014: 303), Verbal clauses (and to a lesser extent Mental ones) 'play an important role in academic discourse, making it possible to quote and report from various scholars while at the same time indicating the writer's stance with verbs like *point out, suggest, claim, assert*'. This points to other distinctions that might be made in the semantic space of Cognition and Communication. Martin and White (2005: 134), for example, subsume Verbal processes, and some Mental processes, in a network of choices in the field of Engagement. This makes a primary distinction between 'contracting' the dialogic space (making disagreement less possible) and 'expanding' the space (making disagreement more possible). These are semantic categories and the resources used in each comprise a variety of lexicogrammatical forms. The 'expand the dialogic space' option includes all forms of attribution, including reporting, and this is divided between 'acknowledge [that someone holds an opinion]' ('argues that'; 'believes that; 'states that') and 'distance [oneself from the opinion]' ('claims that').

A whole other set of distinctions within Verbal processes with a projected clause (i.e. a reporting verb followed by a that-clause) is proposed by Charles (2006). She notes that such clauses may be used by a writer to assert their own propositions, as well as to attribute propositions to others. Using a systemic-type network of choices, she makes a primary distinction between clause subjects that are Human, Non-human or *it*. Within each, there is the option that the source of proposition is 'self' or 'other'. Instances of 'self' as source are shown in examples (12)–(14), which instances of 'other' as source are shown in examples (15)–(17) (all examples from Charles 2006).

(12) I argue that . . .

(13) My interpretation of Mazzini will imply that . . .

(14) In Chapter 3 it was stated that . . .

(15) Armstrong notes that . . .

(16) A recent study has found that . . .

(17) It has been shown that . . .

Charles uses these distinctions to compare two corpora, consisting of postgraduate theses: one in the social science field of Politics and one in the physical science field of Materials Science. The two differ considerably in the frequency of the various choices made. Politics makes more use of human subjects while Materials Science makes more use of *it* as subject. However, Materials Science makes more use of the 'self' as source. In Politics, it is more common to have 'other' as source, but the 'others' to whom propositions are attributed are less likely to be other researchers and more likely to be actors in the political field. If the lens is reversed, and the category of 'self-sourced reports' is observed, in the Politics corpus, the self is expressed as human or as *it* in most cases, while in the Materials Science corpus, the self is mostly expressed through *it* and then through non-human subjects. Charles (2006) goes on to show how these differentials in frequency contribute to the community values of the social sciences and physical sciences respectively.

The point of this brief discussion of some different approaches to the broad area covered by the notions of Cognition and Communication is to highlight similarities and differences. All the researchers cited focus on choice between the resources available to express something. In some cases these choices are presented as a network (Martin and White 2005; Charles 2006; Halliday and Matthiessen 2014), in others as a scale (Semino and Short 2004). They demonstrate the consequences of the choices made in ideological or societal impact. The different focuses of the research, however, means that the general meanings of communicating and cognising are divided up very differently to meet the aim of the research. In the following section, the approach taken in this study will be described.

7.3 Cognition and Communication in This Study

This book is concerned with Verb Argument Constructions only, so omits constructions that centre around nouns and that express speech or thought, such as 'the thought/idea/ hope that' or 'the assertion/argument/proposition that'. It also excludes attribution using prepositional phrases, such as 'according to'. Constructions that indicate that someone thinks, feels, or perceives something are included in the Cognition category. Note that this includes perception verbs (SEE, HEAR, etc.) that are not included in Semino and Short's (2004) definition of 'thought' but which are included in Halliday and Matthiessen's (2014) class of Mental processes. It also includes instances where the verb used is more conventionally a Material process, used metaphorically, as in examples (18) and (19). In these examples, the Senser (underlined) is not the subject of the clause.

(18) He struck her as an interesting person.

(19) A clever thought came to her.

A total of 154 constructions have been identified as expressing the Cognition semantic field.

Constructions that indicate that someone writes, says, or signs something are included in the Communication field, as are constructions that indicate paralinguistic communication such as gestures or facial expressions. As with the Cognition field, this includes metaphoric use of conventionally Material process verbs, as in example (20).

(20) He skated around the topic.

Omitted from the set are intransitive constructions without prepositional complementation, such as 'he spoke' or 'she mused'. These are instances of the pattern **V**, which is excluded from this study. Thus, examples such as (7), from Semino and Short's (2004) category of 'Narrative Report of Voice' are not included. The pattern **V with quote** is also excluded, meaning that Semino and Short's (2004) 'Direct Speech' category, as in example (11) is not included in the study. This is because it was considered that the pattern **V with quote** required no further interpretation in terms of construction. Omitting it does mean, however, that the Communication semantic field is somewhat under-represented in terms of constructions. The category of Free Indirect Speech (example (10)) is not represented in this study because it is not connected with construction choice. A total of 103 constructions have been identified as expressing the Communication semantic field.

As noted in Chapter 2, the pattern **V n** is particularly diverse in the meanings it expresses and the range and number of verbs that are used in it. The constructions that draw on that pattern are listed on the Transitivity-Net website in four different files. Two of these are relevant to this chapter: **V n (Cognition)** and **V n (Communication)**. In some of the figures, these are abbreviated to **V n (Cog)** and **V n (Comm)**.

7.4 From Construction to Network: Cognition

In line with Halliday and Matthiessen's (2014) modelling of mental processes, the constructions expressing cognition are divided into Emotion, Thought, and Perception. No separate Desiderative category is proposed; instead, desiderative meanings are subsumed under Emotion. Each of the three is described separately.

Cognition: Emotion

The term 'Emotion' refers to constructions which describe an emotion that someone experiences. There are 53 constructions that express this meaning, drawing on 27 verb complementation patterns.

The Systemic Network. The Systemic Network is shown in Figure 7.1. It identifies three simultaneous choices: between the elements; between the subject types; and between time references. The first of these relates to the number of elements specified in the construction. All the constructions include a 'Senser' element i.e. the person who feels the emotion. In most cases, they also include a 'Target' element i.e. the thing about which the emotion is felt. Other elements that are less frequent are 'Proxy', 'Reason', and 'Cause'. Examples of each of these elements are shown as examples (1)–(5):

(1) She admired his courage. (Senser)

(2) He worried about the future. (Target)

(3) She feared for her daughter. (Proxy)

(4) She admired him for his courage. (Reason)

(5) Her story shook him out of his apathy. (Cause)

To represent these elements as a series of choices, a distinction is made between 'simple' constructions that express the Senser alone, or the Senser and Target, but no other elements, and 'complex' constructions that include one of the other elements. These choices are shown in bold at the top of Figure 7.1.

The next choice is between which element is realised in the Subject of the clause. In the most congruent constructions, the Subject is the Senser. In other constructions, it is the Target of the emotion, the Emotion itself or the Cause of the emotion. Examples of each of these are shown as examples (6)–(9):

(6) She admired his courage. (Subject is Senser)

(7) The prospect appealed to him. (Subject is Target)

(8) Jealousy gnawed at him. (Subject is Emotion)

(9) Her story shook him out of his apathy. (Subject is Cause)

These choices are shown in italics in the middle of Figure 7.1.

Finally, there is a choice in the time that is referenced by the verb. Time reference is usually unspecified lexically, but in some cases there is a specific

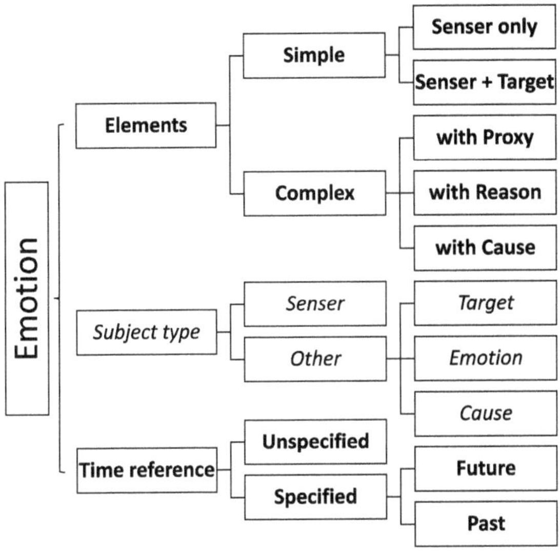

Figure 7.1 Cognition Emotion Systemic Network

indication of future time (e.g. 'anticipate') or of past time (e.g. 'remember'). Examples are shown in examples (10)–(12).

(10) She likes swimming. (unspecified time reference)

(11) She wants to go swimming. (future time reference)

(12) She remembers going swimming. (past time reference)

These choices are shown in bold at the bottom of Figure 7.1.

The Meaning Network. The Meaning Network for Cognition: Emotion draws on all the distinctions described earlier. It is shown in Figure 7.2, but the figure is broken into parts for legibility. The primary distinction made is between constructions with a target and the few that express no target. Where there is a target, it may be a situation or an entity. These first distinctions are shown in Figure 7.2, which also shows the 'no target' set of patterns and constructions. Note that in Figure 7.2d it becomes clear that what is referred to as 'target' in Figure 7.2 is more accurately 'another entity, which may be a target or proxy'.

Figure 7.2b shows more detail where the target is a situation. Here the distinction between 'general' (or unspecified), 'future', and 'past' time references is made. The patterns and constructions in each condition are shown.

Figure 7.2c focuses on constructions where the target is an entity. It distinguishes between four types of Subject: Senser, Target, Emotion, and Causer.

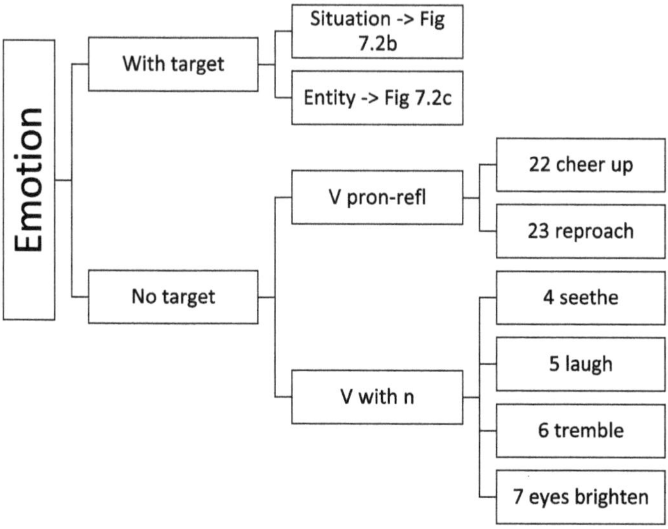

Figure 7.2a Cognition Emotion Meaning Network

The Senser as Subject is treated in greater detail in Figure 7.2d, while the other Subject types are detailed in Figure 7.2e.

Figure 7.2d shows the network for constructions where the target is an entity and the Subject is the Senser. The first distinction made is between constructions which specify a reason for the emotion and those that do not. Within the 'without reason' choice, the distinction between time references again becomes relevant, and there is also a distinction made between constructions that specify a Target and the few that specify a Proxy.

Figure 7.2e shows the network for the other types of Subject, again where the Target is an entity. There are no further distinctions except for the patterns and constructions.

Here is a prose version of all these meaning and form distinctions, with examples invented to maximise simplicity and clarity.

The primary distinction is between constructions that specify a target and those that do not.

- With target. The target may be a situation or an entity.
  - Target is a situation (Figure 7.2b). The time reference may be general, future, or past.
    - General (non-specific) time reference
      - V that Cx13 e.g. 'I hate that he ignores me'. [Note: predominantly US usage.]

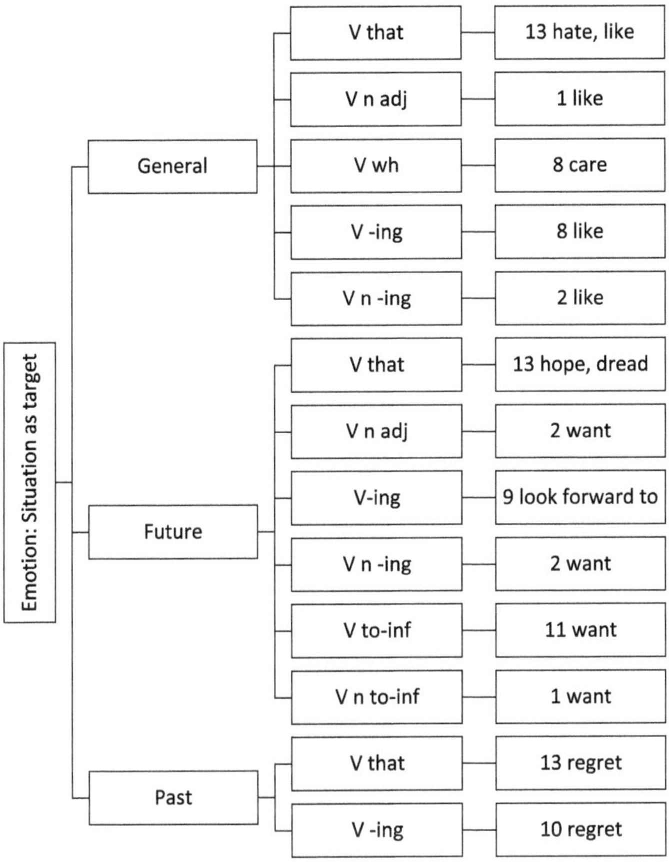

Figure 7.2b Cognition Emotion: the situation as target network

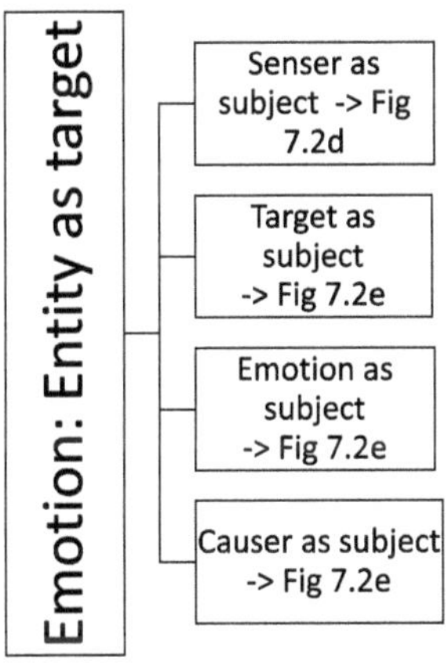

Figure 7.2c Cognition Emotion: the entity as target network

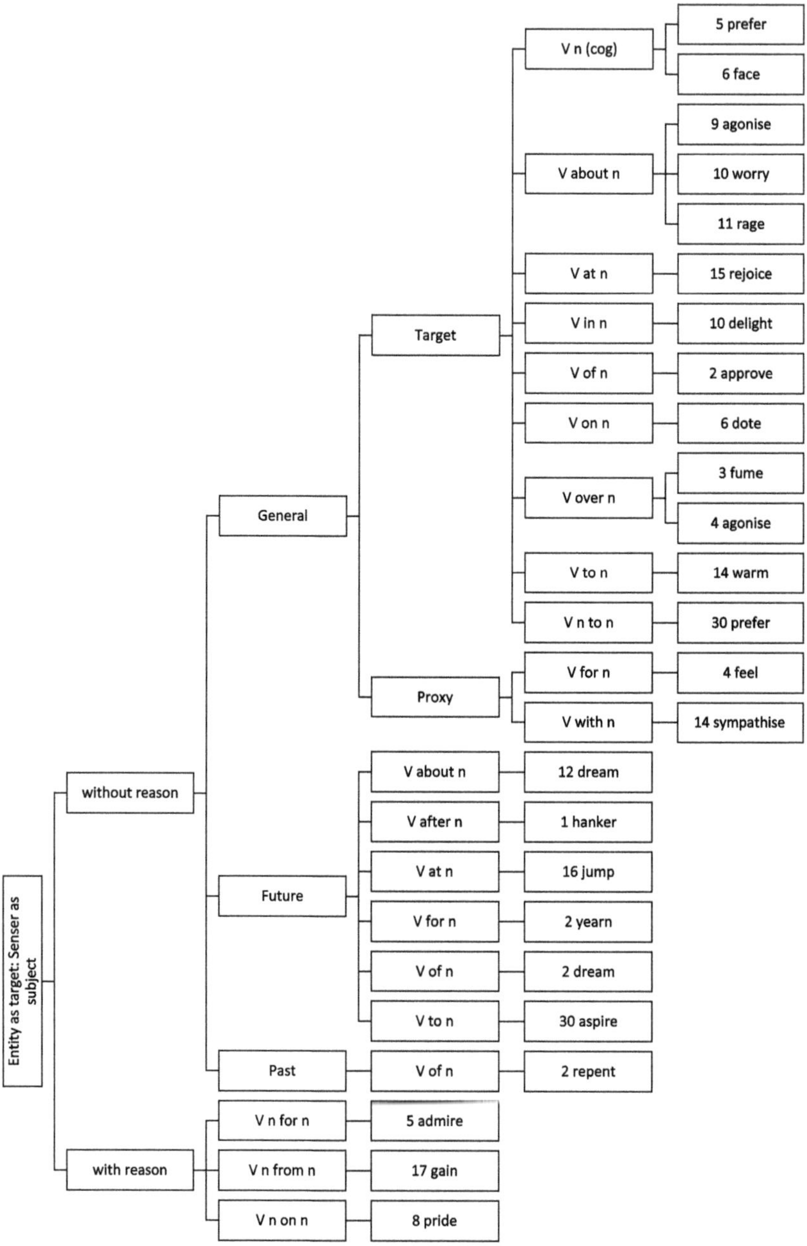

Figure 7.2d Cognition Emotion: the entity as target network, showing senser as subject choices

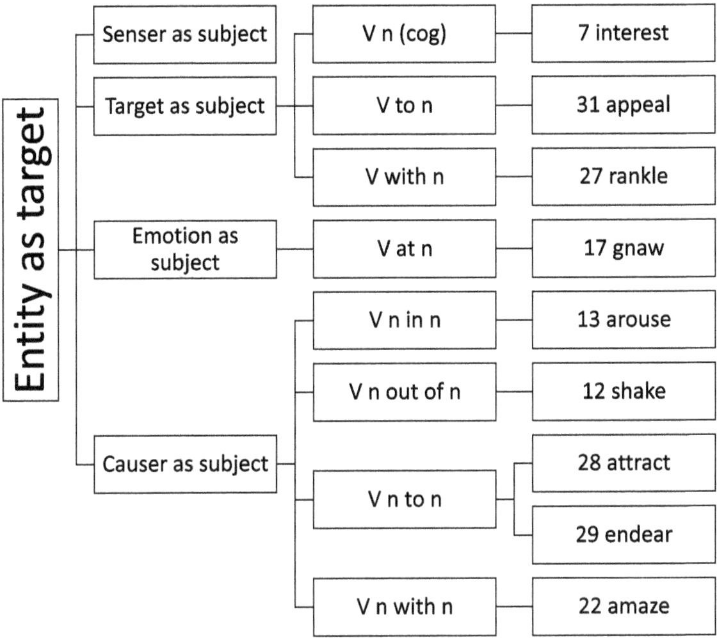

Figure 7.2e Cognition Emotion: the entity as target network, showing target and causer as subject choices

- V n adj Cx1 e.g. 'Emma likes her tea sweet'.
- V wh Cx8 e.g. 'Joe doesn't care who washes the clothes'.
- V -ing Cx8 e.g. 'Emma likes planting bulbs'.
- V n -ing Cx2 e.g. 'Emma hates Joe ignoring her'.

▪ Future time reference
  - V that Cx13 e.g. 'Cathy hopes the parcel will arrive in time'.
  - V n adj Cx2 e.g. 'Cathy wants her coffee hot'.
  - V -ing Cx9 e.g. 'Emma is looking forward to visiting the Christmas market'.
  - V n -ing Cx2 e.g. 'Emma wants the car working properly'.
  - V to-inf Cx11 e.g. 'Cathy wants to celebrate with her family'.
  - V n to-inf Cx1 e.g. 'Joe wants Michael to wash the clothes'.

▪ Past time reference
  - V that Cx13 e.g. 'Joe regrets that he was not kinder'.
  - V -ing Cx10 e.g. 'Joe regrets not being kinder'.

◦ Target is an entity (Figure 7.2c). The subject of the clause may be the Senser, the Target, an Emotion, or a Cause.

- Senser as subject of the clause (Figure 7.2d). A reason may be unspecified or specified.
  - No reason specified. The time reference may be general, future, or past.
    - General (non-specific) time reference. Either a Target or a Proxy may be specified.
      - with a Target
        - V n (Cognition) Cx5 e.g. 'Cathy prefers tea.' and Cx6 e.g. 'Emma couldn't face coffee'.
        - V about n
          - Cx9 e.g. 'Joe agonised about his decision'.
          - Cx10 e.g. Joe worried about the future'.
          - Cx11 e.g. 'Joe raged about the delay'.
        - V at n Cx15 e.g. 'Emma rejoiced at the result'.
        - V in n Cx10 e.g. 'Emma delighted at Cathy's success'.
        - V of n Cx3 e.g. 'Joe approved of the decorations'.
        - V on n Cx6 e.g. 'Cathy doted on the kitten'.
        - V over n Cx3 e.g. 'Joe fumed over the delay.' and Cx4 e.g. 'Joe agonised over the decision'.
        - V to n Cx14 e.g. 'Cathy warmed to the idea'.
        - V n to n Cx30 e.g. 'Emma preferred the kitten to the puppy'.
      - with a Proxy
        - V for n Cx4 e.g. 'Joe felt for the victims'.
        - V with n Cx14 e.g. 'Joe sympathised with the victims'.
    - Future time reference
      - V about n Cx12 e.g. 'Emma dreamt about a career as a vet'.
      - V after n Cx1 e.g. 'Emma hankered after a career as a vet'.
      - V at n Cx16 e.g. 'Emma would jump at a career as a vet'.
      - V for n Cx2 e.g. 'Emma yearned for a career as a vet'.
      - V to n Cx30 e.g. 'Joe aspired to success as a dancer'.
    - Past time reference
      - V of n Cx2 e.g. 'Joe repented of his criminal past'.
  - Reason specified
    - V n for n Cx5 e.g. 'Emma admired Cathy for her poise'.
    - V n from n Cx17 e.g. 'Emma gained courage from Cathy's attitude'.
    - V n on n Cx8 e.g. 'Emma prided herself on her courage'.
- Target as Subject of the clause (Figure 7.2e)
  - V n (Cognition) Cx7 e.g. 'The book interested Joe'.
  - V to n Cx31 e.g. 'The book appealed to Joe'.
  - V with n Cx27 e.g. 'Cathy's remarks rankled with Joe'.
- Emotion as Subject of the clause (Figure 7.2e)
  - V at n Cx17 e.g. 'Remorse gnawed at Cathy'.

    - Causer as Subject of the clause (Figure 7.2e)
        - V n in n Cx13 e.g. 'The book aroused fear in Joe'.
        - V n out of n Cx12 e.g. 'The book shook Joe out of his complacency'.
        - V n to n Cx28 e.g. 'Emma's courage attracted Joe to her.' and Cx29 e.g. 'Emma's courage endeared her to Joe'.
        - V n with n Cx22 e.g. 'Emma amazed Joe with her courage'.
- No target (Figure 7.2a)
    - V pron-refl Cx22 e.g. 'Cathy cheered herself up.' and Cx23 e.g. 'Joe reproached himself'.
    - V with n
        - Cx4 e.g. 'Joe seethed with anger'.
        - Cx5 e.g. 'Cathy laughed with glee'.
        - Cx6 e.g. 'Emma trembled with fear'.
        - Cx7 e.g. 'Cathy's eyes brightened with joy'.

Cognition: Perception

The term 'Cognition: Perception' refers to constructions that indicate how someone perceives something, using senses such as sight or hearing. There are nine constructions with this meaning, drawing on eight verb complementation patterns.

The Systemic Network. The Systemic Network, shown in Figure 7.3, identifies three independent choices: the type of clause Subject, the type of target of the perception, and the sense type. The Subject of the clause is usually the Senser, but in a few cases it is a body part, such as the eyes. Included here is one construction (e.g. 'The third day saw the storms increase') which personifies time as something that 'sees'. Although this is not strictly speaking perception, as there is no animate Senser, the metaphoric use of 'see' warrants its inclusion. The target type is either an entity or a situation. Although it is shown here as an independent choice, in practice 'situation' is an option only when the Subject of the clause is a Senser. The choice of sense type plays no role in the Meaning Network, because constructions indicating perception are mostly used with all senses. However, when the Subject is an indicator of time, the sense must be sight.

The Meaning Network. The Meaning Network is shown in Figure 7.4. It prioritises the type of Subject as the primary distinction. Where the Subject is the Senser, there is a further distinction between constructions where the target is an entity and those where it is a situation. All other distinctions are between patterns and constructions.

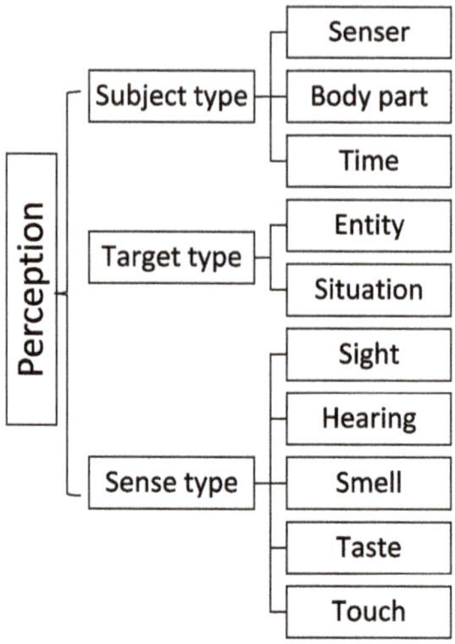

Figure 7.3 Cognition Perception Systemic Network

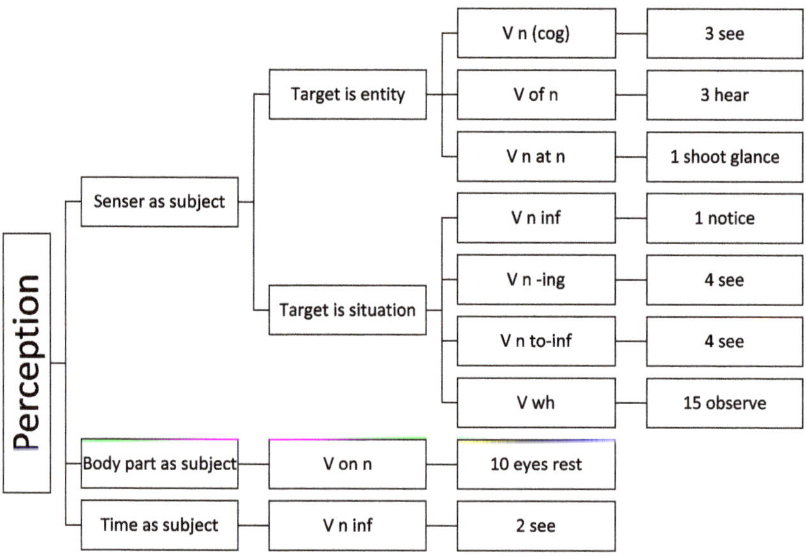

Figure 7.4 Cognition Perception Meaning Network

Here is a prose version of all these meaning and form distinctions, with examples invented to maximise simplicity and clarity.

The primary distinction involves the subject of the clause, whether it is the Senser, a body part, or time.

- Senser as Subject. The target of perception may be an entity or a situation.
  - The target of perception is an entity
    - V n (Cognitive) Cx3 e.g. 'Alan saw the picture'.
    - V of n Cx3 e.g. 'Ella was hearing of disturbances'.
    - V n at n Cx1 e.g. 'Alan shot a glance at his accomplice'.
  - The target of perception is a situation
    - V n inf Cx1 e.g. 'Ella notice Alan cross the road'.
    - V n -ing Cx4 e.g. 'Ella saw Alan crossing the road'.
    - V n to-inf Cx4 (passive only) e.g. 'Alan was seen to have crossed the road'.
    - V wh Cx15 e.g. 'Ella observed what Alan did'.
- Body part as Subject
  - V on n Cx10 e.g. 'Ella's eyes rested on the picture'.
- Time as Subject
  - V n inf Cx2 e.g. 'The second day saw them arrive at the shrine'.

Cognition: Thought

The term 'Thought' refers to constructions which describe the process of thinking. There are 92 constructions that express this meaning, drawing on 31 verb complementation patterns.

The Systemic Network. The Systemic Network for Thought, shown in Figure 7.5, identifies three distinctions between constructions: the Subject type, the Object type, and the process type. Although the figure shows these as simultaneous choices, the process type is an issue only when the Subject is the Senser, and the Object type is an issue only when the Subject is a Causer.

The Subject type choices are shown in bold at the top of Figure 7.5. The most congruent Subject type is the Senser (a person thinks something), as in example (1). Other possible Subject types are an Entity and a Causer of thought. These express the process of thought more obliquely. Three kinds of Entity Subjects are identified: evidence for an idea, the Target of the thought, or a noun indicating an idea. These are illustrated in examples (2)–(4). A Causer of thought is very similar to evidence, but a construction with Causer includes a verb that implies causation. An example is given in example (5).

(1) He thought it was Monday. (Sense as Subject)

(2) The photo suggested that it had been raining. (Evidence as Subject)

(3) The picture claimed his attention. (Target as Subject)

(4) The thought hit him that it might have been raining. (Idea as Subject)

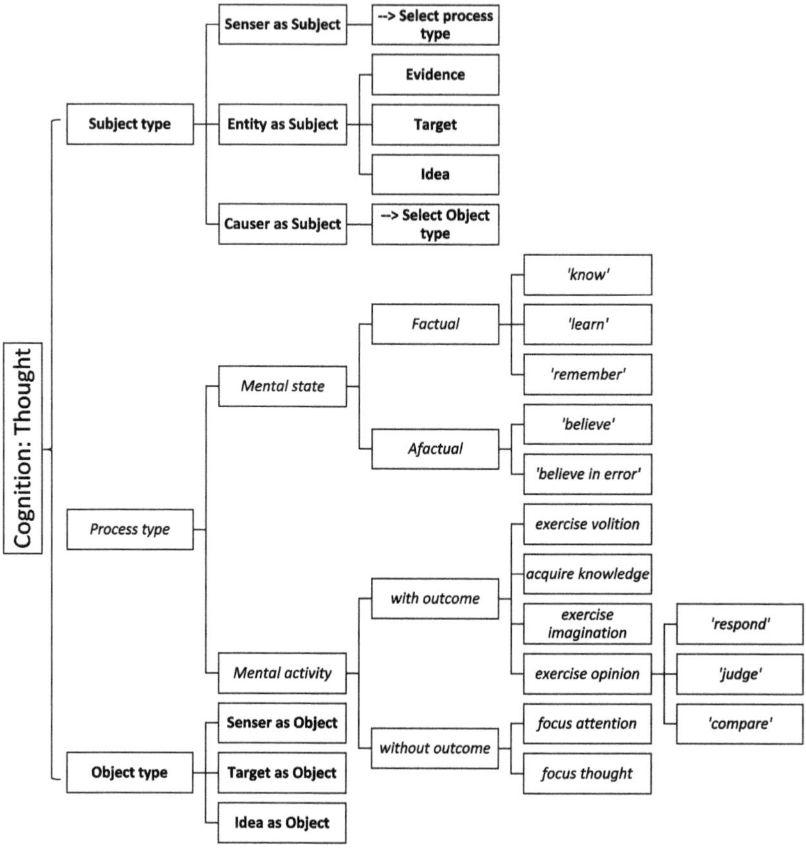

Figure 7.5 Cognition Thought Systemic Network

(5) These events convinced her that she should act. (Causer as Subject)

The process type choices are shown in italics in the middle of Figure 7.5. All the process types identified assume the Senser as Subject, and all are what might broadly be described as mental processes. Taking that for granted, the Process type network makes a primary distinction between verbs indicating a mental state, where there is no process of change or of mental exertion, and those indicating mental activity, which implies mental exertion of some kind. There are five mental state categories, divided into 'factual', implying that what is known or remembered is factually true, and 'afactual', which implies that the target of thought is either uncertain or incorrect. There are six mental activity categories, divided into those 'with an outcome', where the process of thought has a result, and those 'without an outcome', where the thought occurs without a result being specified. Note that in this network, a distinction is made between 'learn', where the action of learning requires no effort and belongs to mental state, and 'acquire knowledge', which does imply exertion and belongs to mental activity. This is the difference between learning something because one is told it, for example, and making an effort to learn historical dates. The category 'exercise opinion' is further divided into responding to another's opinion, making a judgement, and making a comparison between two things. All these options are illustrated in examples (6)–(18).

(6) He knew how much it cost. (Mental state, factual)

(7) He learned how much it cost. (Mental state, factual)

(8) He remembered how much it cost. (Mental state, factual)

(9) She believed him to be her son. (Mental state, afactual)

(10) She mistook the stranger for her son. (Mental state, afactual)

(11) She intended to help them. (Mental activity, with outcome, exercise volition)

(12) She found out how best to help them. (Mental activity, with outcome, acquire knowledge)

(13) She imagined herself helping them. (Mental activity, with outcome, exercise imagination)

(14) He agreed with those comments. (Mental activity, with outcome, exercise opinion)

(15) He judged himself worthy of a prize. (Mental activity, with outcome, exercise opinion)

(16) He compared her to a summer's day. (Mental activity, with outcome, exercise opinion)

(17) She concentrated on her work. (Mental activity, without outcome)

(18) She thought about her work. (Mental activity, without outcome)

Finally, in those cases where the Subject of the clause is a Causer, the Object of the clause may be the Senser, the Target of thought, or a noun indicating an idea. These choices are shown in bold at the bottom of Figure 7.5. They are exemplified in examples (19)–(21).

(19) The results decided him on a course of action. (Senser as Object)

(20) The shape determined the picture's value. (Target as Object)

(21) The book casts doubt on the theory. (Idea as Object)

The Meaning Network. The Meaning Network is shown in Figure 7.6. Because so many patterns and constructions are involved it is shown in segments to make it more legible. The Meaning Network largely follows the Systemic Network in prioritising the Subject type, as shown in Figure 7.6.

Here is a prose version of all these meaning and form distinctions, with examples invented to maximise simplicity and clarity.

The primary distinction involves the nature of the subject of clause, which may be the Senser, and entity, or the Causer.

- The Subject of the clause is a Senser. The basic network is shown in Figure 7.6b. The verb may indicate a mental state or a mental activity.
    - Verb describes a mental state. This is shown in Figure 7.6c. The verb may be factual or afactual.
        - Factual. The factual verbs are of three types: 'know', 'learn' and 'remember'.
            - 'know' type

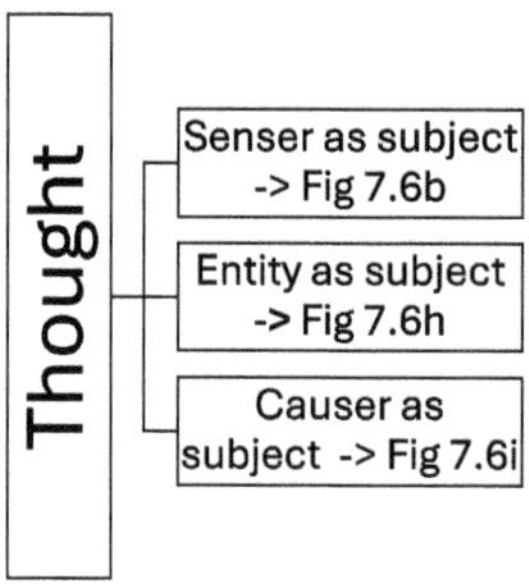

Figure 7.6a Cognition Thought Meaning Network

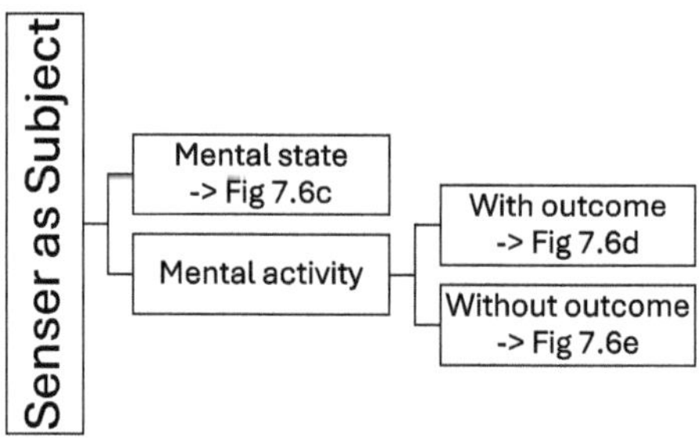

Figure 7.6b Cognition Thought: the senser as subject network

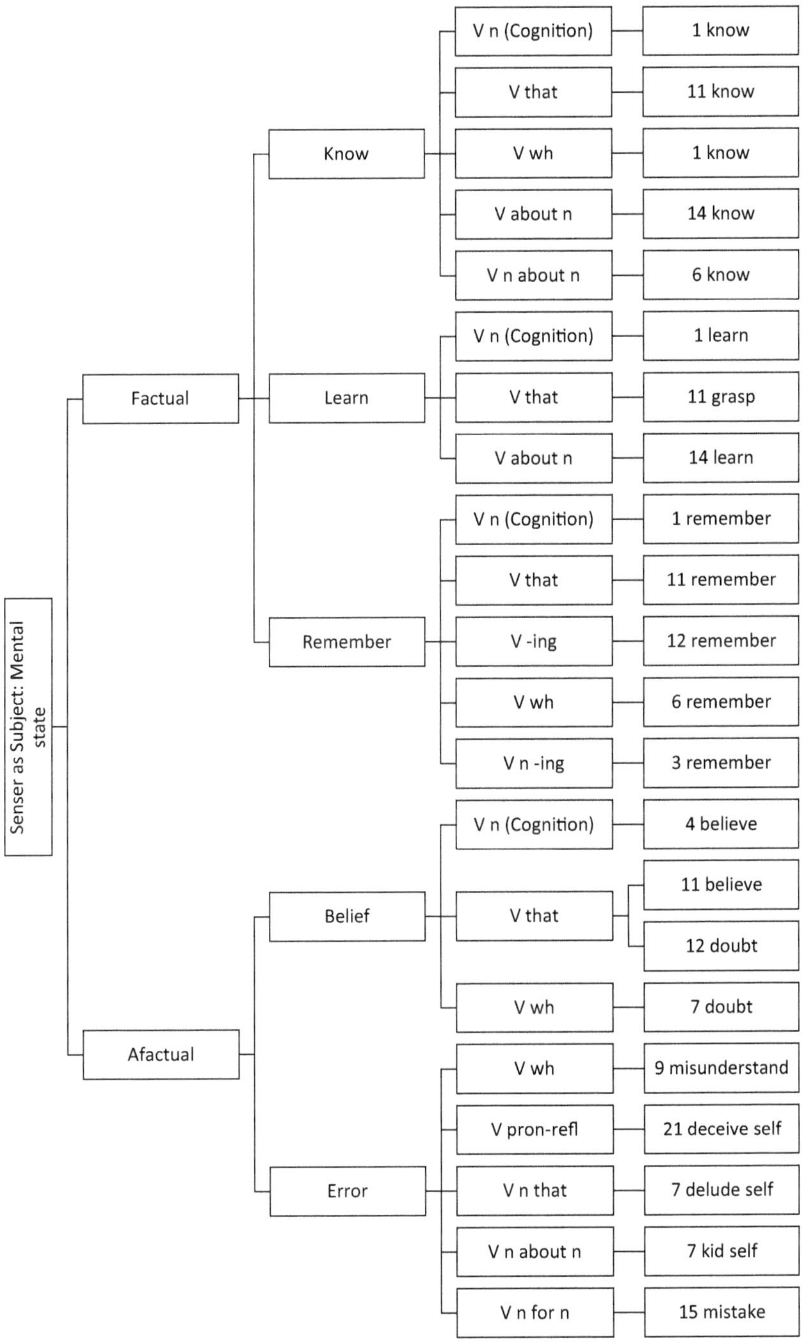

Figure 7.6c Cognition Thought: the senser as subject network, showing mental state choices

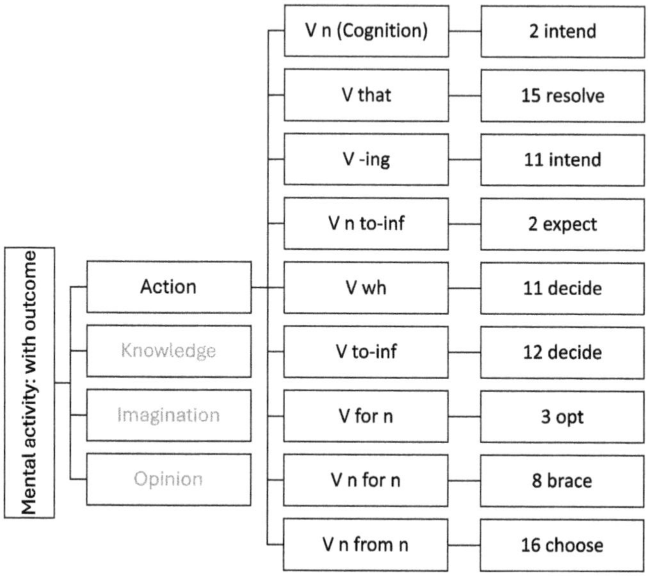

Figure 7.6d Cognition Thought: the senser as subject, mental activity network, showing with outcome, action choices

  - V n (Cognitive) Cx1 e.g. 'Alice knew the facts of the case'.
  - V that Cx11 e.g. 'Alice knew that Jim had stolen the money'.
  - V wh Cx1 e.g. 'Alice knew who had stolen the money'.
  - V about n Cx14 e.g. 'Alice knew about the stolen money'.
- 'learn' type
  - V n (Cognitive) Cx1 e.g. 'Alice learned the facts of the case'.
  - V that Cx11 e.g. 'Alice grasped that Jim stole the money'.
  - V about n Cx14 e.g. 'Alice learned about the theft'.
- 'remember' type
  - V n (Cognition) Cx1 e.g. 'Alice remembered the theft'.
  - V that Cx11 e.g. 'Alice remembered that the money was stolen'.
  - V -ing Cx12 e.g. 'Jim remembered stealing the money'.
  - V wh Cx6 e.g. 'Alice remembered who stole the money'.
  - V n -ing Cx3 e.g. 'Alice remembered Jim stealing the money'.

▪ Afactual. The afactual verbs are of two types: 'believe' and 'error'.
- 'believe' type
  - V n (Cognition) Cx4 e.g. 'Alice believed the story'.
  - V that Cx11 e.g. 'Alice believed that Jim was innocent.' and Cx12 e.g. 'Alice doubted that Jim was guilty'.
  - Vwh Cx7 e.g. 'Alice doubted whether Jim was guilty'.

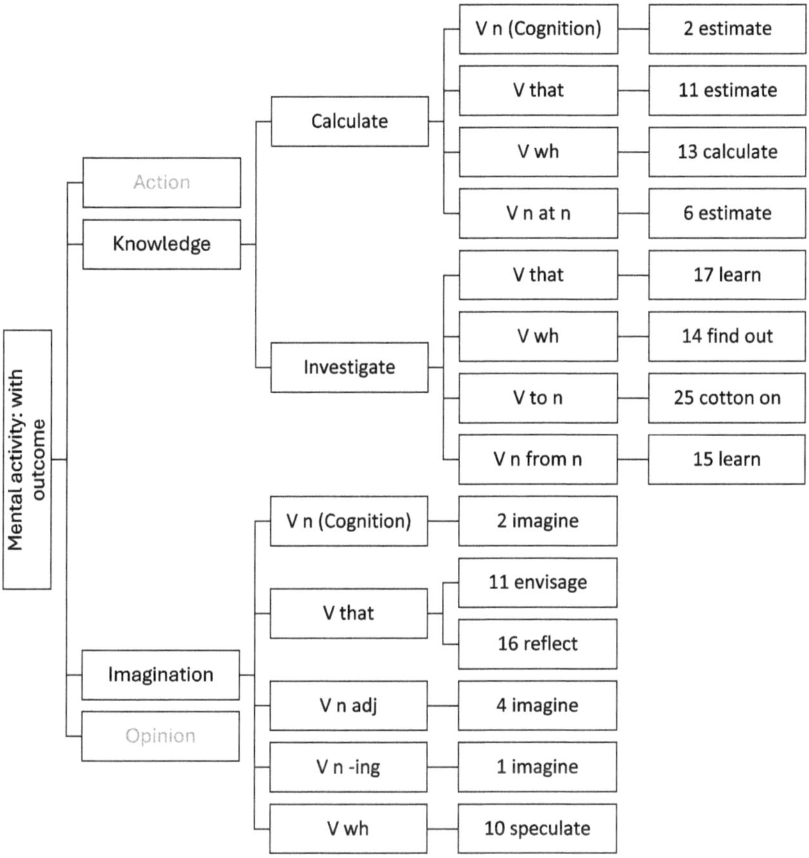

Figure 7.6e Cognition Thought: the senser as subject, mental activity network showing with outcome, knowledge and imagination choices

- 'believe in error' type
  - V wh Cx9 e.g. 'Alice misunderstood what had happened'.
  - V pron-refl Cx21 e.g. 'Alice was deceiving herself'.
  - V n that Cx7 e.g. 'Alice deluded herself that it was true'.
  - V n about n Cx7 e.g. 'Alice kidded herself about the theft'.
  - V n for n Cx15 e.g. 'Alice mistook Jim for the thief'.

◦ Verb describes a mental activity. The construction may specify the outcome of the activity or not.

- Activity has an outcome. This is shown in Figures 7.6d–f. Four kinds of activity are specified: a mental action, acquiring knowledge, using the imagination, and having an opinion.

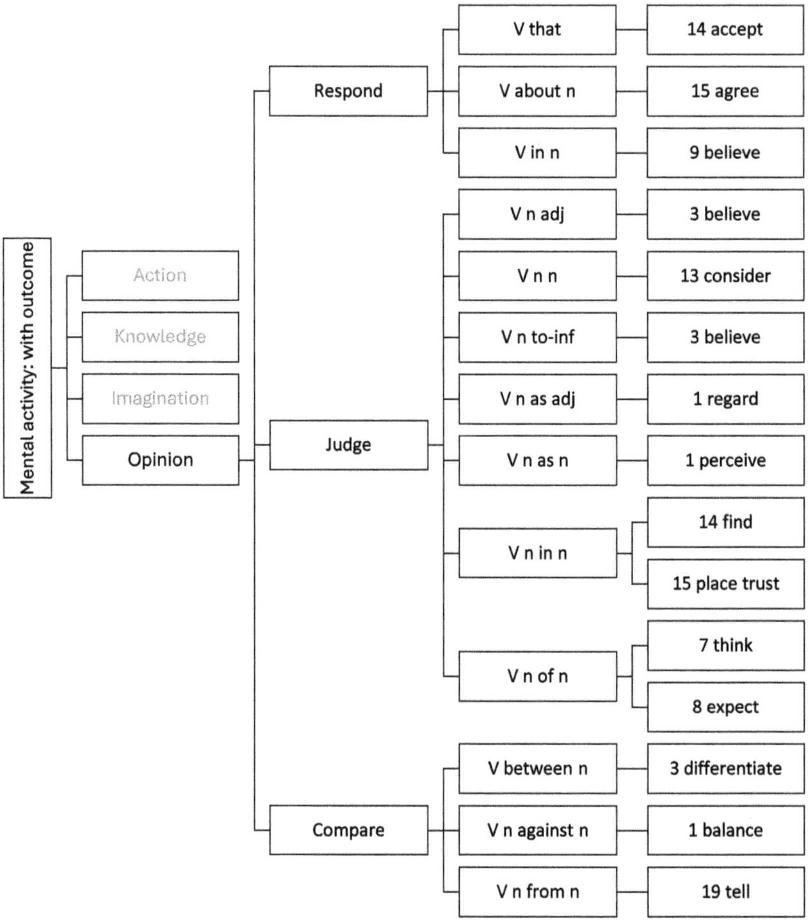

Figure 7.6f Cognition Thought: the senser as subject, mental activity network, showing with outcome, opinion choices

- Mental action (Figure 7.6d)
  - V n (Cognitive) Cx2 e.g. 'Jim intended no harm'.
  - V that Cx15 e.g. 'Jim resolved that he would do no harm'.
  - V -ing Cx11 e.g. 'Jim intended doing no harm'.
  - V n to-inf Cx2 e.g. 'Alice expected Jim to return'.
  - V wh Cx11 e.g. 'Jim decided what he would do'.
  - V to-inf Cx12 e.g. 'Jim decided to steal the money'.
  - V for n Cx3 e.g. 'Alice opted for a red dress'.
  - V n for n Cx8 e.g. 'Alice braced herself for criticism'.

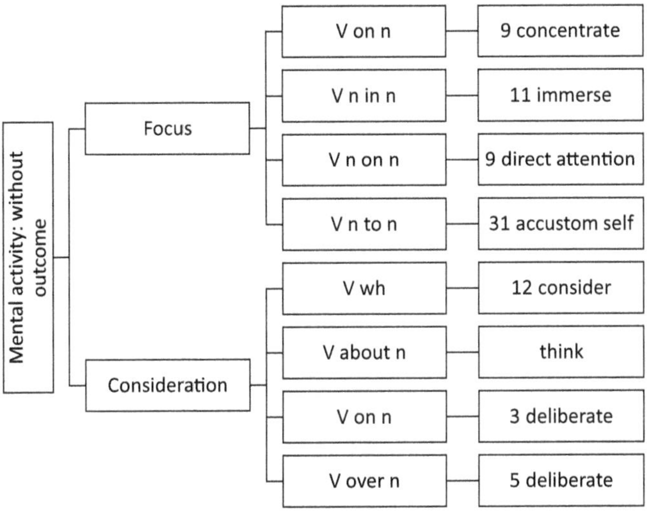

Figure 7.6g Cognition Thought: the senser as subject, mental activity network, showing without outcome choices

    - V n from n Cx16 e.g. 'Alice chose a puppy from the litter'.
- Acquire knowledge (Figure 7.6e). The knowledge may be acquired through calculation or through investigation.
    - Acquire knowledge through calculation
        - V n (Cognitive) Cx2 e.g. 'Alice estimated the value'.
        - V that Cx11 e.g. 'Jim estimated that the train would arrive at 2pm'.
        - V wh Cx13 e.g. 'Alice estimated what the result would be'.
        - V n at n Cx6 e.g. 'Jim estimated that vase at £20'.
    - Acquire knowledge through investigation
        - V that Cx17 e.g. 'Alice learned that the train was late'.
        - V wh Cx14 e.g. 'Alice found out when the train would arrive'.
        - V to n Cx25 e.g. 'Alice cottoned on to the truth'.
        - V n from n Cx15 e.g. 'Jim learned the facts from Alice'.
- Use imagination (Figure 7.6e)
    - V n (Cognitive) Cx2 e.g. 'Pat could imagine the scene'.
    - V that Cx11 e.g. 'Pat envisaged that a problem would arise.' and Cx16 e.g. 'Pat reflected that this would be a problem'.
    - V n adj Cx4 e.g. 'Alice imagined the tree bare of leaves'.
    - V n -ing Cx1 e.g. 'Pat imagined the tree falling'.
    - V wh Cx10 e.g. 'Alice speculated what Jim would do'.
- Have opinion (Figure 7.6f). A distinction is made between responding to another's opinion, making a judgement, and making a comparison.

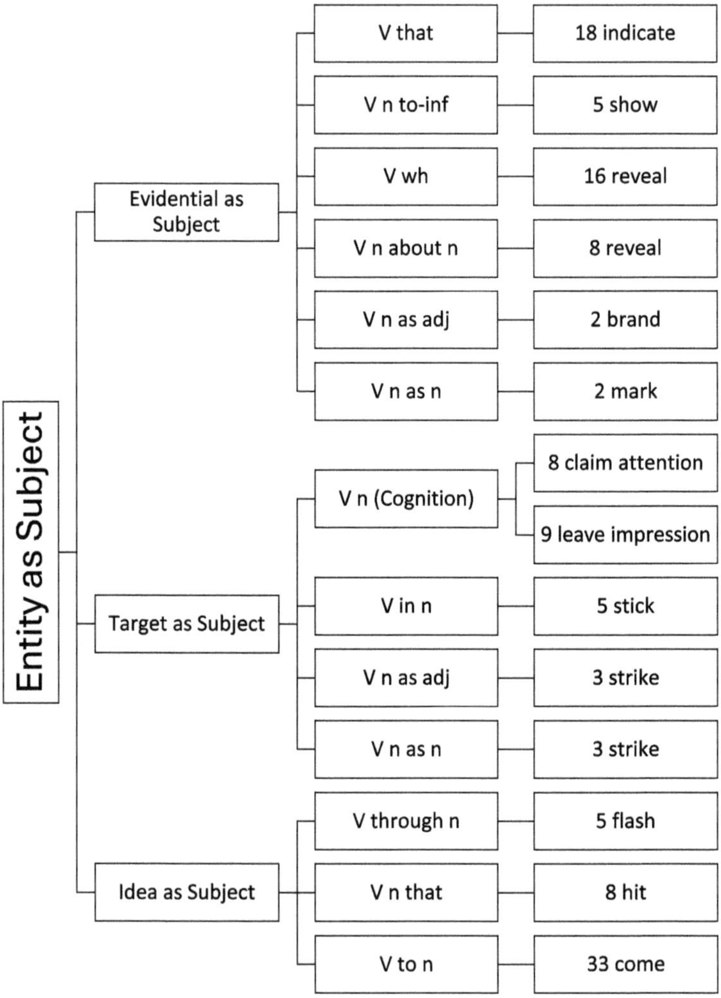

Figure 7.6h Cognition Thought: the entity as subject network

- Respond to another
  - V that Cx14 e.g. 'Pat accepted that Jim had stolen the money'.
  - V about n Cx15 e.g. 'Pat agreed about the circumstances of the theft'.
  - V in n Cx9 e.g. 'Pat believed in Jim's guilt'.
- Make a judgement

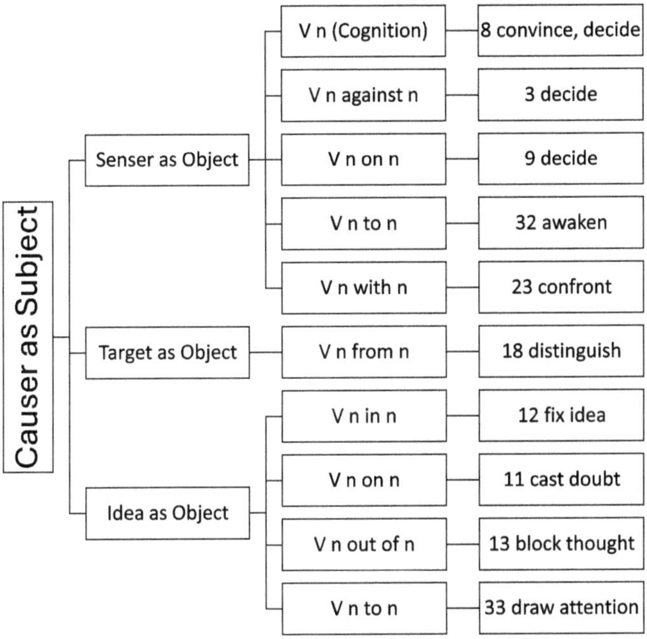

Figure 7.6i Cognition Thought: the causer as subject network

- V n adj Cx3 e.g. 'Pat believed him guilty'.
- V n n Cx13 e.g. 'Alice considered Jim a thief'.
- V n to-inf Cx3 e.g. 'Alice believed Jim to be a thief'.
- V n as adj Cx1 e.g. 'Pat regarded Jim as guilty'.
- V n as n Cx1 e.g. 'Pat regarded Jim as a thief'.
- V n in n Cx14 e.g. 'Alice found comfort in Pat's friendship.' and Cx15 e.g. 'Alice placed trust in Pat's friendship'.
- V n of n Cx7 e.g. 'Alice thought a lot of Jim.' and Cx8 e.g. 'Alice expected a lot of Jim'.

◦ Make a comparison
- V between n Cx3 e.g. 'Jim differentiated between his friends'.
- V n against n Cx1 e.g. 'Jim balanced the chance of success against the possibility of failure'.
- V n from n Cx19 e.g. 'Alice could not tell lies from the truth'.

- Activity has no outcome. This is shown in Figure 7.6g. The construction may indicate that someone focuses the mind or that they give consideration to something.
  - A person focuses the mind

    - V on n Cx9 e.g. 'Pat concentrated on the test'.
    - V n in n Cx11 e.g. 'Pat immersed himself in the test'.
    - V n on n Cx9 e.g. 'Jim directed his attention on the test'.
    - V n to n Cx31 e.g. 'Jim accustomed himself to exam conditions'.
  - A person gives consideration to something
    - V wh Cx12 e.g. 'Alice considered what the answer should be'.
    - V about n Cx? e.g. 'Alice thought about the answer'.
    - V on n Cx3 e.g. 'Alice deliberated on the answer'.
    - V over n Cx5 e.g. 'Alice deliberated over the answer'.

- The subject of the clause is an Entity. This is shown in Figure 7.6h. The subject may be evidence for a conclusion, the target of thought, or a thought or idea.
  - Subject is evidence for the conclusion
    - V that Cx18 e.g. 'Fingerprints indicate that Jim was the thief'.
    - V n to-inf Cx5 e.g. 'The fingerprints showed Jim to be the thief'.
    - V wh Cx16 e.g. 'The fingerprints revealed who the thief was'.
    - V n about n Cx8 e.g. 'The evidence revealed a lot about the crime'.
    - V n as adj Cx2 e.g. 'Pat's clothes branded him as vain'.
    - V n as n Cx2 e.g. 'Pat's clothes marked him as a detective'.
  - Subject is the target of thought
    - V n (Cognitive) Cx8 e.g. 'The picture claimed their attention.' and Cx9 e.g. 'The picture left a deep impression'.
    - V in n Cx5 e.g. 'The picture stuck in their minds'.
    - V n as adj Cx3 e.g. 'The picture struck her as odd'.
    - V n as n Cx3 e.g. 'The picture struck her as something unusual'.
  - Subject is a thought or idea
    - V through n Cx5 e.g. 'A clever thought flashed through her mind'.
    - V n that Cx8 e.g. 'The idea hit Pat that Jim might have stolen the money'.
    - V to n Cx33 e.g. 'A clever thought came to Alice'.
- The subject of the clause is a Causer. This is shown in Figure 7.6i. Distinctions are made between the types of object: a Senser, a target of thought, or a thought or idea.
  - The object of the clause is a Senser
    - V n (Cognitive) Cx8 e.g. 'The new evidence convinced Alice'.
    - V n against n Cx3 e.g. 'The new evidence decided Alice against Jim's guilt'.
    - V n on n Cx9 e.g. 'The new evidence decided Alice on a course of action'.
    - V n to n Cx32 e.g. 'The new evidence awakened Alice to another possibility'.
    - V n with n Cx23 e.g. 'The new evidence confronted Alice with another possibility'.

- The object of the clause is a target of thought
  - V n from n Cx18 e.g. 'The size of the ears distinguishes the African elephant from the Indian elephant'.
- The object of the clause is a thought or idea
  - V n in n Cx12 e.g. 'The book fixed a new idea in Alice's mind'.
  - V n on n Cx11 e.g. 'The book cast doubt on the culprit's identity'.
  - V n out of n Cx13 e.g. 'The football match blocked all thoughts of love from Pat's mind'.
  - V n to n Cx33 e.g. 'The match drew attention to Pat's failings'.

This concludes the proposed networks for the Cognition semantic field. Section 7.5 focuses on Communication.

7.5 From Construction to Network: Communication

Communication Overview

The field of communication covers all forms of language, whether spoken, written, or signed. For simplicity's sake, in this description, language is treated as spoken, but in most cases it could include other media. Communication also includes paralanguage. Other than the distinction between language and paralanguage, the primary distinction that is made in this study is between 'giving and asking for information' and 'asking someone to do something or committing oneself to doing something'. This reflects Halliday's distinction between 'information' and 'goods and services' (Halliday and Matthiessen 2014: 135). For ease of presentation, following this overview, the field is divided into 'Communication: Information' and 'Communication: Action'.

The Systemic Network. The systemic network, shown in Figure 7.7, makes the primary distinction mentioned earlier between 'language' and 'paralanguage'. The term 'paralanguage' is used here only for a few constructions where there is non-verbal communication without content see example (1) in the following. Other instances, where a gesture, for example, is used to communication content, as in example (2), are treated as instances of language.

(1) Joe smiled at Annie. (Paralanguage)

(2) Joe gestured to Annie to open the door. (Language)

Within the option of 'language' there are two areas of choice: the type of content communicated; and the direction of the exchange. The type of content can be information or goods and services: see examples (3) and (4).

(3) Joe told Annie the story of his life. (Information)

(4) Joe asked Annie to write his biography. (Goods and services: Action)

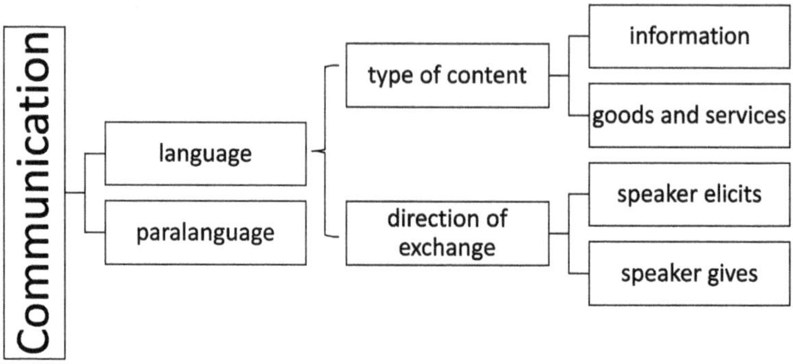

Figure 7.7 Communication Systemic Network

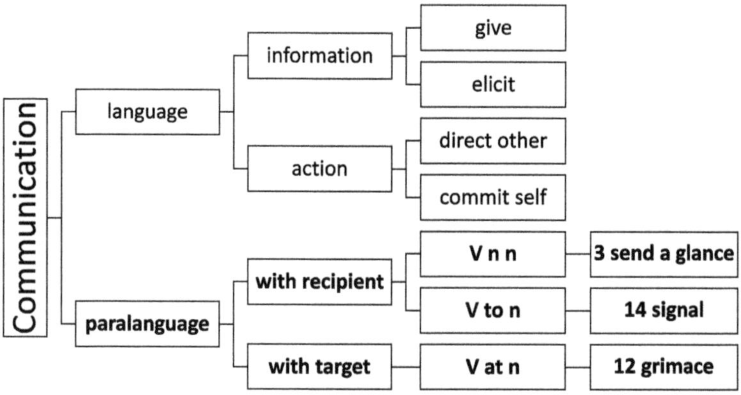

Figure 7.8 Communication Meaning Network

The direction of exchange is either from speaker to hearer – the speaker gives information or commits themselves to an action – or from hearer to speaker – the speaker requests information or requests an action. This distinguishes between examples (5) and (6).

(5) Joe asked Annie to write the book. (Requesting Action)

(6) Joe promised Annie that he would write the book. (Promising Action)

The Meaning Network. The Communication Meaning Network in Figure 7.8 reworks the Systemic Network, showing the 'information' and 'action' options within 'Language'. It also adds the pattern and construction detail to the 'Paralanguage' option, shown in bold on the figure.

Here is a prose version of the Meaning Network.

The primary distinction is between language and paralanguage.

- Language. The construction may related to the exchange of information or action.
  - Information is exchanged.
    - The speaker gives information.
    - The speaker elicits information.
  - Action is promised or requested.
    - The speaker tells/asks the hearer to do something.
    - The speaker commits to doing something.
- Paralanguage. The construction may specify a recipient or a target.
  - The construction specifies a recipient of the communication.
    - V n n Cx3 e.g. 'Annie sent Brenda a withering glance'.
    - V to n Cx14 e.g. 'Annie signalled to Brenda'.
  - The construction specifies a target of the communication.
    - V at n Cx12 e.g. 'Annie grimaced at Brenda'.

The remainder of this chapter is divided between 'Communication: Action' and 'Communication: Information'.

Communication: Action

The term 'Communication: Action' refers to constructions that construe a communicative act that relates to a future action. There are 21 verb argument constructions that express this semantic field, drawing on 14 verb complementation patterns.

The Systemic Network. The Systemic Network, shown in Figure 7.9, specifies three distinctions: who the Actor is in the future action; the nature of the future action; and whether the recipient of the communicative act is indicated in the construction or not.

Taking the first of these, the Actor may be another person or the speaker themselves. This distinguishes between examples (1) and (2).

(1) Anne promised to leave. (Actor is the speaker)

(2) Anne asked John to leave. (Actor is another person)

In terms of the future action itself, there are three independent choices: degree of specification, speech act type, and polarity. The action is usually specified, as in example (3).

(3) Eric told Bert to bring a cup of tea. (Action is specified)

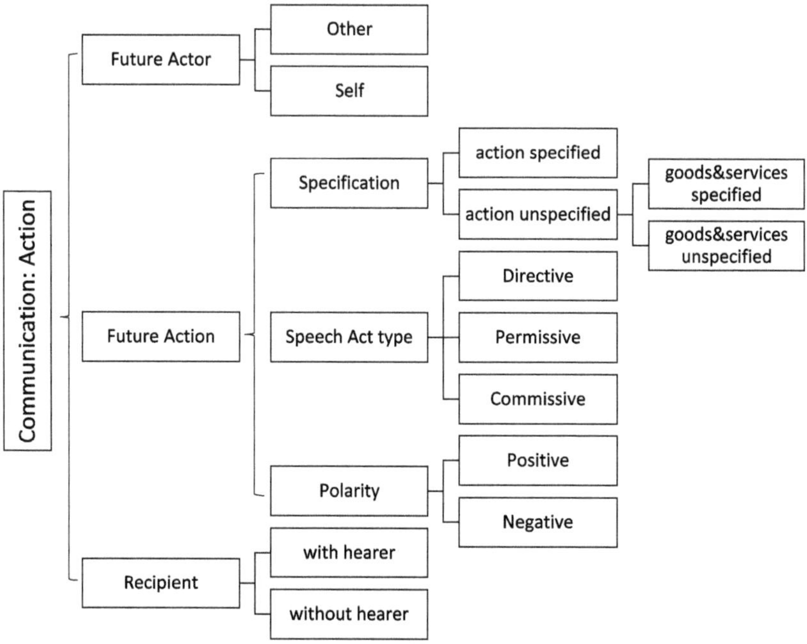

Figure 7.9 Communication: Action Systemic Network

There are ways of being less specific, however. Goods and services might be specified, implying an action (example (4)), or the action may be totally unspecified, as in example (5).

(4) Eric asked for tea. (Action implied)

(5) Eric pleaded with Bert. (Action unspecified)

The speech act may be Directive (issuing an order), Permissive (asking for permission), or Commissive (issuing a promise). Examples (6)–(8) illustrate these distinctions.

(6) Eric told Bert to bring tea. (Directive)

(7) Eric asked to have tea. (Permissive)

(8) Bert promised to bring tea. (Commissive)

In terms of polarity, this may be positive or negative, that is, ordering or forbidding an action. Examples (9) and (10) illustrate this.

(9) Eric told Bert to bring tea. (Positive polarity)

(10) Eric forbad Bert to bring tea. (Negative polarity)

Finally, the construction may or may not include an element that indicates the recipient of the communicative act. This choice is illustrated in examples (11) and (12).

(11) Eric asked Bert to bring tea. (Hearer is indicated)

(12) Eric asked that tea be brought. (Hearer is not indicated)

The Meaning Network. The Meaning Network for Communication: Action shows which of the systemic choices co-occur in practice. The network is shown in Figure 7.10 and is described in prose, with examples that as before are invented for simplicity and clarity. Figure 7.10 gives the overall outline of the network.

- Other as Actor. This is shown in Figure 7.10b
  - The action is specified in the construction.
    - The hearer is indicated in the construction.
      - The directive is positive.
        - V n to-inf
          - Cx9 e.g. 'Eric asked Bert to open the envelope'.
          - Cx10 e.g. 'Eric commanded Bert to open the envelope'.
          - Cx11 e.g. 'Eric dared Bert to open the envelope'.
        - V n into n. Cx7 e.g. 'Eric talked Bert into treason'.
        - V n to n. Cx26 e.g. 'Eric suggested treason to Bert.' and Cx25 e.g. 'Eric challenged Bert to a duel'.

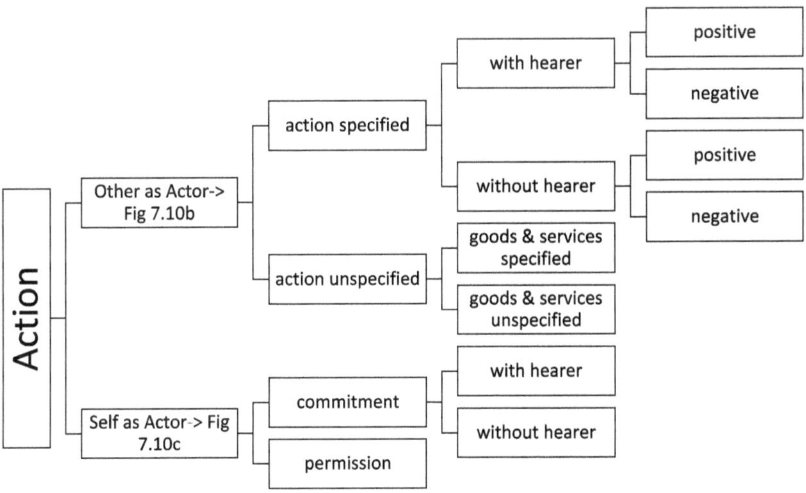

Figure 7.10a Communication: Action Meaning Network

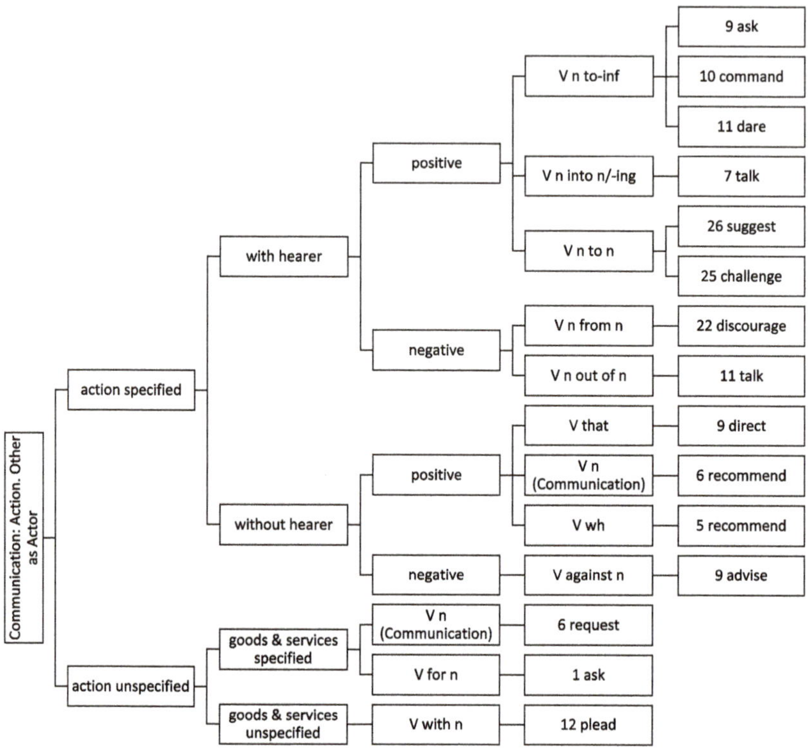

Figure 7.10b Communication: Action, the other as actor network

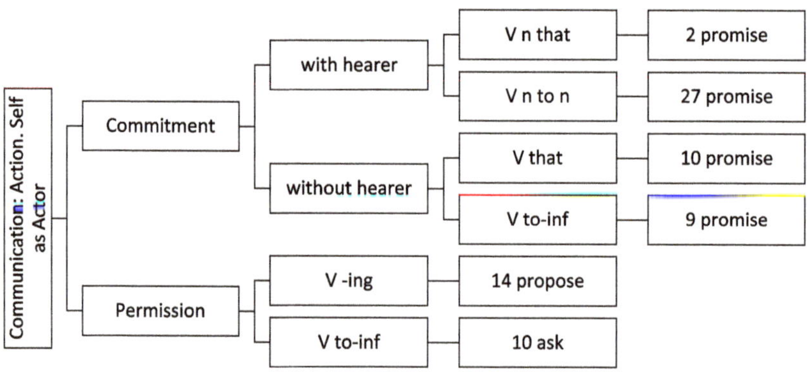

Figure 7.10c Communication: Action, the self as actor network

- The directive is negative.
  - V n from n. Cx22 e.g. 'Bert discouraged Eric from drinking tea'.
  - V n out of n. Cx11 e.g. 'Bert talked Eric out of opening the envelope'.
- The hearer is not indicated in the construction.
  - The directive is positive.
    - V that. Cx9 e.g. 'Eric directed that tea be brought'.
    - V n (Communication). Cx6 e.g. 'Eric recommended a tea break'.
    - V wh Cx5 e.g. 'Eric recommended what they should drink'.
  - The directive is negative.
    - V against n. Cx9 e.g. 'Eric advised against drinking the tea'.
- The action is not specified in the construction.
  - Goods and services are specified in the construction.
    - V n (Communication). Cx6 e.g. 'Eric requested tea'.
    - V for n. Cx1 e.g. 'Eric asked for tea'.
  - Goods and services are not specified in the construction.
    - V with n. Cx12 e.g. 'Eric pleaded with Bert'.
- Self as Actor. This is shown in Figure 7.10c.
  - The speech act is one of commitment to a future action.
    - The hearer is specified in the construction.
      - V n that. Cx2. 'Bert promised Eric that he would walk the dog'.
      - V n to n. Cx27. 'Bert promised assistance to Eric'.
    - The hearer is not specified in the construction.
      - V that. Cx10. 'Bert promised that he would walk the dog'.
      - V to-inf. Cx9. 'Bert promised to walk the dog'.
  - The speech act is one of asking permission or agreement to perform a future action.
    - V -ing. Cx14 e.g. 'Bert proposed visiting the coast'.
    - V to-inf. Cx10 e.g. 'Bert asked to see the picture'.

Communication: Information

The term 'Communication: Information' refers to those constructions that construe an act of communication in which information is exchanged. There are 82 constructions belonging to this semantic field, drawing on 26 verb complementation patterns.

The Systemic Network. The Systemic Network is shown in Figure 7.11. It represents four independent choices, relating to: the **direction** of the communication; the **participants** in the communication; the presence or absence of **content**; and other **circumstances** that may be expressed by the constructions. Whereas some of the choices are between the type of entity

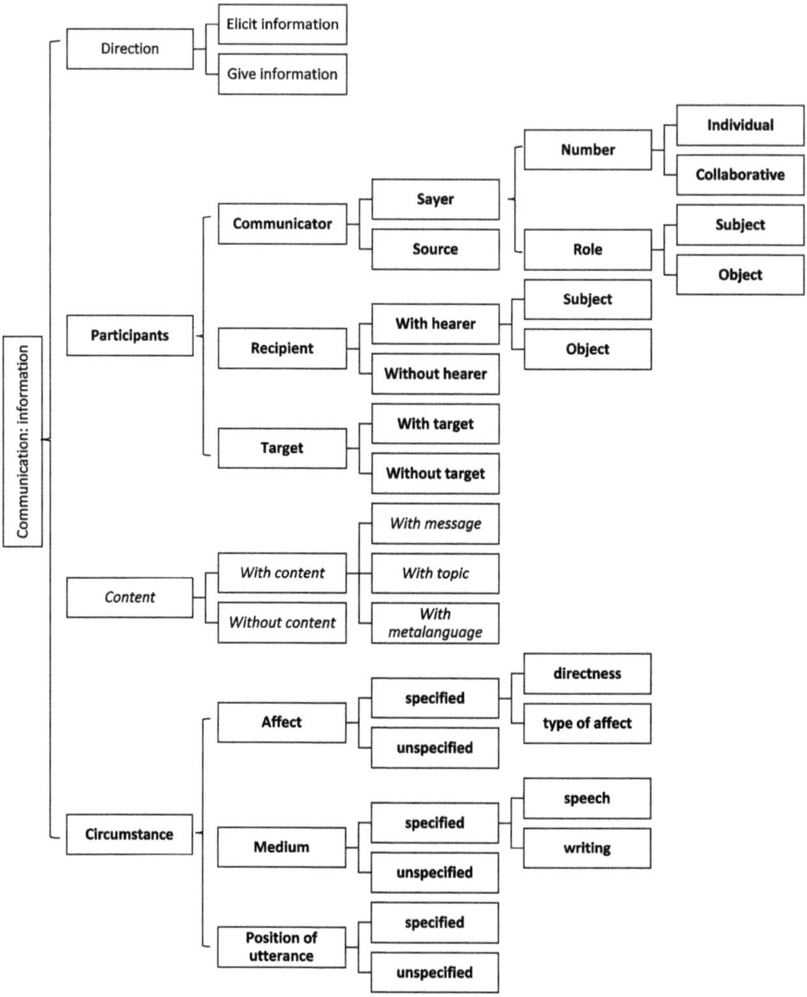

Figure 7.11 Communication: Information Systemic Network

expressed – for example, whether the communicator is a Sayer or a Source – in many cases, the choice is between 'presence' and 'absence'; for example, there may or may not be a Recipient or a Target. In many cases also the choices are strongly skewed in terms of the number of constructions that express each choice. For example, very few constructions have a Source as the communicator.

The communication **direction** choice is shown in plain text at the top of Figure 7.11. This is a choice between eliciting and giving information, illustrated in examples (1) and (2).

(1) Ann asked the customer her name. (Eliciting information)

(2) The customer told Ann her name. (Giving information)

The choice network related to **participants** is shown in bold towards the top of Figure 7.11. There are three relevant participants: the communicator, the recipient of the communication, and the target of the communication.

In relation to the communicator, there is a choice of communicator type: Sayer and Source (examples (3) and (4)). Where there is a Sayer, there are then choices relating to number and to grammatical role. Most constructions do not specify how many people are speaking, but a few specify that the communication is collaborative or reciprocal. This is shown in Figure 7.11 as a choice between 'individual' and 'collaborative', though of course, the 'individual' Sayer constructions may involve several people talking (see examples (5) and (6)). In terms of grammatical role, most constructions construe the communicator as Subject, when the construction is in active voice, but in a few constructions it is the Object (see examples (7) and (8)).

(3) Tim suggested the bones belonged to a dinosaur. (The communicator is a Sayer.)

(4) Analysis of the bones suggested they belonged to a dinosaur. (The communicator is a Source.)

(5) One man was shouting slogans. OR The crowd were shouting slogans. (The communicator may be individual.)

(6) The politicians bandied words with each other. (The communication must be collaborative.)

(7) Ann talked to Jim. (The communicator is the Subject.)

(8) Ann listened to Jim. (The communicator is the Object.)

The second participant in communication is the recipient or hearer. This participant may be present or absent in the construction (see examples (9) and (10)). Where there is a recipient, there are choices in the grammatical role. In most constructions, the recipient is the Object, but it may be the Subject (examples (11) and (12)).

(9) Ann told the children a story. (Recipient is present: With hearer.)

(10) Ann told a story. (Recipient is not present: Without hearer.)

(11) Ann talked to Jim. (Recipient is Object)

(12) Ann listened to Jim. (Recipient is Subject)

The third possible participant in the communication is a Target, which may be present or not: see examples (13) and (14).

(13) The teacher shouted at the children. (With target)

(14) The teacher shouted orders. (Without target)

In terms of **content**, there is a choice between expressing or not expressing the content of the communication. This is shown in italics in the middle of Figure 7.11. Most constructions indicate specific content as an independent element, but a few do not. In example (15), for instance, the content is indicated by the verb, not by a separate element. If content is indicated as an element of the construction, it may be a message, a topic, or metalanguage: see examples (16)–(18).

(15) Amy thanked Tim. (Without content)

(16) Tim said that he was leaving at six. (With content: Message)

(17) Tim talked about his departure. (With content: Topic)

(18) Tim made a prediction. (With content: Metalanguage)

In most cases, constructions are not distinguished by aspects of **circumstance**. In some cases, however, constructions are distinguished by Affect, Medium, or the position of the utterance in relation to others. The Affect may specify the level of directness or whether the Affect is positive or negative. These choices are illustrated in examples (19)–(22).

(19) Amy hinted that Jim was at fault. (Affect specified: directness)

(20) Amy criticised Jim. (Affect specified: negative Affect)

(21) Jim wrote a speech. (Medium specified: writing)

(22) Amy added a few comments. (Position of utterance specified)

These choices are shown in bold at the bottom of Figure 7.11.

The Meaning Network. The Meaning Network is shown in Figure 7.12, which is divided into sections for legibility. This network combines several aspects of the Systemic Network, specifying distinctions where these are relevant in context.

Here is a prose version of Figure 7.12, with invented examples to illustrate the constructions. The first part of the network (Figure 7.12) shows the distinction between eliciting and giving information.

- Information is elicited. This is shown in Figure 7.12b.
  - The construction specifies a Hearer.
    - The construction also specifies a message.

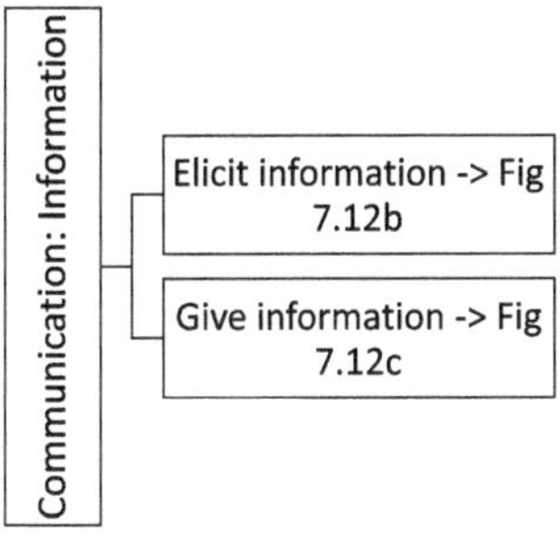

Figure 7.12a Communication: Information Meaning Network

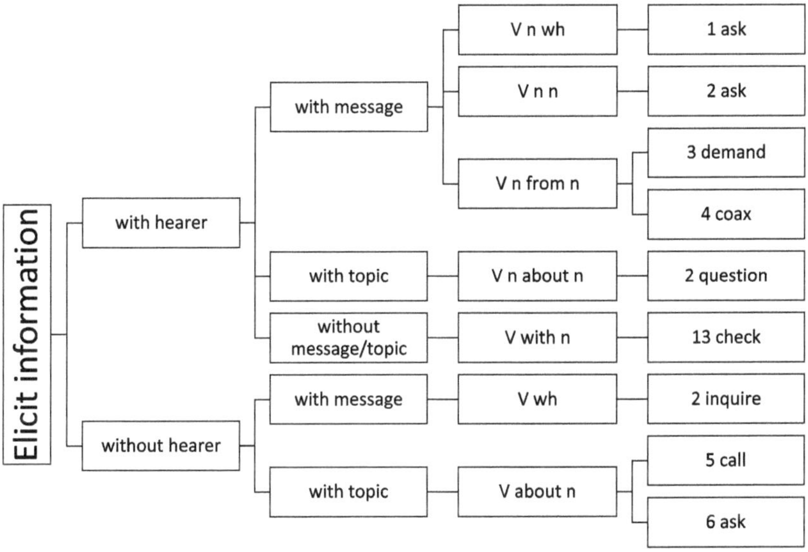

Figure 7.12b Communication: Information, the elicit information network

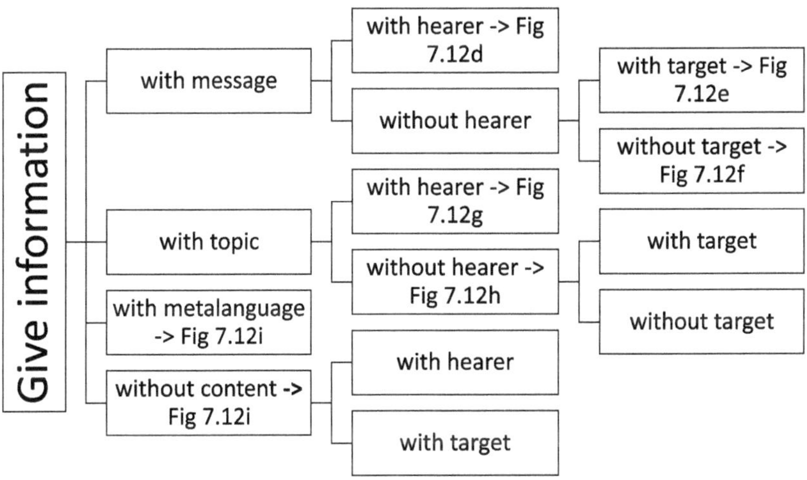

Figure 7.12c Communication: Information, the give information network

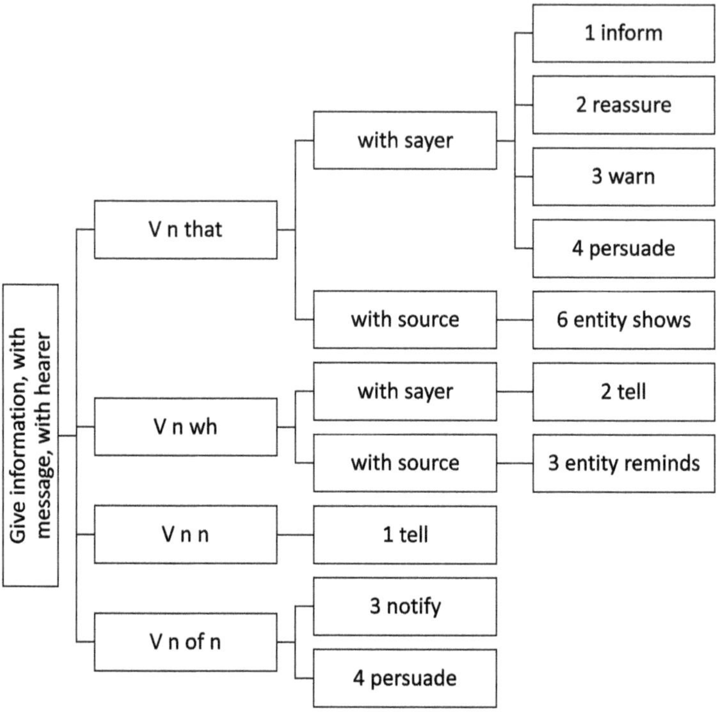

Figure 7.12d Communication: Information, the give information network, showing with message and hearer choices

- V n wh. Cx1 e.g. 'Cindy asked Jake what he wanted to eat'.
- V n n. Cx2 e.g. 'Cindy asked Jake his name'.
- V n from n. Cx3 e.g. 'Cindy demanded information from Jake.' and Cx4 e.g. 'Cindy coaxed information from Jake'.
  - The construction also specifies a topic.
    - V n about n. Cx2 e.g. 'Cindy questioned Jake about his preferences'.
  - The construction does not specify any other element.
    - V with n. Cx13 e.g. 'Cindy checked with Jake'.
- The construction does not specify a Hearer.
  - The construction specifies a message.
    - V wh. Cx2 e.g. 'Cindy inquired what Jake wanted to eat'.
  - The construction specifies a topic.
    - V about n. Cx5 e.g. 'Cindy called about their dinner plans.' and Cx6 e.g. 'Cindy asked about their dinner plans'.
- Information is given. This is shown in Figure 7.12c and subsequent figures.

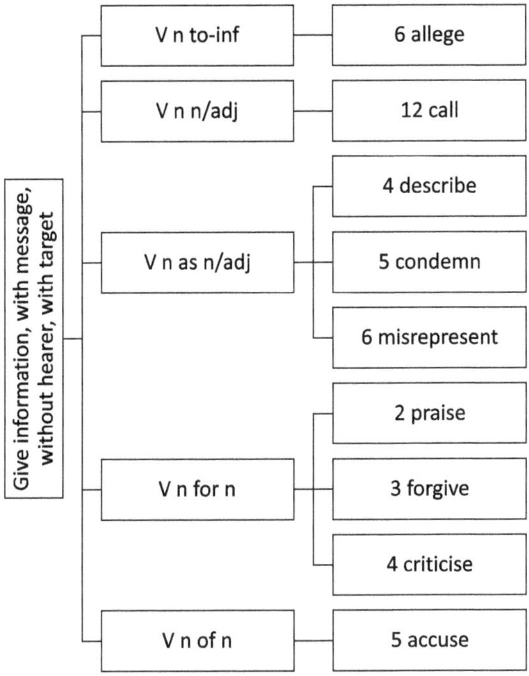

Figure 7.12e Communication: Information, the give information network, showing with message, without hearer, with target choices

- The construction specifies a message.
  - The construction indicates the hearer. This is shown in Figure 7.12d.
    - V n that
      - The communicator is a Sayer.
        - Cx1 e.g. ‘Selma informed Dilip that she wanted chips’.
        - Cx2 e.g. ‘Dilip reassured Selma that chips were available’.
        - Cx3 e.g. ‘Selma warned Dilip that the food was hot’.
        - Cx4 e.g. ‘Dilip persuaded Selma that salad was a better option’.
      - The communicator is a Source.
        - Cx6 e.g. ‘The tests showed Dilip that he should eat less salt’.
    - V n wh
      - The communicator is a Sayer.
        - Cx2 e.g. ‘Selma told Dilip what he should eat’.
      - The communicator is a Source.
        - Cx3 e.g. ‘The tests reminded Dilip what he should eat’.
    - V n n. Cx1 e.g. ‘Dilip told Selma the outcome of the experiment’.

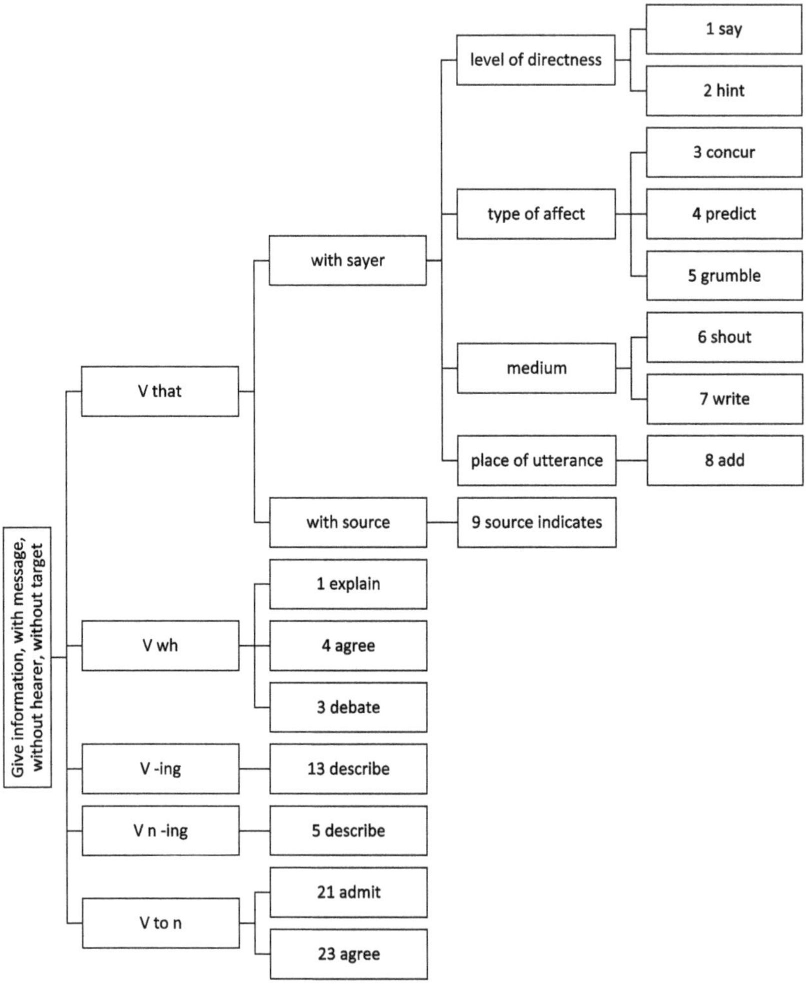

Figure 7.12f Communication: Information, the give information network, showing with message only choices

- V n of n. Cx3 e.g. 'Dilip notified Selma of the results.' and Cx4 e.g. 'Dilip persuaded Selma of the need to exercise more'.
- The construction does not indicate the hearer.
  - The construction indicates a target. This is shown in Figure 7.12e.
    - V n to-inf. Cx6 e.g. 'Phil alleged the dog to be the source of the outbreak'.
    - V n n/adj. Cx12 e.g. 'Phil called his friend an idiot'.

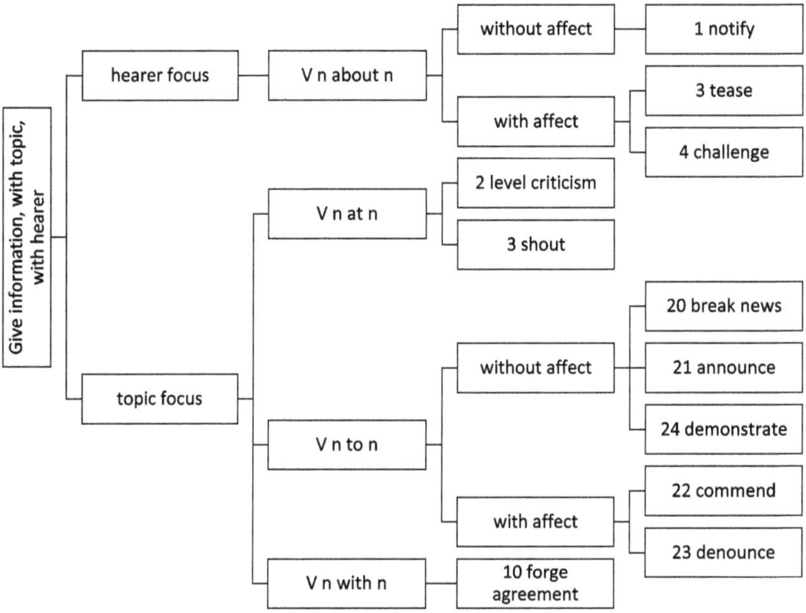

Figure 7.12g Communication: Information, the give information network, showing with topic and hearer choices

- V n as n/adj.
  - Cx4 e.g. 'Phil described his friend as an idiot'.
  - Cx5 e.g. 'Phil condemned his friend as an idiot'.
  - Cx6 e.g. 'Phil misrepresented his friend as an idiot'.
- V n for n
  - Cx2 e.g. 'Amy praised the driver for her courage'.
  - Cx3 e.g. 'Amy forgave the driver for her mistake'.
  - Cx4 e.g. 'Amy criticised the driver for her mistake'.
- V n of n. Cx5 e.g. 'Phil accused his friend of stupidity'.

- The construction does not indicate a target. This is shown in Figure 7.12f.
  - V that
    - The communicator is a Sayer.
      - The level of directness is specified. Cx1 e.g. 'Amy said that the driver was brave.' and Cx2 e.g. 'Amy hinted that the driver caused the accident'.
      - The type of affect is specified.
        - Cx3 e.g. 'Amy concurred that she was to blame'.
        - Cx4 e.g. 'Amy predicted that the cost would be high'.
        - Cx5 e.g. 'Amy grumbled that the cost would be high'.

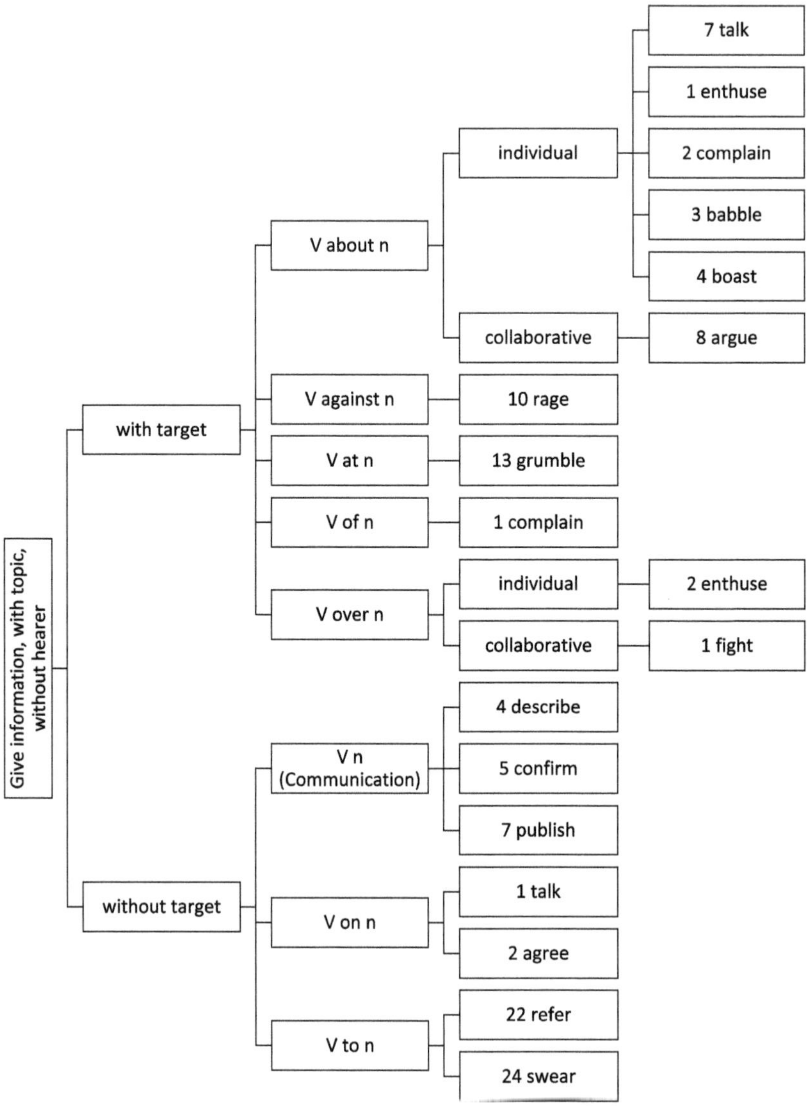

Figure 7.12h Communication: Information, the give information network, showing with topic, without hearer choices

- The medium is specified. Cx6 e.g. ‘Phil shouted that the cost was too high.’ and Cx7 e.g. ‘Phil wrote that the cost was too high’.

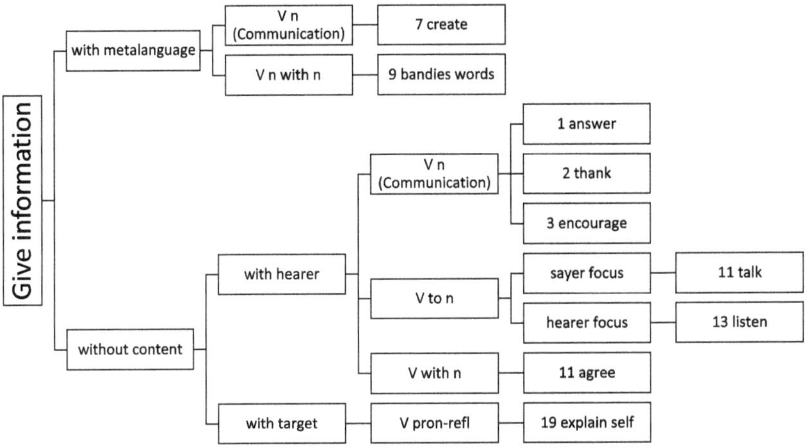

Figure 7.12i Communication: Information, the give information network, showing with metalanguage choices and without content choices

- The position of the utterance is specified. Cx8 e.g. 'Amy added that the cost was too high'.

▪ The communicator is a Source. Cx9 e.g. 'The findings indicated that it had been an accident'.

◦ V wh
  ▪ Cx1 e.g. 'Sara explained what they should do'.
  ▪ Cx4 e.g. 'They all agreed what they should do'.
  ▪ Cx3 e.g. 'They debated what they should do'.
◦ V -ing. Cx13 e.g. 'Sara described seeing the accident'.
◦ V n -ing. Cx5 e.g. 'Sara described the car disappearing'.
◦ V to n. Cx21 e.g. 'Phil admitted to the crime.' and Cx23 e.g. 'Phil agreed to a fine'.

◦ The construction specifies a topic.
  ▪ The construction also indicates the hearer. This is shown in Figure 7.12g.
    • Hearer focus: the noun following the verb indicates the hearer.
      ◦ V n about n
        ▪ Affect is not specified. Cx1 e.g. 'Sara notified Phil about the fine'.
        ▪ Affect is specified. Cx3 e.g. 'Sara teased Phil about the fine.' and Cx4 e.g. 'Sara challenged Phil about the fine'.

    • Topic focus: the noun following the verb indicates the topic.
      ◦ V n at n. Cx2 e.g. 'Jake levelled criticism at Mo.' and Cx3 e.g. 'Jake shouted insults at Mo'.
      ◦ V n to n

    - Affect is not specified.
      - Cx20 e.g. ‘Mo broke the news to Jake’.
      - Cx21 e.g. ‘Mo announced his promotion to the group’.
      - Cx24 e.g. ‘Mo demonstrated his commitment to his employers’.
    - Affect is specified. Cx22 e.g. ‘Mo commended Jake to his employers.’ and Cx23 e.g. ‘Mo denounced Jake to his employers’.
      - V n with n. Cx10 e.g. ‘Mo forged an agreement with Jake’.
  - The construction does not indicate the hearer. This is shown in Figure 7.12h.
    - The construction indicates a target.
      - V about n.
        - Individual communication
          - Cx7 e.g. ‘Jake talked about his enemies’.
          - Cx1 e.g. ‘Jake enthused about his new job’.
          - Cx2 e.g. ‘Jake complained about his new job’.
          - Cx3 e.g. ‘Jake babbled about his enemies’.
          - Cx4 e.g. ‘Jake boasted about his new job’.
        - Collaborative communication. Cx8 e.g. ‘They argued about the accident’.
      - V against n. Cx10 e.g. ‘Jake raged against his enemies’.
      - V at n. Cx13 e.g. ‘Jake grumbled at his duties’.
      - V of n. Cx1 e.g. ‘Jake complained of his duties’.
      - V over n.
        - Individual communication. Cx2 e.g. ‘Jake enthused over his new job’.
        - Collaborative communication. Cx1 e.g. ‘Jake and Mo fought over the cause of the accident’.
    - The construction does not indicate a target.
      - V n (Communication)
        - Cx4 e.g. ‘Mo described the picture’.
        - Cx5 e.g. ‘Mo confirmed the decision’.
        - Cx7 e.g. ‘Mo published a book of poetry’.
      - V on n. Cx1 e.g. ‘Sara talked on a new topic.’ and Cx2 e.g. ‘Sara and Jake agreed on the best way forward’.
      - V to n. Cx22 e.g. ‘Sara referred to Mo’s book.’ and Cx24 e.g. ‘Sara swore to the truth of her statement’.
- The construction specifies metalanguage. This is shown in Figure 7.12i.
  - V n (Communication). Cx7 e.g. ‘Mo created a poem’.
  - V n with n. Cx9 e.g. ‘Mo bandied words with Jake’.
- The construction does not specify content. This is also shown in Figure 7.12i.

- The construction indicates the hearer.
  - V n (Communication)
    - Cx1 e.g. ‘Sara answered Dilip’.
    - Cx2 e.g. ‘Sara thanked Dilip’.
    - Cx3 e.g. ‘Sara encouraged Dilip’.
  - V to n
    - The Sayer is the Subject. Cx11 e.g. ‘Dilip talked to Sara’.
    - The Hearer is the Subject. Cx13 e.g. ‘Sara listened to Dilip’.
  - V with n. Cx11 e.g. ‘Dilip agreed with Sara’.
- The construction indicates a target.
  - V pron-refl. Cx19 e.g. ‘Jake explained himself’.

7.6 Conclusion

This chapter has proposed networks that show the relationship between constructions expressing two major semantic fields: Cognition and Communication. It has demonstrated the usefulness of concepts drawn from SFG in deriving such networks that might be termed a partial constructicon. The most significant contribution is the use of systemic networks that work separately from but alongside the more familiar taxonomic networks. The Meaning Networks themselves are very busy, accounting as they do for dozens of constructions. The Systemic Networks offer a more abstract version of the same information that identify which language features are important in the semantic field and the main oppositions that contribute to the taxonomic network.

Interestingly, identifying the constructions within the target fields, and locating them in the networks, becomes most difficult when there is a degree of metaphor involved. One example is ‘skate around a topic’, where the image of an ice-skate moving around but not touching a central point is transferred to a speaker failing to address a topic of importance. In other cases, the subject of the clause is an element other than the speaker, thinker, or hearer. Examples would include ‘a novel thought struck him’ or ‘the results told us that … ’. These examples impose an interpretation of animacy on ‘a thought’ and ‘the results’ as the subjects of STRIKE and TELL respectively. Halliday’s concept of grammatical metaphor is useful in interpreting these as ‘he thought that … ’ and ‘we concluded that … ’.

In this chapter, the semantic fields associated with the process types of Mental and Verbal have been discussed. In Chapter 8, semantic fields associated with Material and Relational processes are outlined in a similar way.

8 Semantic Fields: Material and Relational

8.1 Introduction

Chapter 6 showed in some detail how the networks for the Causation semantic field were derived. Chapter 7 did the same for the Cognition field and the Communication field. It was argued that a taxonomic Meaning Network is the most efficient way to show the progression from semantic field to specific constructions, while the Systemic Network summarises the information as a set of alternatives between features. The distinction between taxonomy and system is drawn from Matthiessen (2023).

This chapter summarises the meaning and systemic networks for six further semantic fields. These are semantic fields rather than process types, but they are inspired by the process type distinctions made in Halliday and Matthiessen (2014). Specifically, three of the fields correspond to meanings that relate to material processes, while the other two correspond to relational processes. The six fields are:

- Material processes: Change (Section 8.2), Creation (Section 8.3), Location change (Section 8.4), and Possession transfer (Section 8.5).
- Relational processes: Equivalence (Section 8.6) and Logical relation (Section 8.7).

Each of the following sections consists of: (a) an explanation of which constructions comprise the field, and a note of how many there are; (b) a description of the systemic network; and (c) a description of the meaning network. The accompanying figures show the two networks. The conclusion to the chapter relates the semantic fields to the process types in Halliday and Matthiessen (2014).

8.2 The Change Semantic Field

The term 'Change' refers to those constructions which indicate that an entity changes in some way, so that there is an end point that is different from the start point.

There are 44 constructions that express this meaning, drawing on 11 verb complementation patterns.

The Systemic Network. The Systemic Network, shown in Figure 8.1, comprises simultaneous choices of meaning and of form. In terms of **meaning**, three main independent distinctions are identified. The most important of these is the distinction between constructions where the cause of change is expressed in the construction (described here as 'caused change') and those where it is not ('autonomous change'). This distinction is illustrated in examples (1) and (2).

(1) Joe pushed the door open. (caused change)

(2) The door slammed shut. (autonomous change)

Then, the entity that is changed can be physical or abstract. This is shown in examples (3) and (4).

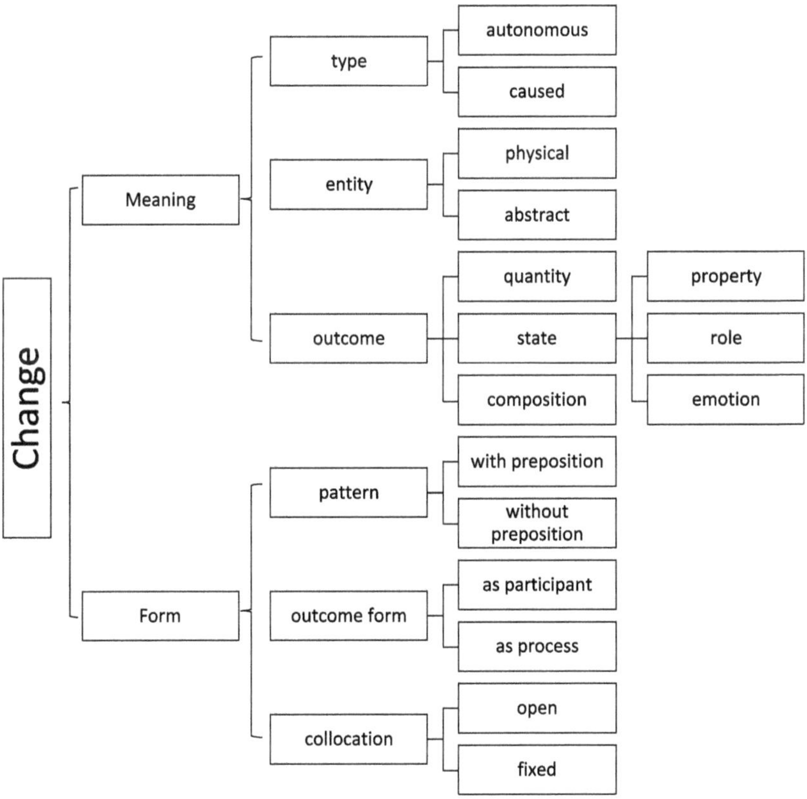

Figure 8.1 Change Systemic Network

(3) Joe repaired the bicycle. (physical changed entity)

(4) Maria solved the problem. (abstract changed entity)

Finally, there is a distinction between the types of outcome to the process: whether the change results in a different state, quantity, or composition. This is illustrated in examples (5)–(7).

(5) The magician turned the watch into a dove. (change of state)

(6) The price increased to £10. (change of quantity)

(7) Joe divided the cake into three parts. (change of composition)

In turn, 'state' can be divided into three types: 'property' (e.g. 'fade into darkness'), 'role' (e.g. 'progress to sainthood'), and 'emotion' (e.g. 'burst into tears').

Turning to **form**, three independent distinctions are identified. One is simply the pattern used in the construction. In Figure 8.1, patterns are notionally divided into those with a preposition and those without. Because some constructions have fixed collocations and others have more open ones, a second distinction shows a choice between open and fixed collocations. This is illustrated in examples (8) and (9).

(8) The puppy made its new owner happy. (The collocation between 'made' and 'happy' is relatively open.)

(9) She wiped the table clean. (The collocation between 'wiped' and 'clean' is relatively fixed.)

Finally, there is an important distinction between constructions that express the outcome of the change in the verb element, or 'process' element, of the construction and those which express the outcome as a non-verb element, or 'participant'. This distinction is illustrated in examples (10) and (11).

(10) Joe repaired the car. (The outcome is expressed in the process 'repair'.)

(11) Joe divided the cake into three parts. (The outcome is expressed in the participant 'three parts'.)

The Meaning Network. The Meaning Network combines choices from 'meaning' and 'form' and is shown in Figure 8.2. Figure 8.2 shows the overall network; the primary distinction made is between 'autonomous change' and 'caused change'. Within each of these is the distinction between 'outcome as participant' and 'outcome as process'. Each of the four resulting sets is shown in Figures 8.2b–e. Figure 8.2 is described in the next subsection, under the headings of 'Autonomous Change' and 'Caused Change'.

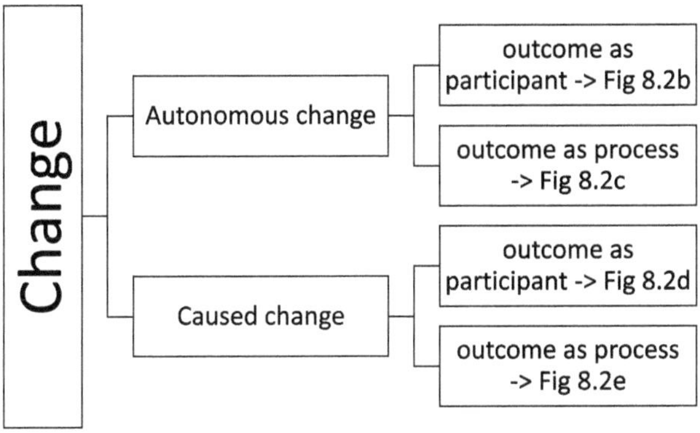

Figure 8.2a Change Meaning Network

The 'Autonomous Change' Meaning Network: Choices and Examples

The outcome of the change may be expressed as a participant or in the process.

- The outcome of change is expressed as a participant in the construction (Figure 8.2b)
  - V adj
    - Cx8 e.g. 'The door slammed shut'.
    - Cx9 e.g. 'The prisoner broke free'.
    - Cx10 e.g. 'The next athlete jumped higher'.
    - Cx11 e.g. 'The stock market closed higher'.
    - Cx12 e.g. 'The lake froze solid'.
  - V into n
    - The outcome is a change in property. Cx7 e.g. 'The tadpole turned into a frog.' and Cx8 e.g. 'The apparition faded into shadow'.
    - The outcome is a change in composition. Cx9 e.g. 'The road divided into two lanes'.
    - The outcome is a change in emotion. Cx12 e.g. 'The child burst into tears.' and Cx13 e.g. 'They lapsed into gloom'.
  - V to n
    - The collocation is relatively open
      - Cx1 e.g. 'She converted to Buddhism'.
      - Cx3 e.g. 'He progressed to a leadership position'.
      - Cx4 e.g. 'They switched to solar energy'.
    - The collocation is relatively fixed
      - Cx38 e.g. 'The victim bled to death'.
      - Cx39 e.g. 'The vehicle ground to a halt'.
      - Cx40 e.g. 'The child dropped off to sleep'.

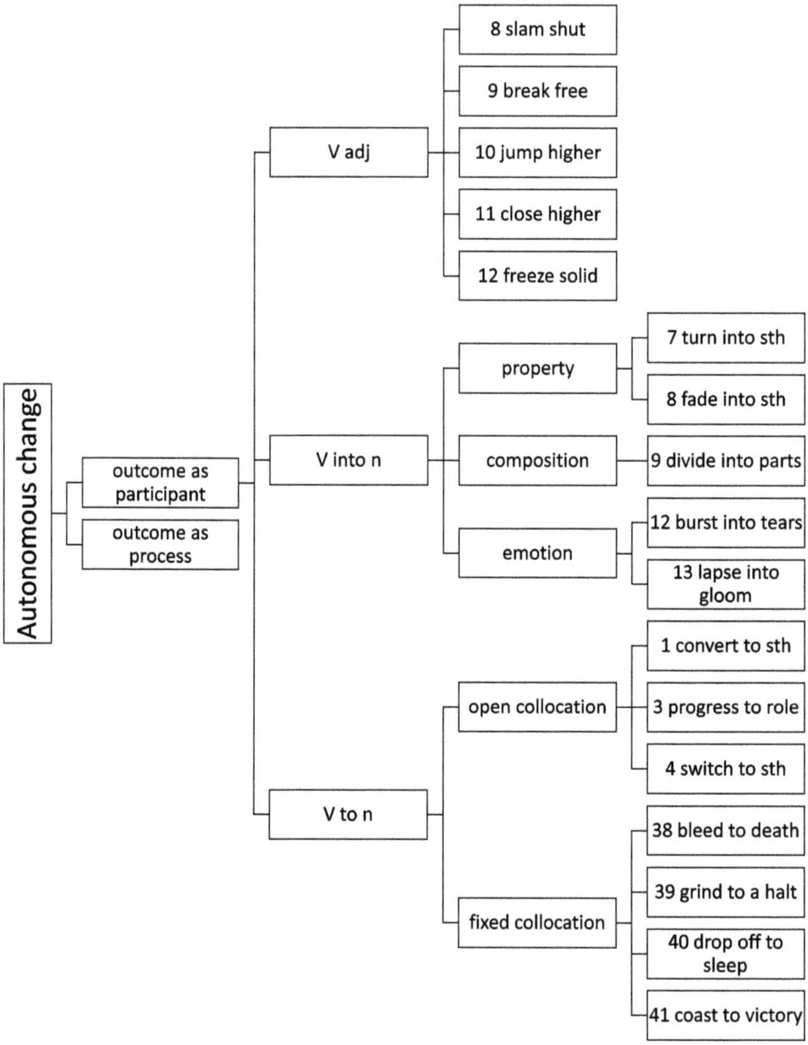

Figure 8.2b Change: autonomous change, the outcome as participant network

- Cx41 e.g. 'Our candidate coasted to victory'.

- The outcome of change is expressed in the process (Figure 8.2c)
  - V pron-refl Cx2 e.g. 'She killed herself.' and Cx10 e.g. 'They disguised themselves'.
  - V in n Cx15 e.g. 'Crimes have increased in quantity'.
  - V to n Cx2 e.g. 'Prices increased to their highest level'.

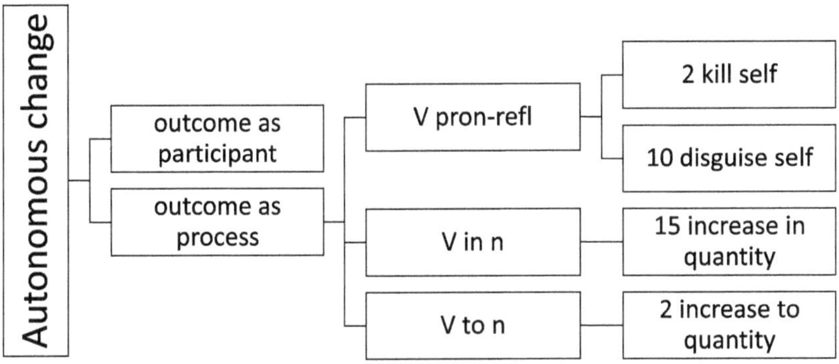

Figure 8.2c Change: autonomous change, the outcome as process network

The 'Caused Change' Meaning Network: Choices and Examples

The outcome of the change may be expressed as a participant or in the process.

- The outcome of change is expressed as a participant in the construction (Figure 8.2d).
  - V n adj
    - The collocation is relatively open. Cx7 e.g. 'She made the stew spicy'.
    - The collocation is relatively fixed.
      - Cx8 e.g. 'He pushed the door shut'.
      - Cx9 e.g. 'He wiped the table clean'.
      - Cx11 e.g. 'She cranked the volume higher'.
      - Cx12 e.g. 'The child coloured the trees blue'.
      - Cx15 e.g. 'The gangsters shot him dead'.
  - V in n Cx1 e.g. 'She divided the loaf into three.' and Cx10 e.g. 'He drilled a hole in the wall'. (Note: The wall is changed by this action. This construction also appears as an instance of 'Creation', because the hole is created.)
  - V in into n
    - The outcome is a change in the state of the entity.
      - Cx1 e.g. 'He changed the frog into a princess'.
      - Cx2 e.g. 'They condensed the gas into liquid'.
      - Cx3 e.g. 'She translated the book into Spanish'.
    - The outcome is a change in the composition of the entity.
      - Cx5 e.g. 'She amalgamated the departments into one'.
      - Cx6 e.g. 'He chopped the onions into small pieces'.

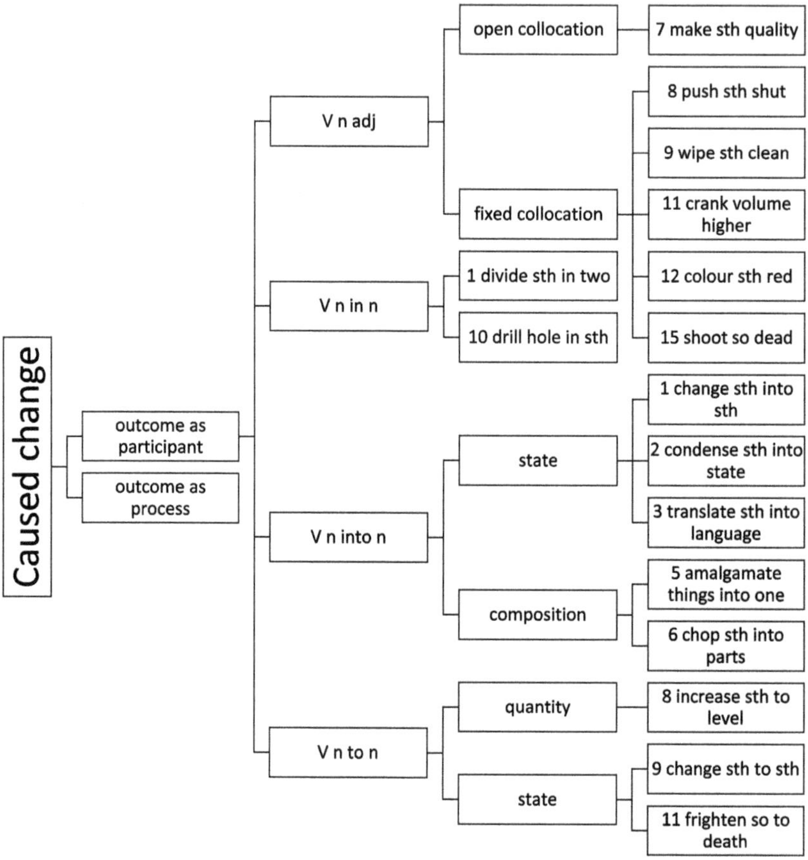

Figure 8.2d Change: caused change, the outcome as participant network

- V n to n
  - The outcome is a change in the quantity of the entity. Cx8 e.g. 'He increased the concentration of the liquid to 80 per cent'.
  - The outcome is a change in the state of the entity.
  - Cx9. 'He changed the princess to a frog.' and Cx11 e.g. 'The ghost frightened him to death'.
- The outcome of change is expressed in the process (Figure 8.2e). The entities may be physical or abstract.
  - V n (Material)
    - The entities are physical.
      - Cx4 e.g. 'Joe broke the mirror'.
      - Cx5 e.g. 'Joe repaired the car'.

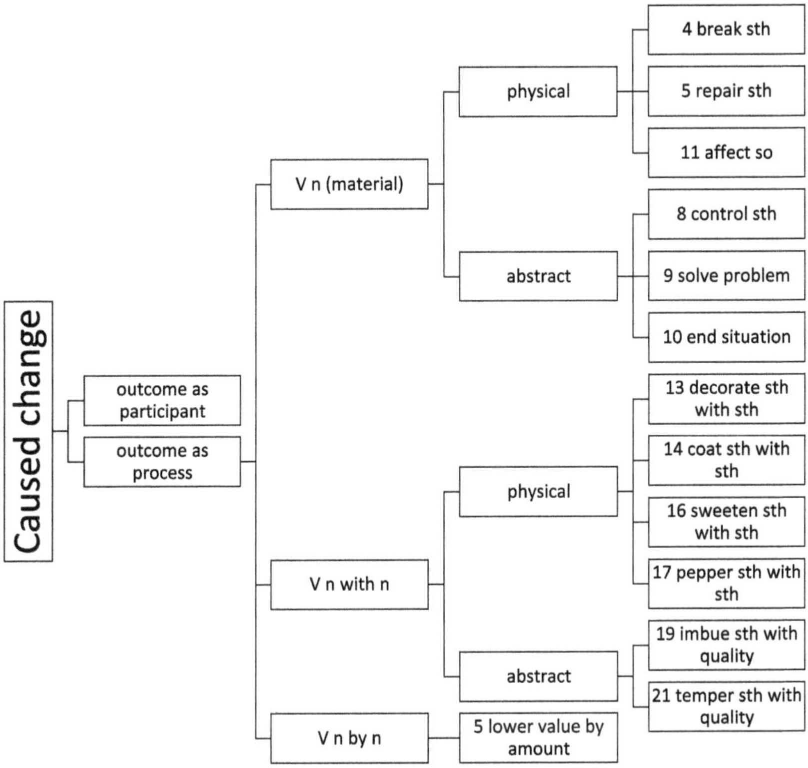

Figure 8.2e Change: caused change, the outcome as process network

- Cx6 e.g. 'Joe decorated the room'.
- Cx11 e.g. 'The polluted air affected his lungs'.

▪ The entities are abstract.

- Cx8 e.g. 'He controlled the network'.
- Cx9 e.g. 'She solved the problem'.
- Cx10 e.g. 'They ended the affair'.

◦ V n with n

▪ The entities are physical.

- Cx13 e.g. 'She decorated the windows with stickers'.
- Cx14 e.g. 'They coated the walls with creosote'.
- Cx16 e.g. 'He sweetened the tea with honey'.
- Cx17 e.g. 'He peppered the steak with spices'.

▪ The entities are abstract. Cx19 e.g. 'His character imbued the situation with menace.' and Cx21 e.g. 'She tempered the announcement with kindness'.

◦ V n by n Cx5 e.g. 'They lowered the price by a few pounds'.

8.3 The Creation Semantic Field

The term 'Creation' refers to constructions which indicate that an action brings an entity into being.

There are 10 constructions that express this meaning, drawing on 6 verb complementation patterns.

The Systemic Network. The Systemic Network is shown in Figure 8.3. It shows simultaneous choices between meaning and form. The only **meaning** distinction identified is between created entities of different types: physical and abstract. Prototypical physical entities are physical objects as in instances such as 'build a house' or 'knit a sweater', but the action may be more distributed as in 'publish a book', and the category includes communicative acts such as 'give a speech'. The abstract category includes thoughts as in 'form an opinion' and completely abstract notions as in 'form a bond' or 'hold an event'. In terms of **form**, the primary distinction is between constructions that specify only two participants, as in 'build a house' or 'drill a hole', and those that specify an additional participant. The additional participant can be a beneficiary, a location, or constituents. These are shown in examples (1)–(3). The verb complementation patterns specified here do not include multiple prepositional phrases, but in practice, these can be chained to include more participants, as in example (4).

(1) They built Mary a house. (includes a beneficiary)

(2) They drilled a hole in the wall. (includes a location)

(3) They built a house out of bricks and mortar. (includes constituents)

(4) They built Mary a house out of bricks and mortar. (includes a beneficiary and constituents)

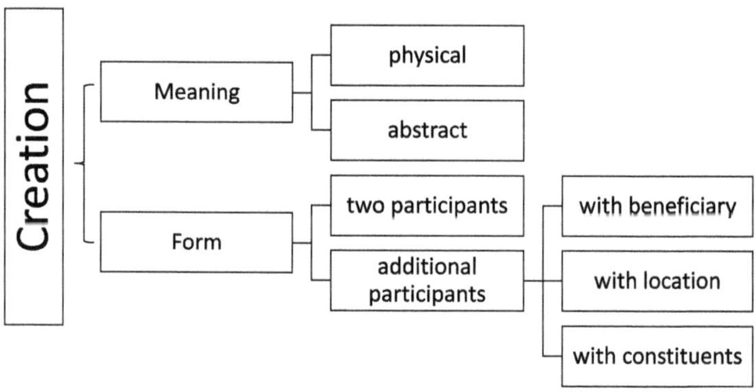

Figure 8.3 Creation Systemic Network

The Meaning Network. The Meaning Network prioritises the form distinction and makes a distinction between 'simple constructions', which have two participants only, and 'complex constructions', which have three. Within the simple constructions only there is a choice between physical and abstract entities. The Meaning Network can be seen in Figure 8.4 and is described here.

- Simple constructions
  - V n (Material)
    - The entities are physical. Cx1 e.g. 'Joe built a house'.
    - The created entity is abstract. Cx2 e.g. 'Emma formed an opinion.' and Cx3 e.g. 'We held an event'.
  - V n (Communication) Cx8 e.g. 'She published her first book.' and Cx9 e.g. 'Emma gave a speech'.
- Complex constructions
  - With beneficiary
    - V n n Cx10 e.g. 'She made him dinner'.

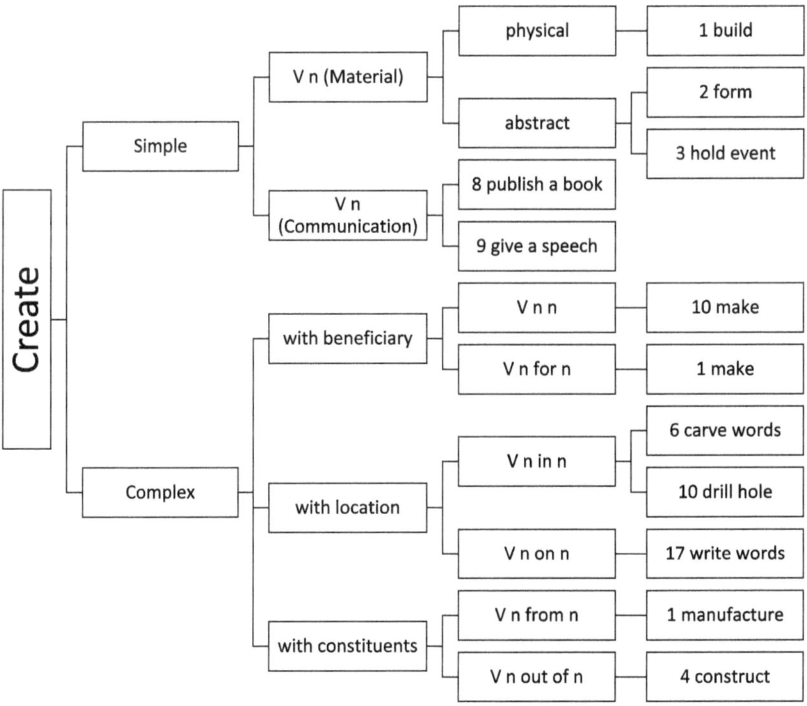

Figure 8.4 Creation Meaning Network

    - V n for n Cx1 e.g. 'She made dinner for him'.
      Note: Constructions that include a beneficiary are not restricted to verbs that express the Creation meaning.
  - With location
    - V n in n Cx6 e.g. 'They carved their initials in the tree.' and Cx10 e.g. 'They drilled a hole in the wood'.
    - V n on n Cx17 e.g. 'She wrote three words on the paper'.
  - With constituents
    - V n from n Cx1 e.g. 'They manufactured radios from recycled parts'.
    - V n out of n Cx4 e.g. 'They constructed radios out of recycled parts'.

8.4 The Location Change Semantic Field

The term 'Location change' refers to those constructions which indicate that an entity moves from one location to another. The name 'Movement' can also be used for this field, though 'Location change' is more precise.

There are 31 constructions that express this meaning, drawing on 13 verb complementation patterns.

The Systemic Network. The Systemic Network is shown in Figure 8.5. It shows independent choices between meaning and form. The form distinctions comprise choices in the nature of the process ('process types') and in how the direction of movement is expressed ('direction indicator'). The two **process types** are 'autonomous', meaning that the construction construes the entity moving itself, or 'caused', meaning that the construction construes the movement as being caused by something. This is illustrated in examples (1) and (2).

(1) The crowd converged on the notice board. (The movement is autonomous.)

(2) The player kicked the football into the goal. (The movement is caused.)

The **direction indicator** may be the verb in the construction or the preposition. This is illustrated in examples (3) and (4).

(3) The guest brought a present. (The direction ('to here') is indicated by the verb.)

(4) The player kicked the ball into the net. (The direction indicated by the prepositional phrase.)

Figure 8.5 shows these two choices as independent; however, when the process type is 'autonomous', only the preposition as direction indicator is available. It should be noted, however, that if the constructions identified in this book were extended to include verbs without complementation (i.e. the intransitive 'V' pattern), then some constructions would comprise autonomous

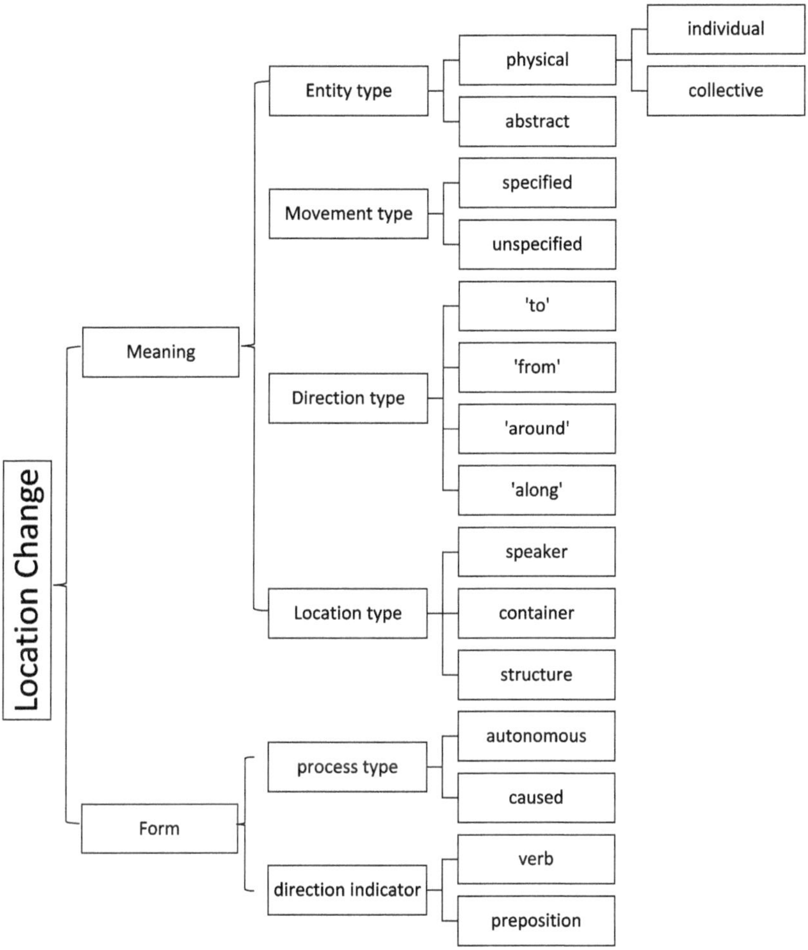

Figure 8.5 Location change Systemic Network

location change with the direction indicated by the verb e.g. 'She left' and 'He approached'.

The meaning distinctions comprise choices in the nature of each of the participants in the constructions: the entity that moves, the movement itself, the direction type, and the 'target' type. More detail is given here:

The **entity that moves** may be physical or abstract, as illustrated in examples (5) and (6). Physical entities may be individual or collective. That is, the nature of the activity may require there to be more than one person or thing involved, or not. The verb CROWD, for example, requires that more than one person moves (see example 8). In other instances, such as the verb BARGE, there may be more than one person involved but there does not need to be (see example 7).

(5) Joe kicked the ball into the net. ('the ball' is a physical entity.)

(6) Emma breathed life into the situation. ('life' is an abstract entity.)

(7) Emma barged through the crowd. ('Emma' is an individual.)

(8) The fans crowded around the film star. ('the fans' act collectively.)

The **nature of the movement** may be specified or unspecified. The difference is often between verbs used in the same construction, as in examples (9) and (10).

(9) She brought a dog into the room. (The nature of the movement is unspecified.)

(10) She dragged a dog into the room. (The nature of the movement is specified.)

The **direction type** may be specified by the preposition, and there are as many directions as there are prepositions. However, four primary directions may be identified: 'to' (which includes 'into' and 'on'), 'from' (which includes 'out of'), 'around' (which can include 'on' with some verbs), and 'along' (which includes 'through'). These directions are illustrated in examples (11)–(14).

(11) The fans crowded into the stadium.

(12) They deported him from the USA.

(13) The fans crowded around the singer.

(14) Emily barged through the crowd.

The **location** where the entity moves to or from can be described as: the speaker, a container (which may be an enclosed space, an abstract space, or a geographical space) or a structure. These are illustrated in examples (15)–(17).

(15) Joe brought a cake. (The location, indicated by the verb, is the speaker, or a space into which the speaker projects themselves.)

(16) They were deported to a third country. (The location is a geographical space: a third country.)

(17) Joe detached the door from the barn. (The location is a structure: the barn.)

The Meaning Network. The Meaning Network is shown in Figure 8.6 and is described in this section. It combines choices from 'meaning' and 'form'. The primary distinction is between 'autonomous location change' and 'caused location change'. This is shown in Figure 8.6. More detail of the 'autonomous' constructions is shown in Figure 8.6b and detail of the 'caused' constructions is shown in Figure 8.6c.

The Location Change Meaning Network: Choices and Examples

- Autonomous Location Change. See Figure 8.6b.
  - V around n
    - Cx4 e.g. 'The lions circled around the encampment'.
    - Cx5 e.g. 'The fans crowded round the singer'.
    - Cx6 e.g. 'The crowds moved around the square'.
  - V pron-refl from n Cx6 e.g. 'Joe absented himself from the meeting'.
  - V into n
    - Cx1 e.g. 'The fans crowded into the stadium'.
    - Cx2 e.g. 'Emma barged into the room'.
    - Cx3 e.g. 'The students filtered into the classroom'.
  - V off n Cx1 e.g. 'Light reflected off the polished surface'.
  - V on n Cx13 e.g. 'The fans converged on the stadium'.
  - V out of n Cx7 e.g. 'The fans cleared out of the room'.
  - V through n Cx e.g. 'Emma barged through the crowd'.
  - V to n Cx34 e.g. 'Emma journeyed to her destination.' and Cx35 e.g. 'The fans flocked to the stadium'.
- Caused Location Change. See Figure 8.6c. The entity that moves may be physical or abstract.
  - The entity is physical.
    - V n (Material) Cx17 e.g. 'She brought a cake.' and Cx22 e.g. 'The police moved the crowd along'.
    - V n from n
      - Cx7 e.g. 'They deported him from the USA'.
      - Cx8 e.g. 'He sent the package from his home'.

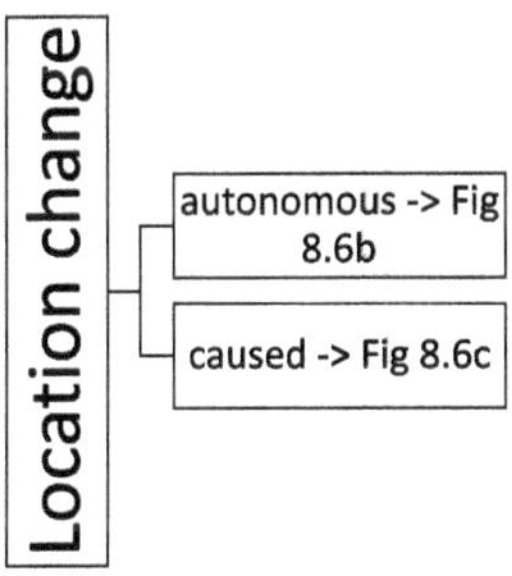

Figure 8.6a Location change Meaning Network

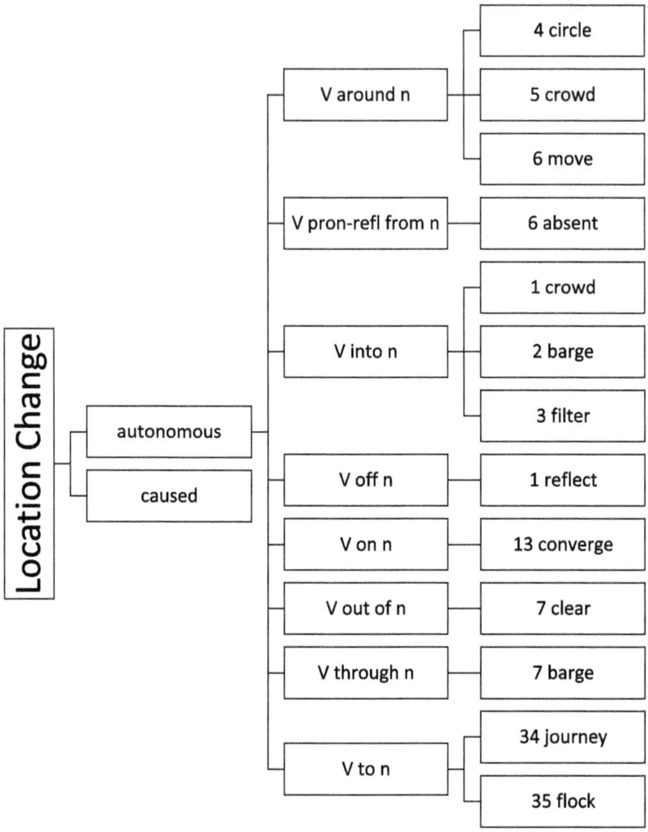

Figure 8.6b Location change: autonomous change

- Cx9 e.g. 'Joe detached the door from the barn'.
- V n in n Cx4 e.g. 'Emma inserted a key in the lock.' and Cx8 e.g. 'Joe shut the pig in the barn'.
- V n into n Cx14 e.g. 'Emma dragged the logs into the barn'.
- V n out of n Cx1 e.g. 'Joe plucked the flower out of his buttonhole.' and Cx2 e.g. 'Emma kicked the ball out of the park'.
- V n to n Cx12 e.g. 'They deported him to the USA'.

◦ The entity is abstract
- V n (Material) Cx19 e.g. 'Emma gathered information'.
- V n from n Cx10 e.g. 'Joe dismissed the idea from his mind'.

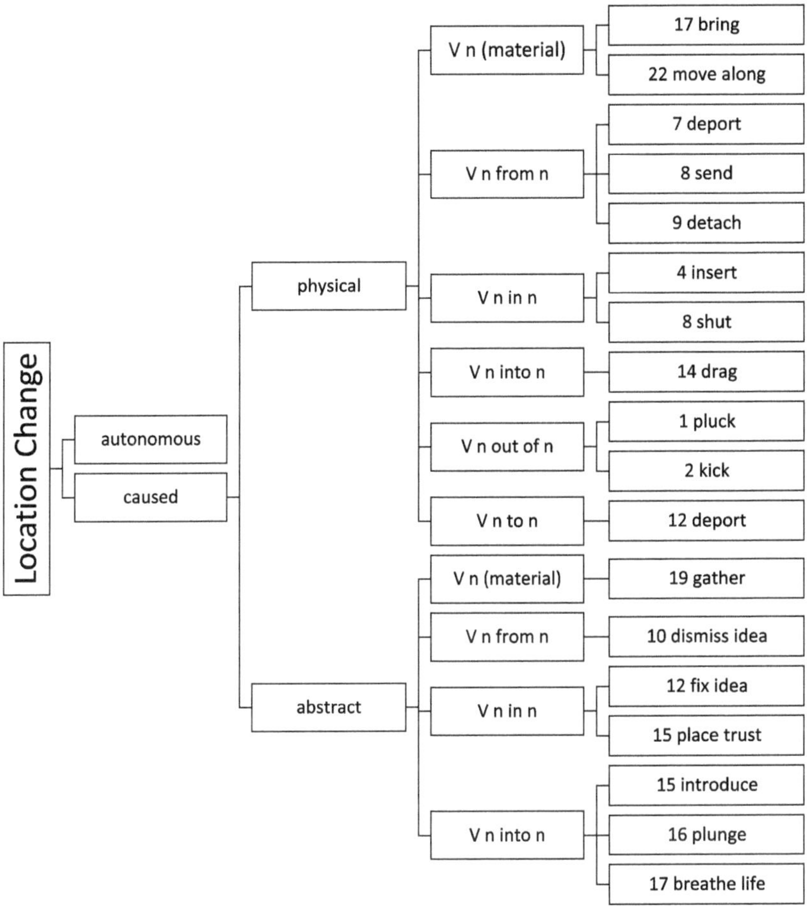

Figure 8.6c Location change: caused change

- V n in n Cx 12 e.g. 'The speech fixed this new idea in her mind.' and Cx15 e.g. 'Joe placed a great deal of trust in Emma'.
- V n into n
  - Cx15 e.g. 'Joe introduced a new topic into the conversation'.
  - Cx16 e.g. 'The war plunged the nation into crisis'.
  - Cx17 e.g. 'Her ideas breathed new life into the discussion'.

8.5 The Possession Transfer Semantic Field

The term 'Possession Transfer' refers to constructions that indicate that an entity is given by one person to another or taken by one person from another. The entity may be something physical, such as 'a book', or something abstract, such as 'permission' or 'a confession'. There are 20 constructions with this meaning, derived from 8 verb complementation patterns.

The Systemic Network. The Systemic Network, shown in Figure 8.7, shows independent choices in meaning and in form. Two simultaneous **meaning** choices are made: the process type and the direction ('give' and 'take'). The process type includes two further simultaneous systems: 'type' ('action' or 'communication') and the degree of physicality ('physical' or 'abstract'). Action process types include examples such as 'provide something' which is physical, and 'grant permission to someone', which is abstract, while communication process types include examples such as 'demand something from someone'. The example 'provide something' also exemplifies the direction 'give', while the example 'demand something from someone' also exemplifies the direction 'take'. Examples (1)–(3) illustrate this.

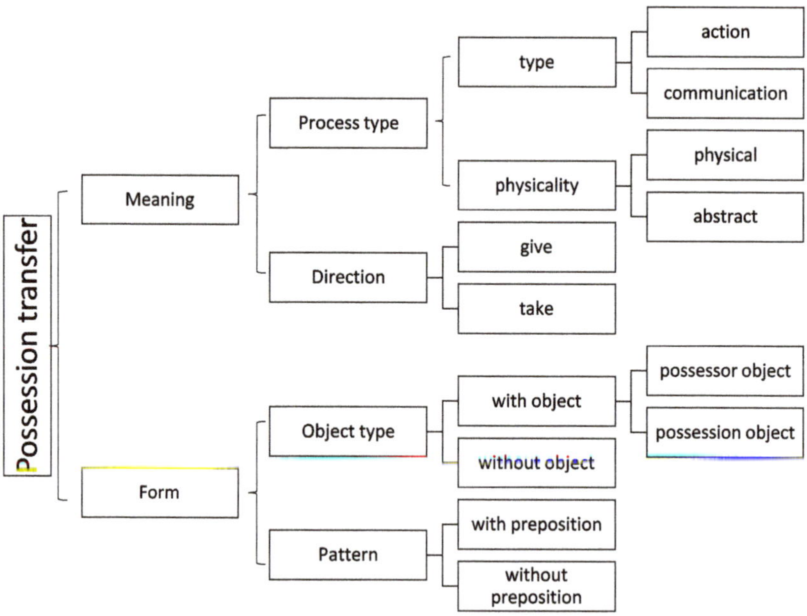

Figure 8.7 Possession transfer Systemic Network

(1) Sara provided extra balloons. (Action process; physical process; 'give' direction)

(2) Sara granted Jenny permission to take the book. (Action process; abstract process; 'give' direction)

(3) Sara demanded respect from her subordinates. (Communication process; abstract process; 'take' direction)

Two simultaneous **form** distinctions are identified. One is the object type, and the other is the pattern. Most constructions include an object element, with one construction ('borrow from someone') having no object. The object can be the possessor or the possession, as shown in examples (4) and (5).

(4) Thieves robbed the baron of all his gold. (The object, 'the baron', is the possessor.)

(5) Thieves stole money from the baron. (The object, 'money', is the possession.)

In terms of pattern, examples (3), (4), and (5) illustrate patterns with prepositions while examples (1) and (2) illustrate patterns without prepositions.

The Meaning Network. The Meaning Network for this semantic field combines choices from both 'meaning' and 'form'. The primary distinction made is between the process types – action and communication – while the other distinctions prioritise form. The meaning network is shown in Figure 8.8. Figure 8.8 shows the process type distinction. Figures 8.8b and 8.8c show the 'by action' constructions. Figure 8.8d shows the 'by communication' constructions.

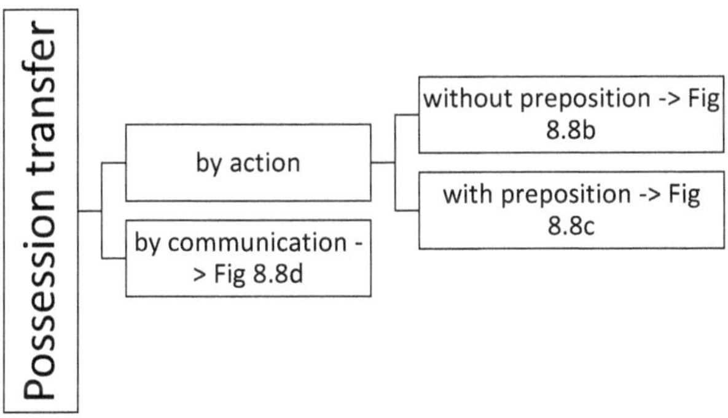

Figure 8.8a Possession transfer Meaning Network

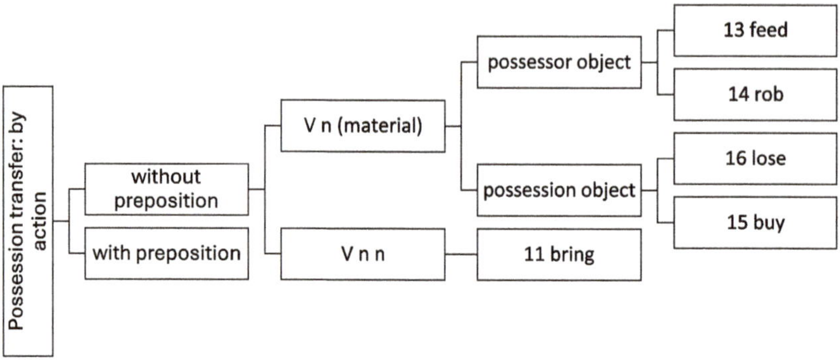

Figure 8.8b Possession transfer: by action, the noun phrase only network

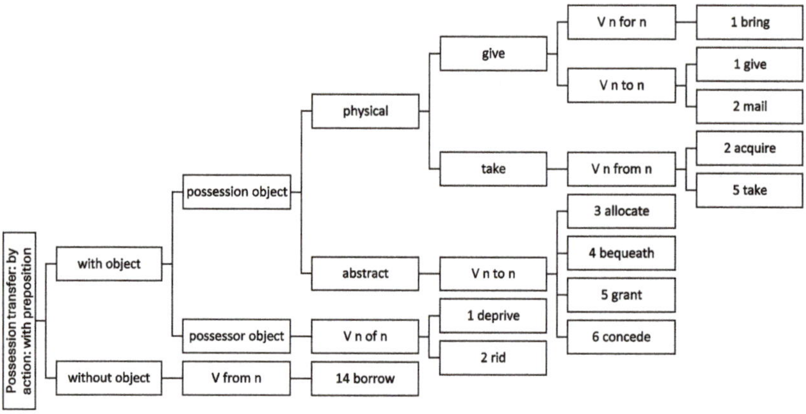

Figure 8.8c Possession transfer: by action, the with prepositional phrase network

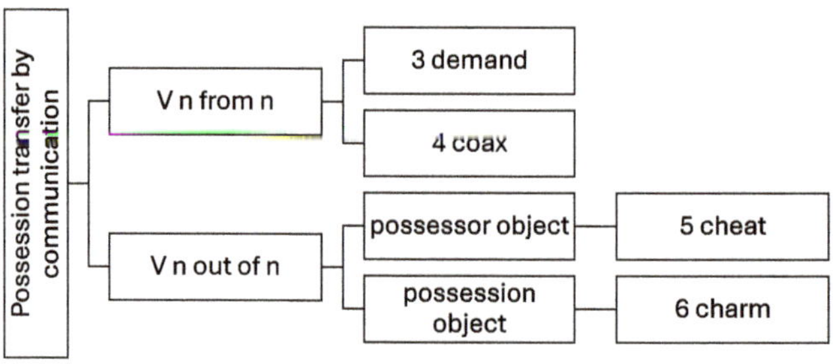

Figure 8.8d Possession transfer: by communication

Figure 8.8 is described here.
The process may construe action or communication.

- Possession Transfer by action
    - Patterns without prepositions (Figure 8.8b). All the constructions have a clause object.
        - V n (Material). The clause object may indicate the possessor or the possession.
            - The object indicates the possessor. The direction of transfer may be 'give' or 'take'.
                - Give Cx13 e.g. 'Emma fed the cat'.
                - Take Cx14 e.g. 'The gang robbed the bank'.
            - The object indicates the possession. The direction of transfer may be 'give' or 'take'.
                - Give Cx16 e.g. 'Emma provided food'.
                - Take Cx15 e.g. 'The gang took the money'.
        - V n n Cx11 e.g. 'He brought her a book'.
    - Patterns with prepositions (Figure 8.8c). The constructions may or may not have a clause object.
        - Constructions with an object. The object may indicate the possessor or the possession.
            - The object indicates the possession.
                - The things transferred are physical entities. The direction of transfer may be 'give' or 'take'.
                    - Give
                        - V n for n Cx1 e.g. 'Emma brought gifts for the children'.
                        - V n to n Cx1 e.g. 'Emma gave gifts to the children.' and Cx2 e.g. 'Emma mailed gifts to the children'.
                    - Take
                        - V n from n Cx2 e.g. 'Joe acquired land from his cousin.' and Cx5 e.g. 'Joe took the gifts from Emma'.
                - The things transferred are abstract entities. The direction of transfer is only 'give'.
                    - V n to n
                        - Cx3 e.g. 'They allocated tasks to the staff'.
                        - Cx4 e.g. 'Joe bequeathed his possessions to Emma'.
                        - Cx6 e.g. 'Emma conceded the argument to Joe'.
            - The object indicates the possessor. The direction of transfer is only 'take'.
                - V n of n Cx1 e.g. 'Emma deprived the children of gifts.' and Cx2 'Emma rid the barn of rats'.
        - Construction without an object.
            - V from n Cx14 e.g. 'Joe borrowed from his father'.

- Possession Transfer by communication (Figure 8.8d). The clause object may indicate the possession or the possessor.
  - V n from n (The object indicates the possession) Cx3 e.g. 'Emma demanded gifts from Joe.' and Cx4 e.g. 'Emma coaxed gifts from Joe'.
  - V n out of n
    - The object indicates the possessor. Cx5 e.g. 'Joe cheated Emma out of her money'.
    - The object indicates the possession. Cx6 e.g. 'Joe charmed some money out of Emma'.

8.6 The Equivalence Semantic Field

The Equivalence semantic field is the first of two that draw on the concept of Relational processes. The canonical form of the Equivalence meaning is 'x is y' (e.g. 'Gemma is sad/a sad person'). In other words, constructions in this field indicate that something has an identity or quality. The canonical participant roles are Carrier and Attribute. In this book, the semantic field of Equivalence is considered to include constructions that go beyond relational processes and beyond the canonical form. For example, it includes constructions which indicate that someone construes an Equivalence relation through something they say or think (e.g. 'Ivan described Gemma as a sad person'). For this reason, many of the constructions in this semantic field also participate in other fields, such as Communication, Cognition, or Causation.

There are 106 constructions that express this meaning, drawing on 26 verb complement constructions.

The Systemic Network. The choices within this semantic field can be considered under the headings of 'meaning' and 'form'. These can be shown as independent choices, as has been done with other semantic fields in this book. However, given that in this case the distinction between meaning and form is particularly arbitrary, it would be more accurate to say that the choices between constructions can be conceptualised as either semantic choices or as form choices. The resulting network is somewhat large, so to make it as legible as possible it is shown here as two figures. Figure 8.9a models the distinctions as meaning choices, while Figure 8.9b models them as choices of form.

Figure 8.9 shows three independent choice systems: the type of representation, the presence or absence of dynamism, and the attribute type.

The **type of representation** distinguishes assertions that something is the case ('integral') from assertions that something is construed by speech, thought or action to be the case ('construed'). The integral representation may or may not be modified by the verb. The 'unmodified' meaning is exemplified by the verb 'be',

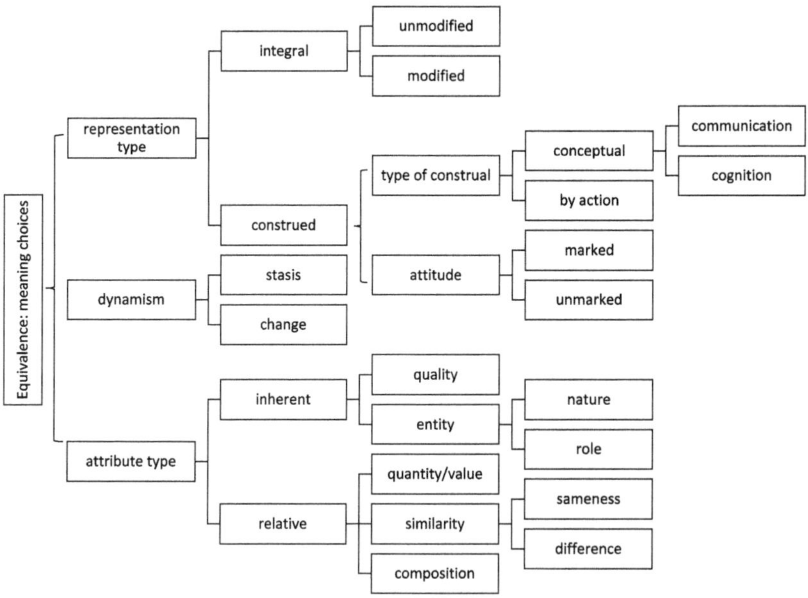

Figure 8.9a Equivalence Systemic Network: meaning choices

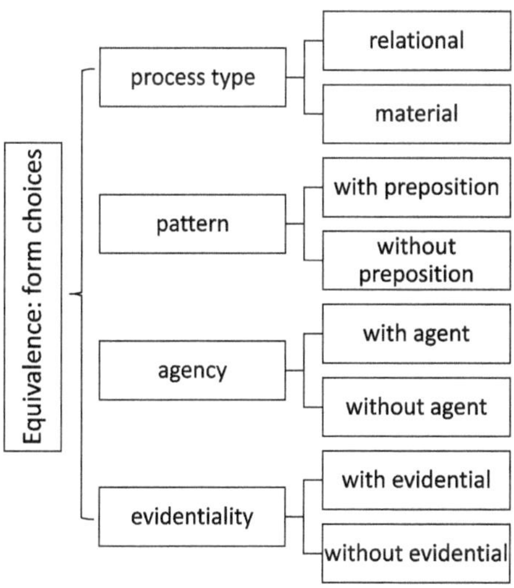

Figure 8.9b Equivalence Systemic Network: form choices

whereas the 'modified' meaning is exemplified by 'seem' or 'appear'. These distinctions are illustrated in examples (1)–(3).

(1) He is foolish. (Representation type: integral: unmodified)

(2) He appeared foolish. (Representation type: integral: modified)

(3) She considered him foolish. (Representation type: construed)

Within the 'construed' system, further independent choices are made of the type of construal and of attitude. The type of construal may be conceptual, i.e. someone construes an equivalence through thought or through speech, or it may be by action i.e. someone does something to bring about an equivalence. This is illustrated in examples (4)–(6).

(4) She called him foolish. (Construal: conceptual: communication)

(5) She considered him foolish. (Construal: conceptual: cognition)

(6) They voted her President. (Construal: action)

Attitude may be marked or unmarked, as illustrated in examples (7)–(9). If the choice is 'unmarked attitude', there is no indication of a judgement of truth or value by either the speaker or the reported person. This is the case in example (4): from the verb CONSIDER, it is not known if the speaker of the clause agrees with 'she' or not, or what value the reported 'she' places on being foolish. If the choice is 'marked', an attitude is indicated. In example (5), the reported person's attitude is expressed. In example (6), the fact that the speaker considers the reported person to be wrong is indicated by the verb MISTAKE.

(7) She considered him foolish. (Attitude: unmarked)

(8) She denounced him as foolish. (Attitude: marked: attitude of reported person)

(9) She mistook him for a fool. (Attitude: marked: attitude of reporter)

Under '**dynamism**', a distinction is made between constructions indicating a state and those indicating a process of change. This is illustrated in examples (10) and (11). '**Attribute type**' distinguishes between attributes that are inherent, such as quality or identity, and those that are relative to other entities, such as quantity, composition or degree of similarity. This is illustrated in examples (12)–(14).

(10) He was old. (Dynamism: stasis)

(11) He became older. (Dynamism: change)

(12) He was a teacher. (Attribute: inherent: entity: role)

(13) He surpassed his rivals in every way. (Attribute: relative: value)

(14) He resembled his brother. (Attribute: relative: similarity: sameness)

The system of form choices, shown in Figure 8.9b, is more straightforward and identifies four simultaneous systems: the process type, the pattern, whether agency is expressed or not and whether there is an evidential or not. The process, agency, and evidentiality choices are illustrated in examples (15)–(20). As with other semantic fields, the pattern system simply distinguishes patterns with a preposition, as in example (19) and those without, as in the other examples.

(15) She became President. (Process: relational)

(16) They elected her President. (Process: material)

(17) The news made him angry. (Agency: with agent)

(18) He became angry. (Agency: without agent)

(19) His shirt identified him as a rapper. (Evidentiality: with evidential)

(20) He was a rapper. (Evidentiality: without evidential)

The Meaning Network. The Meaning Network combines choices from 'meaning' and 'form'. The primary distinction combines the representation and dynamism systems, and distinguishes between 'being', 'construal', and 'becoming'. This is shown in Figure 8.10. The main distinctions are described here, with examples. These are shown under the headings 'Entity is: being'

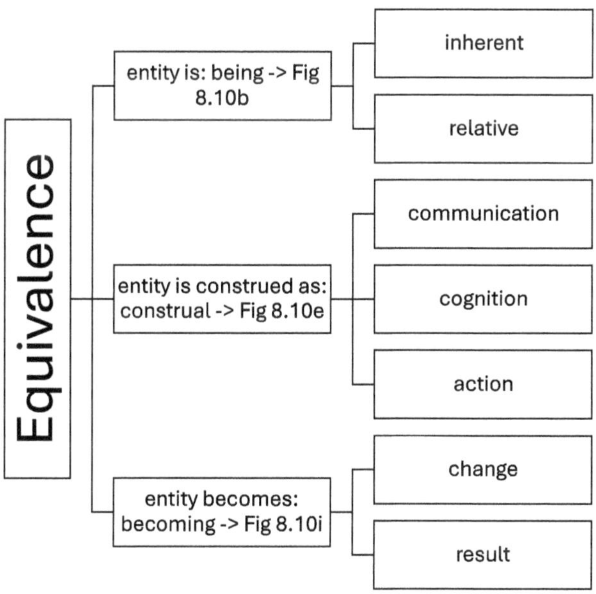

Figure 8.10a Equivalence Meaning Network

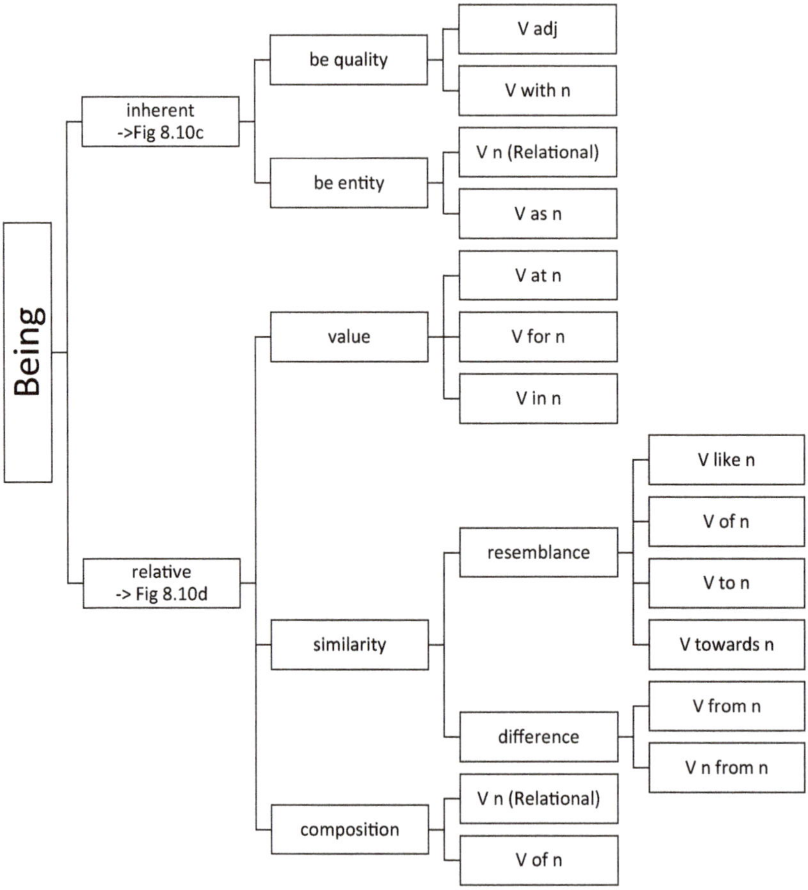

Figure 8.10b Equivalence: being

(Figure 8.10b–d), ‘Entity is construed as: construal’ (Figure 8.10e–h), and ‘Entity becomes: becoming’ (Figure 8.10i–m).

The ‘Equivalence: Being’ Meaning Network
The Attribute (quality or identity) may be inherent or relative.

- The quality or identity is inherent (see Figure 8.10c).
  - The construction indicates a quality.
    - V adj. The construction may modify the truth of the assertion or not.

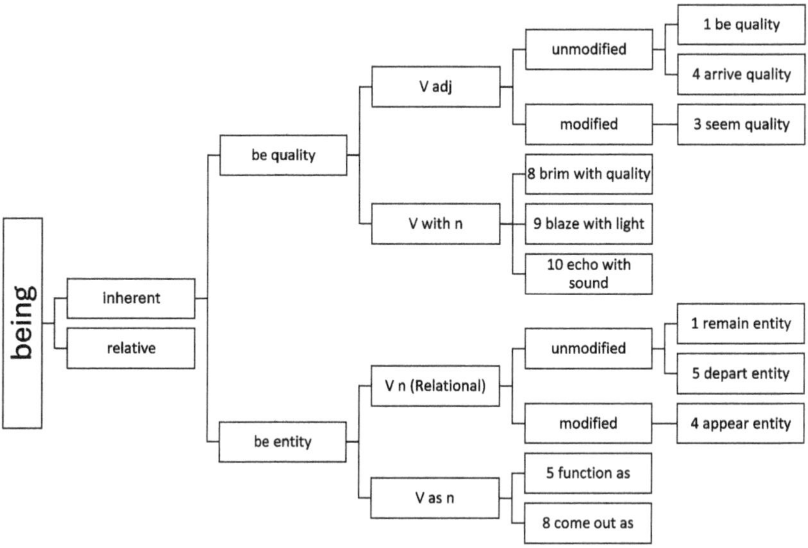

Figure 8.10c Equivalence: being, showing choices of inherent quality

        - Unmodified. Cx1 e.g. 'Sid is clever.' and Cx4 e.g. 'Sid arrived exhausted'.
        - Modified. Cx3 e.g. 'Sid seems clever'.
    - V with n
        - Cx8 e.g. 'The musical brimmed with joy'.
        - Cx9 e.g. 'The room blazed with light'.
        - Cx10 e.g. 'The house echoed with laughter'.
  - The construction indicates an entity.
    - V n (Relational). The construction may modify the truth of the assertion or not.
        - Unmodified. Cx1 e.g. 'Sid remained a recluse.' and Cx5 e.g. 'Sid departed a bitter man'.
        - Modified. Cx4 e.g. 'Sid seemed a bitter man'.
    - V as n. Cx5 e.g. 'The phone box functions as a spaceship.' and Cx8 e.g. 'Sid came out as a devil-worshipper'.

- The quality/identity is relative (see Figure 8.10d). The construction may indicate quantity, similarity, or composition.
  - The construction indicates a value or quantity.
    - V at n. Cx2 e.g. 'The price stands at £200.' and Cx3 e.g. 'The shares sell at £2'.

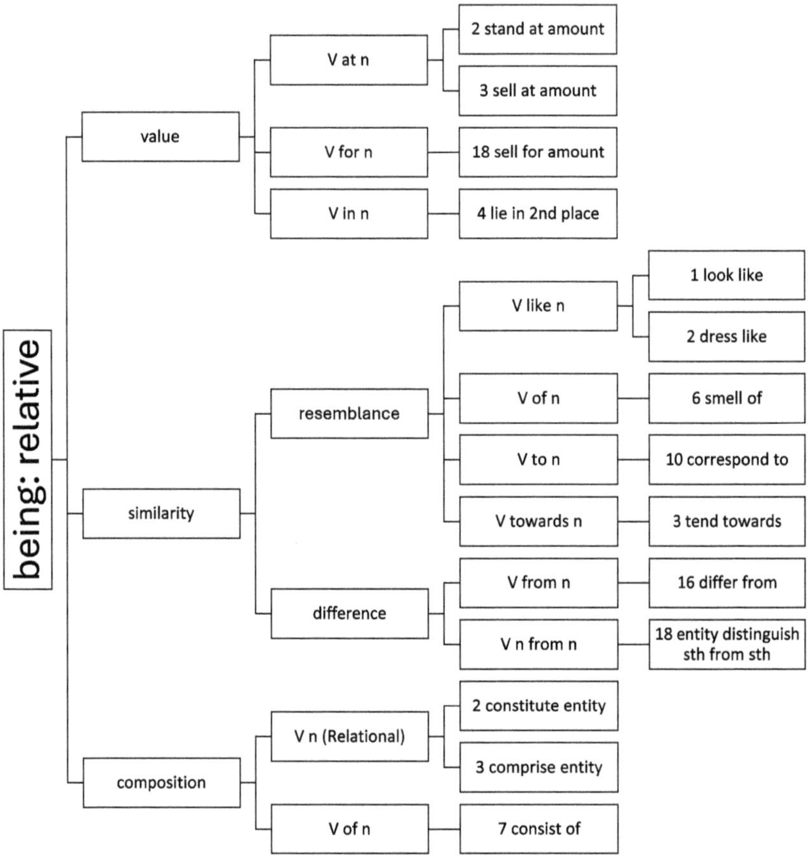

Figure 8.10d Equivalence: being, showing choices of relative quality

    - V for n. Cx18 e.g. ‘The chairs sell for £45 each’.
    - V in n. Cx4 e.g. ‘Becca lay in 2nd place’.
- The construction indicates a degree of similarity. This may be resemblance or difference.
    - The construction indicates resemblance.
        - V like n. Cx1 e.g. ‘Becca looked like a goth.’ and Cx2 e.g. ‘Becca dressed like a goth’.
        - V of n. Cx6 e.g. ‘The perfume smelled of roses’.
        - V to n. Cx10 e.g. ‘The line on the graph corresponds to the increase in prices’.
        - V towards n. Cx3 e.g. ‘The garden tends towards a wilderness’.

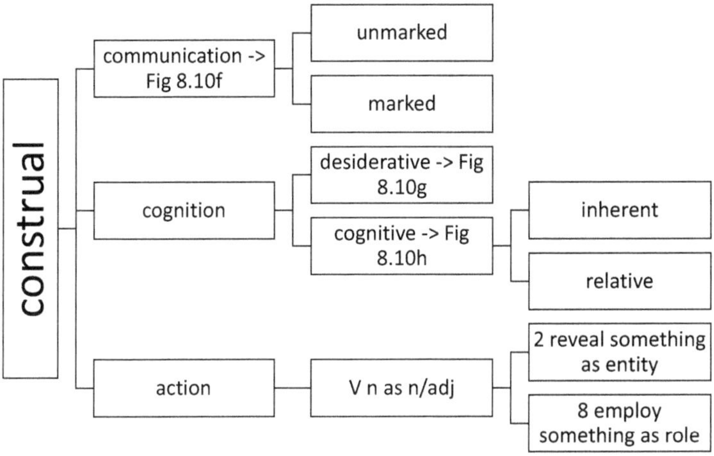

Figure 8.10e Equivalence: construal

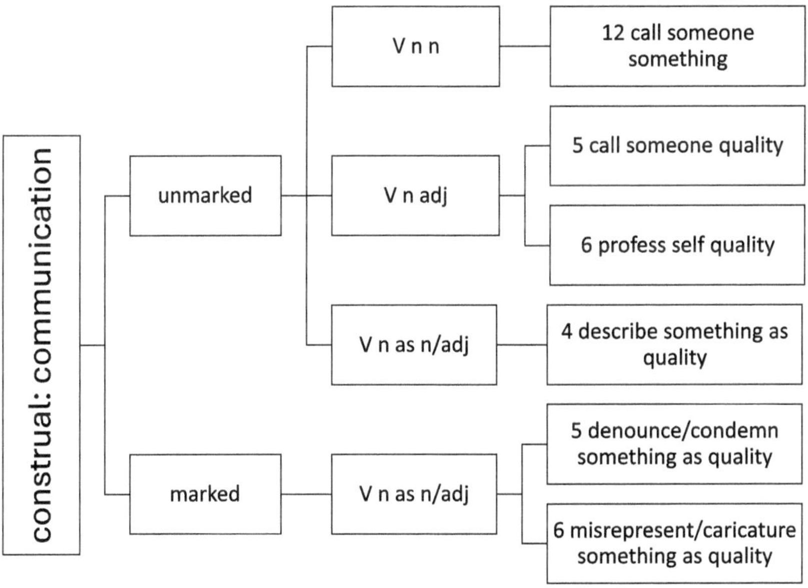

Figure 8.10f Equivalence: construal by communication

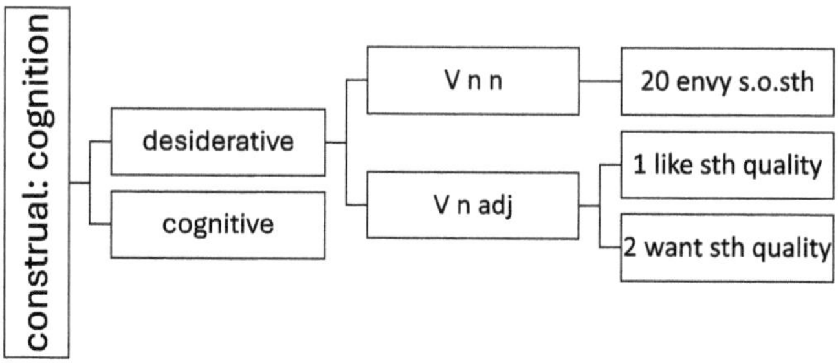

Figure 8.10g Equivalence: construal by cognition, the desiderative network

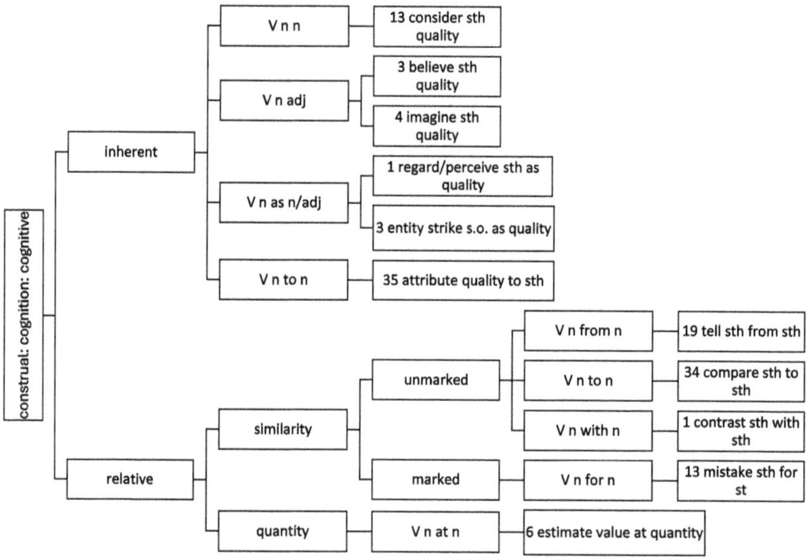

Figure 8.10h Equivalence: construal by cognition, the cognitive network

- The construction indicates difference.
  - V from n. Cx16 e.g. 'The garden differs from a wilderness'.
  - V n from n. Cx18 e.g. 'The presence of cultivated shrubs distinguishes the garden from a wilderness'.
- The construction indicates how something is composed.
  - V n (Relational). Cx2 e.g. 'A collection of tents constitutes the camp.' and Cx3 e.g. 'Several tents comprise the camp'.
  - V of n. Cx7 e.g. 'The camp consists of several tents'.

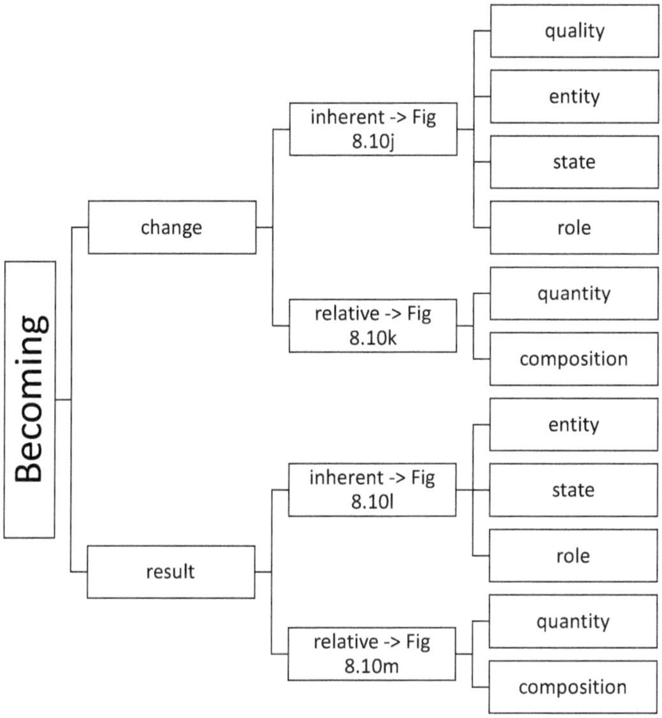

Figure 8.10i Equivalence: becoming

The 'Equivalence: Construal' Meaning Network

The construal may be by communication, by cognition or by action (see Figure 8.10e).

- Construal by communication (Figure 8.10f). The construal may be marked or unmarked.
  - The construal is unmarked.
    - V n n. Cx12 e.g. 'Becca called Sid an idiot'.
    - V n adj. Cx5 e.g. 'Sid called Becca stupid.' and Cx6 e.g. 'Sid professed himself baffled'.
    - V n as n/adj. Cx4 e.g. 'Sid described Becca as the worst driver he had seen'.
  - The construal is marked.
    - V n as n/adj. Cx5 e.g. 'Sid denounced Becca as a terrible driver.' and Cx6 e.g. 'Sid mispresented Becca as a terrible driver'.

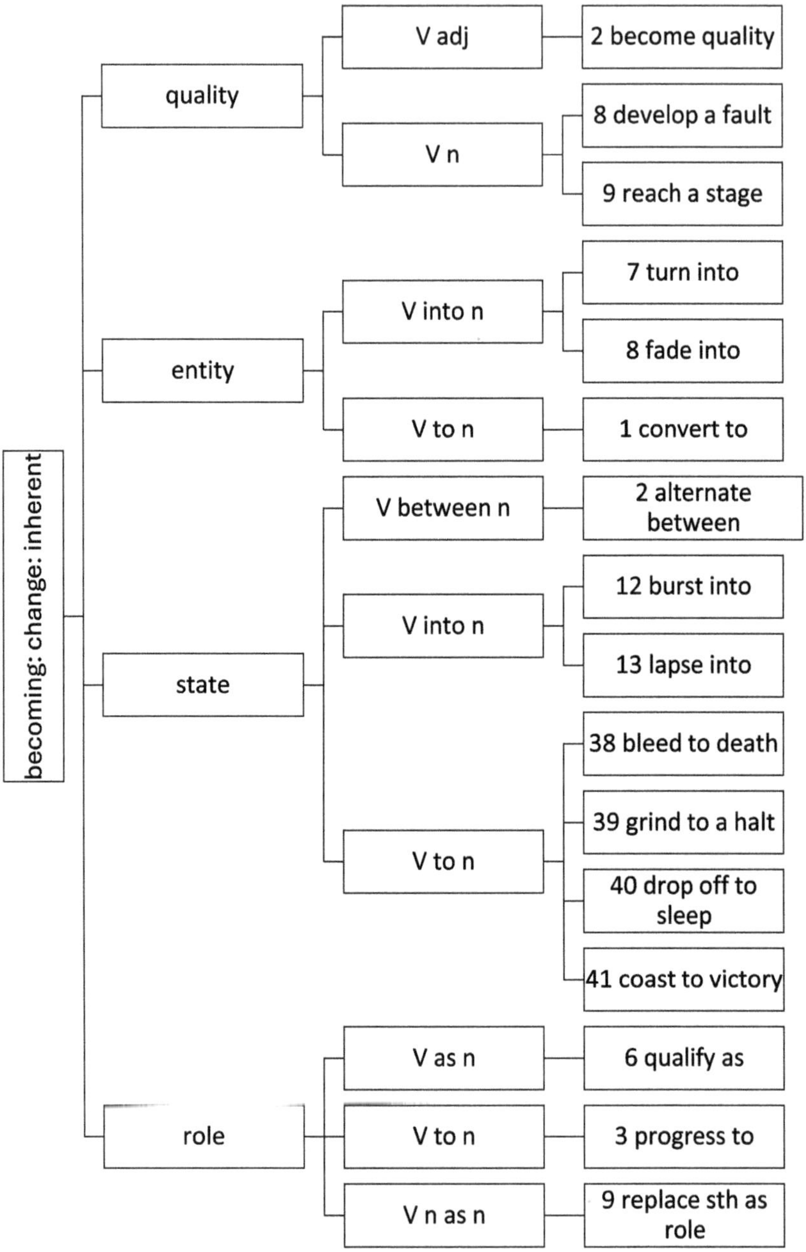

Figure 8.10j Equivalence: becoming, the change network, showing choices of inherent quality

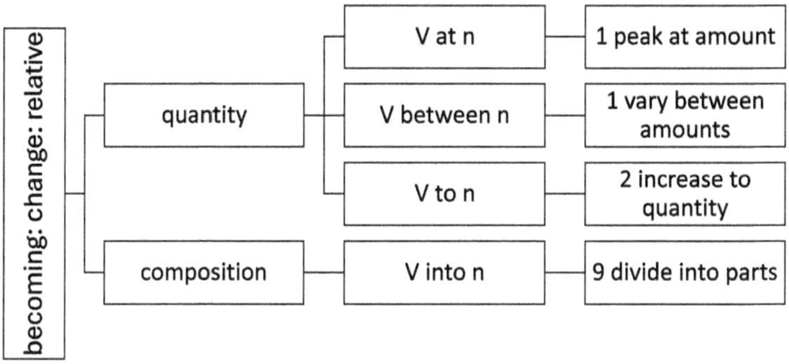

Figure 8.10k Equivalence: becoming, the change network, showing choices of relative quality

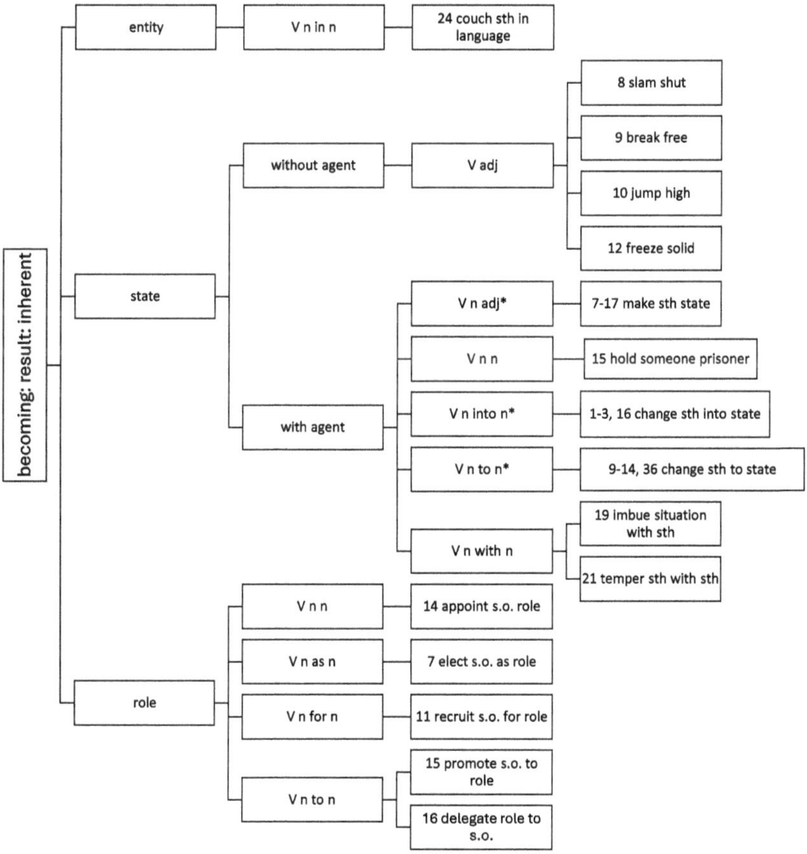

Figure 8.10l Equivalence: becoming, the result network, showing choices of inherent quality

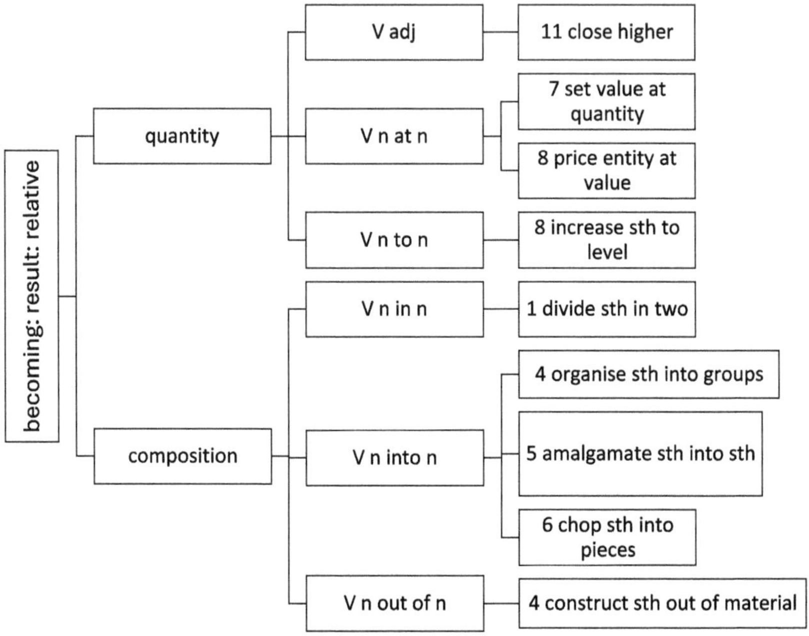

Figure 8.10m Equivalence: becoming, the result network, showing choices of relative quality

- Construal by cognition. The process may be desiderative or cognitive.
  - The process is desiderative (Figure 8.10g).
    - V n n. Cx20 e.g. 'Sid envied Becca her composure'.
    - V n adj. Cx1 e.g. 'Becca liked her tea strong.' and Cx2 e.g. 'Becca wants her tea strong'.
  - The process is cognitive (Figure 8.10h). The quality or identity may be inherent or relative.
    - The quality is inherent.
      - V n n. Cx13 e.g. 'Becca considered Sid an idiot'.
      - V n adj. Cx3 e.g. 'Becca believed Sid stupid.' and Cx4 e.g. 'Becca imagined the house larger'.
      - V n as n/adj. Cx1 e.g. 'Becca regarded Sid as stupid'. And Cx3 e.g. 'Sid struck Becca as intelligent'.
      - V n to n. Cx35 e.g. 'Becca attributed great intelligence to Sid'.
    - The quality is relative. The construed relation may be one of similarity or quantity.
      - The construed relation is one of similarity. It may be marked or unmarked for truth value.

        - The construral is unmarked.
            - V n from n. Cx19 e.g. 'Sid could not tell Becca from a goth'.
            - V n to n. Cx34 e.g. 'Becca compared Sid to a Greek god'.
            - V n with n. Cx1 e.g. 'Sid contrasted the house with a palace'.
        - The construal is marked.
            - V n for n. Cx13 e.g. 'Sid mistook his wife for a hat'.
    - Quantity
        - V n at n. Cx6 e.g. 'Becca estimated the value of the chair at £200'.
- Construal by action (Figure 8.10e)
    - V n as n/adj. Cx2 e.g. 'The party revealed Sid as their candidate.' and Cx8 e.g. 'Sid used his umbrella as a weapon'.

The 'Equivalence: Becoming' Meaning Network

The constructions may indicate change without a cause, or the result of a cause (see Figure 8.10i).

- The constructions indicate change without cause. The quality or identity may be inherent or relative.
    - The quality or identity is inherent (Figure 8.10j). It may be a quality, an entity, a state or a role.
        - Quality
            - V adj. Cx2 e.g. 'Mo became stronger'.
            - V n (Relational). Cx8 e.g. 'The machine developed a fault.' and Cx9 e.g. 'The problem reached a crucial stage'.
        - Entity
            - V into n. Cx7 e.g. 'The caterpillar turned into a butterfly.' and Cx8 e.g. 'The image faded into the background'.
            - V to n. Cx1 e.g. 'Sid converted to Buddhism'.
        - State
            - V between n. Cx2 e.g. 'Becca alternated between fear and anger'.
            - V into n. Cx12 e.g. 'Mo burst into laughter.' and Cx13 e.g. 'Mo lapsed into depression'.
            - V to n.
                - Cx38 e.g. 'The victim bled to death'.
                - Cx39 e.g. 'The train ground to a halt'.
                - Cx40 e.g. 'Mo dropped off to sleep'.
                - Cx41 e.g. 'Mo coasted to victory'.
        - Role
            - V as n. Cx6 e.g. 'Becca qualified as a vet'.
            - V to n. Cx3 e.g. 'Sid progressed to a qualified teacher'.
            - V n as n. Cx9 e.g. 'Mo replaced Sid as the candidate'.

    - The quality or identity is relative (Figure 8.10k). It may be a quantity or composition.
        - Quantity
            - V at n. Cx1 e.g. 'The shares peaked at £2 each'.
            - V between n. Cx1 e.g. 'The price varies between £150 and £200'.
            - V to n. Cx2 e.g. 'The price has increased to £200'.
        - Composition
            - V into n. Cx9 e.g. 'The road divided into two carriageways'.
- The constructions indicate the result of a cause. The quality or identity may be inherent or relative.
    - The quality or identity is inherent (Figure 8.10l). It may be an entity, a state, or a role.
        - Entity
            - V n in n. Cx24 e.g. 'Sid couched the criticism in flowery language'.
        - State. The construction may express an agent or not.
            - The construction may express an agent.
                - V adj
                    - Cx8 e.g. 'The door slammed shut'.
                    - Cx9 e.g. 'The prisoner broke free'.
                    - Cx10 e.g. 'Mo jumped higher'.
                    - Cx12 e.g. 'The lake froze solid'.
            - The construction may not express an agent.
                - V n adj
                    - Cx7 e.g. 'The failure made him stronger'.
                    - Cx8 e.g. 'Mo pushed the door open'.
                    - Cx9 e.g. 'Sid wiped the table clean'.
                    - Cx10 e.g. 'Becca kept the cat safe'.
                    - Cx11 e.g. 'Mo cranked the volume higher'.
                    - Cx12 e.g. 'Sid coloured the clouds grey'.
                    - Cx13 e.g. 'Mo served the soup cold'.
                    - Cx14 e.g. 'The shares began the day higher'.
                    - Cx15 e.g. 'He left the second victim alive'.
                    - Cx16 e.g. 'He captured the second victim live'.
                    - Cx17 e.g. 'He buried his victim alive'.
                - V n n Cx15 e.g. 'Sid held Jake prisoner'.
                - V n into n
                    - Cx1 e.g. 'Jake changed the curtains into blinds'.
                    - Cx2 e.g. 'Jake compressed the dough into a tiny ball'.
                    - Cx3 e.g. 'Mo translated the book into English'.
                    - Cx 16 e.g. 'The decision plunged the meeting into gloom'.
                - V n to n
                    - Cx9 e.g. 'Becca turned the curtains into blinds'.

        - Cx10 e.g. 'Sid attached the tow line to the car'.
        - Cx11 e.g. 'Jake almost frightened Mo to death'.
        - Cx12 e.g. 'The government deported Jake to Canada'.
        - Cx13 e.g. 'The contract shackled Jake to his job'.
        - Cx14 e.g. 'The committee broadened the conversation to a general discussion of the result'.
        - Cx36 e.g. 'The decision brought a sense of relief to the proceedings'.
      - V n with n. Cx19 e.g. 'His failure imbued the atmosphere with gloom.' and Cx21 e.g. 'Sid tempered his remarks with humour'.
  - Role
    - V n n. Cx14 e.g. 'Mo appointed Jake secretary'.
    - V n as n. Cx7 e.g. 'The committee elected Mo chairman'.
    - V n for n. Cx11 e.g. 'Mo recruited Jake for the position of secretary'.
    - V n to n. Cx15 e.g. 'Mo promoted Jake to the position of secretary.' and Cx16 e.g. 'Mo delegated the position of secretary to Jake'.

- The quality or identity is relative (Figure 8.10m). It may be a quantity or composition.
  - Quantity
    - V adj. Cx11 e.g. 'The share price closed higher'.
    - V n at n. Cx7 e.g. 'Becca set the price at £20.' and Cx8 e.g. 'Becca priced the table at £20'.
    - V n to n. Cx8 e.g. 'Sid increased the price to £20'.
  - Composition
    - V n in n. Cx1 e.g. 'Mo divided the apple in two'.
    - V n into n.
      - Cx4 e.g. 'Mo organised the participants into groups'.
      - Cx5 e.g. 'Sid amalgamated the departments into one larger department'.
      - Cx6 e.g. 'Mo chopped the apple into pieces'.
    - V n out of n. Cx4 e.g. 'Becca constructed the hut out of spare timber'.

8.7 The Logical Relations Semantic Field

The term 'Logical Relations' refers to those constructions where the verb expresses the relationship between two entities or two actions or events. In this study, it is limited to those relations that are not covered by the 'Equivalence' Networks or the 'Causation' Networks.

There are 22 constructions that express this meaning, drawing on 12 verb complementation patterns.

The Systemic Network. This network, Figure 8.11, shows simultaneous choices in meaning and form. The form choices are simply choices between patterns. The meaning choices are more interesting. There are simultaneous choices between the type of logical relation expressed and between the type of participant.

The relation types are divided into: dependence, correspondence, evidence, and time. The **time** relation is the simplest; the constructions indicate the sequence of two events. This is illustrated in examples (1) and (2).

(1) The celebrations followed the meeting. (Relation type: time: 'follows')

(2) The meeting preceded the celebrations. (Relation type: time: 'precedes')

The **correspondence** relation comprises constructions that indicate a measure of similarity between two entities or events. It may be simply stated (averred) or it may involve an observer or construer of some kind (attributed). This is illustrated in examples (3) and (4).

(3) The arrows correspond to the decision path. (Relation type: correspondence: averred)

(4) She based her argument on three points. (Relation type: correspondence: attributed)

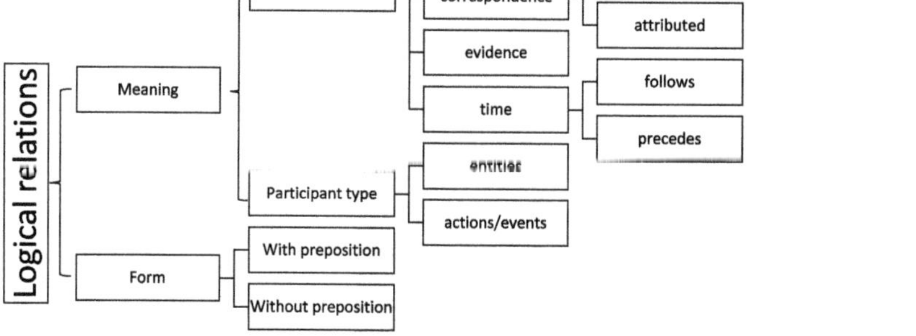

Figure 8.11 Logical Relations Systemic Network

The **evidence** relation refers to constructions where one entity or event provides evidence for the existence of another entity or event, as in example (5).

(5) The witness's testimony pointed to Joe's innocence. (Relation type: evidence)

The **dependence** relation refers to constructions where one entity or event is dependent on another. The dependence may be unidirectional (one thing influences another) or bidirectional (two things influence each other). The unidirectional dependence may work in either direction, with the first-mentioned entity either influencing or being conditional upon the second. This is illustrated in examples (6)–(8).

(6) These working conditions impinged on the effectiveness of their efforts. (Relation type: dependence: unidirectional: influence)

(7) Their effectiveness depends on the working conditions. (Relation type: dependence: unidirectional: condition)

(8) Working well involves working together. (Relation type: dependence: bidirectional)

The types of participants are divided into entities and actions/events. Because all participants can be realised as nouns, however, the distinction is not absolute. The clearest distinctions are illustrated in examples (9) and (10).

(9) Gloom descended over the town. (Participants: entities)

(10) An explosion can result from mixing chemicals. (Participants: event and action)

The Meaning Network. In the meaning network (see Figure 8.12), participant type is prioritised, which means that most of the relation types occur twice in the network. The meanings and patterns are shown here with examples of the constructions.

The construction may indicate relations between entities or between actions/events.

- The constructions indicate relations between entities (see Figure 8.12b). The relation may be one of influence, condition, correspondence, or evidence.
  - The relation is one of influence.
    - V on n Cx21 e.g. 'Stress impinged on her ability to work'.
    - V over n Cx12 e.g. 'Gloom hung over the town'. And Cx13 e.g. 'Gloom descended over the town'.
  - The relation is one of condition.
    - V on n Cx22 e.g. 'They all depended on his kindness'.
  - The relation is one of correspondence. It may be averred or attributed.

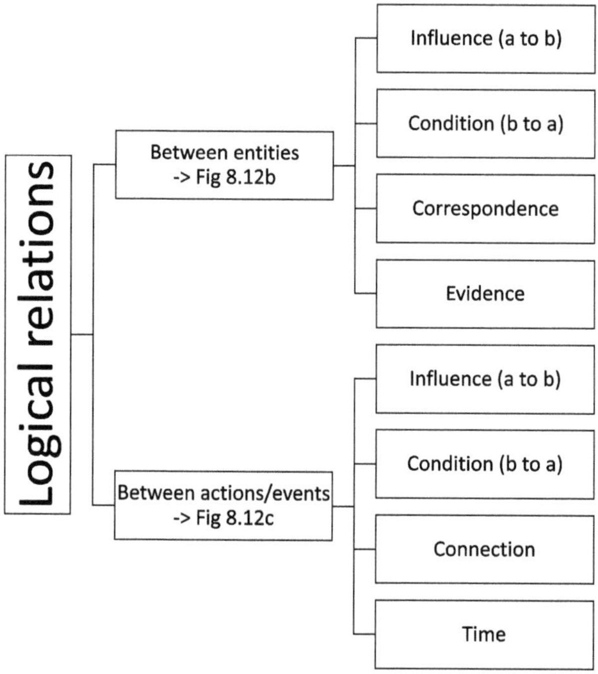

Figure 8.12a Logical Relations Meaning Network

    - The relation is averred
      - V to n Cx10 e.g. 'The arrows correspond to the decision path'.
    - The relation is attributed
      - V n into n Cx18 e.g. 'They built energy efficiency into the design'.
      - V n on n Cx12 e.g. 'They based their ideas on ancient writings.' and Cs13 'They modelled the design on Roman villas'.
      - V n in n Cx24 e.g. 'They couched their teaching in story form'.
  - The relation is one of evidence.
    - V n (Relational) Cx17 e.g. 'The evidence proved his innocence'.
    - V to n Cx9 e.g. 'The evidence pointed to his innocence'.
- The constructions indicate relations between actions/events (see Figure 8.12c). The relation may be one of influence, condition, connection, or time.
  - The relation is one of influence (unidirectional).

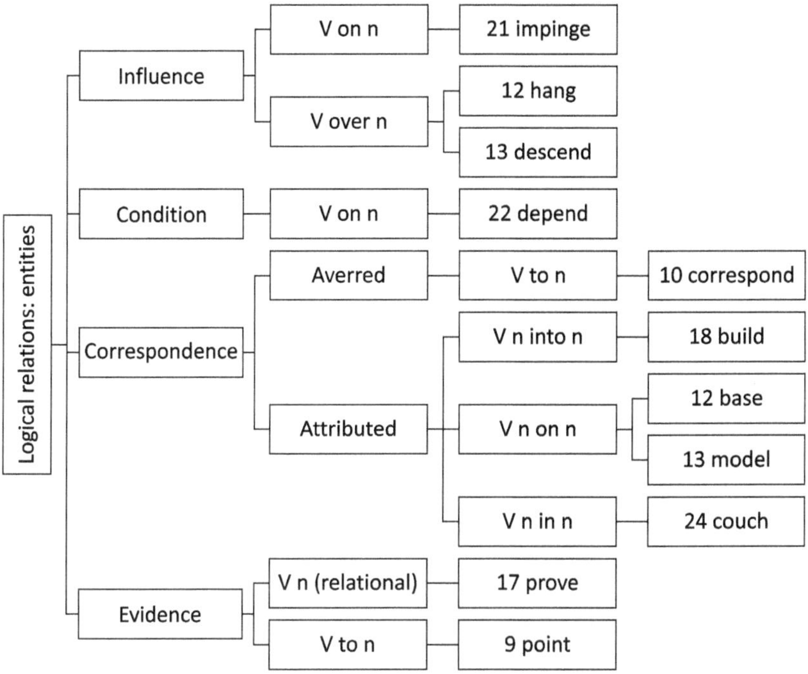

Figure 8.12b Logical Relations: the between entities network

  - V that Cx20 e.g. 'The need to work quickly dictated that some short-cuts were taken'.
  - V n (Relational) Cx18 e.g. 'The short-cuts they took ensured early completion of the work'.
  - V to n Cx37 e.g. 'The short-cuts they took led to early completion of the work'.
  - V wh Cx20 e.g. 'The way they worked determined how quickly the work was finished'.
- The relation is one of condition (unidirectional).
  - V n (Relational) Cx19 e.g. 'Finishing quickly requires absolute concentration'.
  - V n -ing Cx8 e.g. 'Finishing quickly necessitates the craftsman concentrating absolutely'.
  - V from n Cx11 e.g. 'Finishing quickly results from absolute concentration'.
  - V on n Cx22 e.g. 'Finishing quickly depends on absolute concentration'.

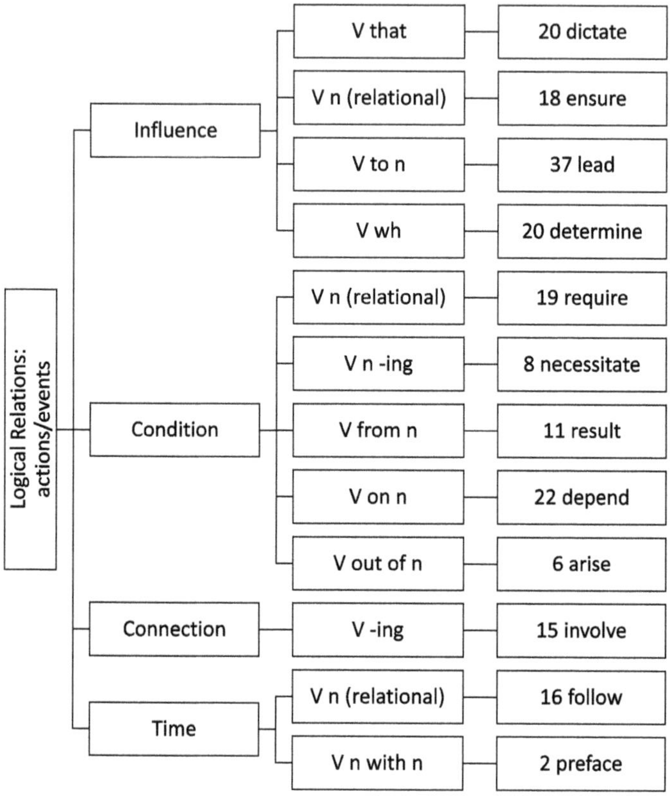

Figure 8.12c Logical Relations: the between actions/events network

  - V out of n Cx6 e.g. 'Her desire to succeed arose out of incidents in her childhood'.
- The relation is one of connection (bidirectional).
  - V -ing Cx15 e.g. 'Scoring goals involves working as a team'.
- The relation is one of time.
  - V n (relational) Cx16 e.g. 'Celebrations followed winning the cup'.
  - V n with n Cx2 e.g. 'He prefaced his remarks with a long digression into the reasons for the meeting'.

8.8 Conclusion

This chapter has presented the proposed meaning taxonomies and systemic networks for six semantic fields, as examples of how such fields might be modelled in terms of constructions and in terms of Systemic Functional Grammar (SFG). In this concluding section, the way that these fields are treated by Halliday and Matthiessen (2014) is briefly outlined.

Halliday and Matthiessen (2014: 234–236) divide material process verbs into two main categories: Creative and Transformative. The 'creative' category is the equivalent of the Creation semantic field as described in this chapter. Transformative verbs are further divided into: Elaborating (equivalent to the Change semantic field); Extending (equivalent to the Possession_transfer semantic field); and Enhancing (equivalent to the Location_change semantic field).

Causation in Halliday and Matthiessen (2014: 483) is a feature of inter-clause relations, and is treated in the context of the clause complex. It is also explained under the heading of hypotaxis in the verbal group (Halliday and Matthiessen (2014: 578–584)), that is, a verb phrase can be extended by the addition of causative verbs such as HELP, FORCE, MAKE, and ENABLE.

Halliday and Matthiessen treat relational processes at length, with a detailed discussion of alternative ways of modelling the various relations between an entity and the attributes, identities, circumstances, or possessions it may have (Halliday and Matthiessen 2014: 265; 279–290). These processes correspond to the Equivalence semantic field, though this is an area where the field covers a great deal more than the process type, as previously noted in this chapter. For example, when the construal of equivalence is attributed to a speaker, the salient process type may be Verbal. Finally, the Logical_relations semantic field corresponds to items discussed under the heading of experiential grammatical metaphor (Halliday and Matthiessen 2014: 707–726).

It is clear that although the study reported in this book is to some extent compatible with the approach of SFG, the two are also to some extent misaligned. This is due to the different starting points and different aims of the two schemas. The degree to which the two can be brought into alignment, and whether it is advantageous to do so, is discussed in Chapter 9.

9 Discussion and Conclusion

9.1 Summary of the Study

This book started with Pattern Grammar, an approach to lexis that is based on the observation of word behaviour in concordance lines and that, inter alia, makes generalisations about the complementation of verbs by clauses and phrases, including prepositional phrases. The Pattern Grammar resources (Francis et al. 1996; http://grammar.collinsdictionary.com/grammar-pattern) list all verb complementation patterns in English, and list all the (or in two cases the most frequent) verbs from the 1995 COBUILD dictionary (Sinclair 1995) that occur with each pattern. Those verbs are divided into 'meaning groups' that demonstrate the connection between form and meaning.

The next stage in this book was to reconcile Pattern Grammar with Construction Grammar. It is apparent that many of the observations that arise from Pattern Grammar can be interpreted in terms of constructions. For example, it may be said that the verb PRAISE occurs in the pattern **V n *for* n** (e.g. *Dr Madok praised the staff for their cooperation*), or it may be said that *praise* occurs in the 'verb someone for an action' construction, where the verb is a spoken response to the action. This observation of the similarity between 'pattern' and 'construction' led to the next phase of the study: the reinterpretation of 50 verb complementation patterns as over 800 proposed constructions. The constructions were obtained through a simple and subjective reworking of the Pattern Grammar meaning groups; as such they are open to refinement or challenge. The constructions form a taxonomy rather than a simple list and the concept of network has been used to show the relationship between constructions at greater and lesser levels of generality. For example, the 'verb someone for an action' construction (meaning 'respond to someone's action in a positive or negative way') may be refined to 'speech-verb someone for an action' (e.g. PRAISE) and 'action-verb someone for an action' (e.g. REWARD). A further level of specificity takes us down to the level of individual verbs: the 'praise someone for an action' construction. This process has been discussed in Chapter 3.

The next stage of the study started with meaning rather than form. It selected nine semantic fields, inspired by the process types identified in Systemic Functional Grammar (e.g. Halliday and Matthiessen 2014), found all the constructions that belong to that field, and labelled the elements of the construction with participant role names, again inspired by SFG. This process has been described in Chapter 4.

The final stage of this study began with the sets of constructions belonging to each of the nine semantic fields and arranged them in networks that showed the choices involved in making the meaning. In each case, two kinds of network are proposed: a taxonomy showing how the constructions in that field relate to one another; and a systemic network that prioritises the features of form and meaning that contribute to construction of the taxonomy (terminology from Matthiessen 2023). In addition, prose descriptions of the taxonomy networks make explicit the choices in meaning and in form that lead to each construction. The networks show routes from the most general meaning to the specific meaning-form matchings of the constructions. They might be said to represent the path from 'grammar' to 'lexis', where 'grammar' is interpreted to be a general process type or semantic field and 'lexis' is a construction. This part of the study has been presented in Chapters 6–8. All the constructions and networks can be seen on transitivity-net.bham.ac.uk. Figure 9.1 summarises the stages of this study.

It should be noted that this book does not claim to present a new theory of lexicogrammar. Instead it attempts to come to an accommodation between different views. The point was made in Chapter 1 that each of the approaches

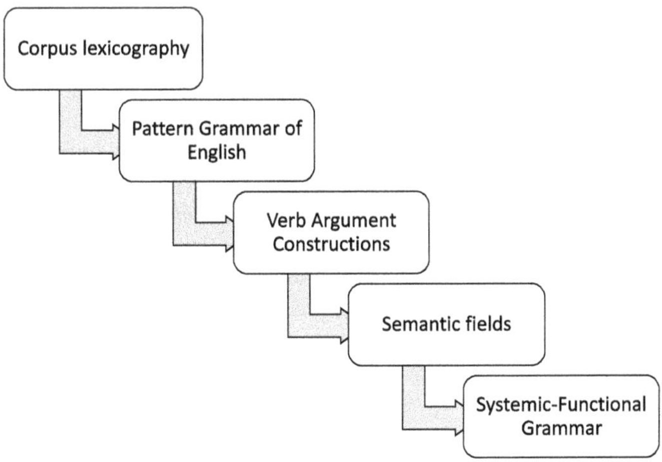

Figure 9.1 The stages of the study

covered in this study comes from a different area of Linguistics, that is, they prioritise different aspects of language. Pattern Grammar is based on an observational approach and seeks to account for language as output. In this book, it is treated as providing the input to two theories of lexis and grammar: SFG and Construction Grammar. Systemic Functional Grammar is based on a concept of language as social semiotic and seeks to account for language as a community resource. Construction Grammar is based on Cognitive Linguistics and seeks to model language in the mind. With these differing views of 'what language is' and 'how language should be studied', it is not surprising that such different models have been developed. On the other hand, given that the same object is being described, it is equally unsurprising that what emerges from the investigations under one approach can be explained in terms of another. Language can be considered as both a social phenomenon and a cognitive phenomenon, the evidence for both coming from observation of output. For some purposes, envisaging language as a mass of constructions is most useful; for others, seeing it as a series of networks is more informative. What this book does do is consider how each approach to language might assist the others. It therefore finds connections and synergies without seeking to replace any one of the approaches with another.

The remainder of this chapter considers the contribution that this study makes to each of the approaches involved and considers possible future developments of the field.

9.2 Contribution to Construction Grammar and Its Applications

Probably the main contribution of this study to Construction Grammar is the demonstration of a systematic approach to identifying constructions of a particular kind in a language. Most accounts of verb arguments in Construction Grammar are confined to familiar instances such as the transitive (**V n**), the ditransitive (**V n n**), those involving causation, such as **V n inf** (e.g. 'make someone move'), or those involving finite clauses, such as **V n to-inf** (e.g. 'tell him to go'). Some constructions with prepositions are investigated, such as the 'causative *into*' construction (**V n *into* -ing**) and the 'oblique predicative' constructions exemplified by 'take her for a friend' (**V n *for* n**) or 'regard him as a genius' (**V n *as* n**) (Stefanowitsch and Gries 2003; Hiltunen 2010; Aarts 2023). Only a small number of such constructions appear in the literature, however. This is because the starting point for Construction Grammar is the identification of form-meaning pairs, with an emphasis on the non-compositional.

The starting point for Pattern Grammar, by contrast, is corpus lexicography, involving a word-by-word study of the thousands of verbs that appear in the Collins COBUILD English Dictionary (Sinclair 1995) and subsequent editions. The purpose of that description was to itemise the grammatical behaviour of each verb in terms of its complementation patterns, irrespective of whether each pattern uniquely identified a meaning. This means that the dictionary contains a description of every pattern and every verb sense, not just those that are striking or noticeable. For example, the **V n *for* n** pattern, as described in Francis et al. (1996: 366–373) includes rather banal examples such as 'schedule an event for a time' and 'search a place for an item' as well as the more idiomatic 'take someone for a fool'. Although the Pattern Grammar resource lacks a great deal of detail (as acknowledged in Chapter 2), it is more comprehensive in its coverage – that is, it accounts for more words – than either the Pattern Dictionary of English Verbs (pdev.org) or FrameNet (https://berkeleyfn.framenetbr.ufjf.br). This comprehensiveness means that more candidate constructions can be identified using Pattern Grammar as a starting point than by using other resources (Perek and Patten 2019).

There are two further caveats to be made concerning the comprehensiveness of the study. One is that for the most part the constructions identified in this book are compositional rather than non-compositional. The meaning of examples such as 'schedule an event for a time' and 'search a place for an item' can be deduced from the meanings of SCHEDULE and SEARCH and an understanding of the kind of entity that might be described as 'an event', 'a place', 'a time', and 'an item'. Only in the case of 'take person for characteristic' (e.g. *took him for a fool*) could the complementation be said to coerce the meaning of TAKE. The argument for the constructions discussed in this book (and those appearing on the Transitivity-Net website) is their frequency rather than what they consist of.

The second caveat is that, of course, only a small proportion of all constructions in English can be derived from the Pattern Grammar resource. The constructions discussed in this book are of one type only and have been referred to in the book as Verb Argument Constructions. There are many other kinds of construction, in English as in other languages. A future development of the work reported in this book would be to extend the study to noun and adjective complementation, using the patterns identified in Francis et al. (1998). For instance, the 'nice of you' construction discussed by Goldberg and Herbst (2021) is an example of an 'Adjective Argument Construction', based on the ***it* v-link ADJ *of* n to-inf** ('*it* + link verb + adjective + *of* noun + to-infinitive clause) pattern (Francis et al. 1998: 501–502). Francis et al.'s description of this pattern notes that the adjective in each case evaluates the action indicated by the to-infinitive clause. The 53 adjectives listed in this pattern are divided into three groups:

- The 'kind' group, comprising general positive adjectives such as *good, kind, lovely, nice*, and *sweet*, together with adjectives with more specific meanings

such as *brave, clever, generous, prudent, smart*, and *thoughtful*. The group includes *big*, which means 'good' only when it is used in this pattern.
- The 'stupid' group, comprising negative adjectives with a wide range of specific meanings such as *absurd, childish, cruel, improper, negligent, rude, silly, unprofessional,* and *wrong*.
- The 'typical' group, comprising three adjectives indicating the degree of typicality: *characteristic, typical*, and *uncharacteristic*.

The implication of Goldberg and Herbst's (2021) work is that these would comprise a single construction, with the specific meaning in context determined by the choice of adjective.

An example of a 'Noun Argument Construction' might be the 'commit to do something' construction, where the pattern is **N to-inf** (noun + to-infinitive clause) and where the noun is one of: *commitment, pledge, promise, threat, undertaking*, and *vow* (Francis et al. 1998: 114). This is one of 12 meaning groups in this pattern identified by Francis et al. (1998), each of which might be the basis for a construction.

If VACs/NACs/AACs are identified as a 'type' of construction, an implication might be that there is a tripartite division of constructions. The most general (or 'grammar-y') constructions are those that are non-specific in terms of lexis, such as the 'past tense' construction or the 'interrogative' construction. The most specific (or 'lexis-y') are those that relate to the idiomatic use of small numbers of lexical items, such as the 'accident waiting to happen' construction, or the 'have your cake and eat it' construction. Midway between the two are the VACs, NACs, and AACs. Researchers in Construction Grammar understandably resist the suggestion that some constructions are core to a language while others lie on the periphery. However, there is a case to be made for specifying construction types, of which the constructions discussed in this book would be one, without assigning priority to any one type.

Another way of looking at this issue of categorisation is to ask a question raised by Herbst (2024): is it possible to identify a cline of generality between 'grammar-like' constructions and 'lexis-like' constructions, or is the 'centre ground' between grammar and lexis more like a cloud, that is, an unordered mass of constructions? The answer suggested by this book is that it is possible to specify clines moving from the most general to the most specific (e.g. from the **V n *for* n** pattern to the 'praise someone for an action or quality' construction). In other words, there is a cloud through which individual pathways might be identified.

This brings us to a key question in Construction Grammar, which is how a constructicon should be modelled (Diessel 2023). A constructicon is an inventory of constructions in a language, arranged to show the relationships between them. It is agreed that a constructicon will be a network, such as the 'hub and spoke' network shown in Perek and Patten (2019). A similar approach is taken in this book, except that a layout based on SFG is used to show relations between more and less general constructions. However, it is argued in this book that one kind of network is insufficient to represent relationships between constructions. As well as the 'form to meaning' networks shown in Chapter 3, there are 'meaning to form' networks, as introduced in Chapter 6. Arguably, it is insufficient to use only one form of network to model the constructions in a language. Instead, a complete constructicon would need to be multidimensional.

Looking to the future, the constructions introduced in this book, and the 800 constructions on the website, have the potential to be the starting point for other studies. The constructions themselves might be refined or reinterpreted. An important extension would be to add a quantitative dimension that is currently lacking, such as the identification of collostructions (Stefanowitsch and Gries 2003), or establishing the relative frequency of constructions in a given semantic field or in a given register (similar to work done by Matthiessen 2006 in the context of SFG). Whereas the study in this book is entirely synchronic, the constructions are available also for diachronic study (suggested by Hans Boas, personal communication). Extensions to other languages are already underway (Song et al. 2024).

Another possibility for future work is that some of the developments in Pattern Grammar studies reported in Hunston and Francis (2000) and in subsequent publications such as Hunston (2008, 2024) can be reinterpreted in terms of constructions, opening up new lines of enquiry. These developments include concepts such as 'semantic sequences' and 'pattern flow', both dealing with how patterns combine to form sentences in running text. The concept of 'semantic sequence' (Hunston 2008) suggests that certain patterns tend to co-occur disproportionately with other elements of meaning. To put this in terms of constructions, a 'node' construction may be found to co-occur disproportionately with a limited range of other constructions. This could be described as a collocation between constructions. For example, what might be called the 'come to terms with [difficult issue]' construction is found to be typically preceded by expressions of difficulty, failure, or obligation, such as 'didn't find it easy to', 'never managed to', or 'had to' (Hunston 2024). If each of those expressions is interpreted as a construction, then there is a found sequence comprising: a construction expressing difficulty, failure, or obligation + the 'come to terms with' construction. This is shown in Table 9.1, with 'come to terms with' shown as the node construction, and the other shown as the collocating constructions. Sequences of constructions of this kind contribute to how texts are made up and to the ideologies that such texts draw on (Hunston 2024).

The concept of 'pattern flow' suggests that sentences or utterances can be analysed as being comprised of a number of catenative patterns (Hunston and

Table 9.1 *Node and collocating constructions: 'come to terms with'*

Collocating construction:	Node construction:
'find it hard to do something' 'fail to' 'have to'	'come to terms with [difficult issue]'

Francis 2000: 207–215). Example (1), taken from the BAWE corpus, illustrates this (see Table 9.2).

(1) Greenhalgh's study of [such] family systems supports the hypothesis that the roots of women's subordination lie in the family system. [BAWE corpus]

Table 9.2 is a diagrammatic representation of the following points:

- Two verbs and three nouns appear in the sentence with complementation patterns: *support* is used in the pattern **V n** (verb + noun phrase); *lie* is used in the pattern **V *in* n** (verb + prepositional phrase with *in*); *study* and *roots* are used in the pattern **N *of* n** (noun + prepositional phrase with *of*); and *hypothesis* is used in the pattern **N that** (noun + that-clause). These verbs and nouns are underlined in the table.
- The two verb patterns follow sequentially after noun patterns. This is another way of saying there is a subject followed by a predicate.
- However, three of the patterns overlap. The noun *hypothesis* forms the second part of the **V n** pattern and itself is the node word of the **N that** pattern. The noun *roots* occurs in the that-clause and is the node word of the **N *of* n** pattern.
- This progression, or 'flow', is an alternative view to the more usual hierarchical representation of the clause as Subject + Verb + Object, where the Object consists of a noun phrase (*the hypothesis that the roots of women's subordination lied in the family system*) with a clause as post-modification.

This progression of elements can equally well be represented as a flow from one construction to another. The lower part of Table 9.2 suggests the constructions involved.

9.3 Contribution to Systemic Functional Grammar

The study in this book has borrowed extensively from SFG. Most obviously, it has used the concept of 'network' in three different ways. Taxonomic networks have been used to demonstrate the relationships between constructions derived

Table 9.2 *'Pattern flow' reinterpreted as catenative constructions*

Greenhalgh's study of Taiwan family systems supports the hypothesis that the roots of women's subordination lie in the family system.

PATTERNS				
The study of systems. . . **N *of* n**				
	. . .supports the hypothesis **V n**			
		. . .the hypothesis that the roots **N that**		
			. . .the roots of subordination **N *of* n**	
				. . .lie in the system. **V *in* n**
CONSTRUCTIONS				
The study of systems. . . 'process *of* entity'				
	. . .supports the hypothesis 'evaluate research entity'			
		. . .the hypothesis that the roots 'idea that'		
			. . .the roots of subordination 'part *of* entity'	
				. . .lie in the system. 'exist in entity'

from the same verb complementation pattern. The same kinds of networks have been used to model the constructions contributing to each of the semantic fields studied. Systemic networks, itemising the features contributing to the taxonomy, have been used as a complementary modelling of the constructions in each field. Other borrowed concepts have also been used to distinguish between sets of constructions, such as the distinction between process types (mental, material, relational, etc.) or between congruent and metaphoric modes of expression. However, this book does not 'do SFG'; rather, it takes an outsider view. As well as borrowing concepts, this study has maintained positions that are at odds with SFG. Most notably, it maintains the descriptive view associated with Pattern Grammar rather than the analytic one adopted by Halliday and Matthiessen (2014). One consequence is that that-clauses, following verbs such as SAY or THINK, are simply recorded as constituting a complementation pattern, rather than being analysed in terms of the grammatical concept of Projection. Even more saliently, prepositional phrases are treated as integral to the behaviour of verbs, and are annotated as Participants, whereas in SFG they are for the most part analysed as Circumstances rather than as Participants. Exceptions include the prepositional phrase with *about* following verbal process verbs (e.g. *they don't talk about your nephews and nieces*), which is coded as Verbiage, though the comment is that 'this type of Verbiage is close in meaning to a circumstance of Matter' (Halliday and Matthiessen 2014: 306). Another distinctive feature of this book is the multiple coding of constructions as exemplifying more than one semantic field simultaneously. For example, 'She thought him a fool' is coded both as an instance of Cognition (what she thought) and as an instance of Equivalence (he is construed as a fool). This is because as well as asking 'what is the best analysis of this instance of text?' this study asks 'what are the various ways that a semantic field can be expressed?'

The main suggested contribution of this study to SFG is to suggest what a version of the lexicogrammar would look like if the end point of the grammar-lexis continuum was considered to be the construction rather than the word. This is at odds with the approach of Hasan (1996/1987) and Matthiessen (2014); the implications of this divergence are worth exploring. Hasan (1996/1987), for example, identifies features that distinguish between near-synonyms such as COLLECT, GATHER, and ACCUMULATE. One system of features is associated with the nature of the action itself, such as the distinction between 'vast (quantity)' and 'unmarked (quantity)': ACCUMULATE is unique in that it only collocates with nouns indicating 'vast' entities, such as 'a lot of money', whereas the other two verbs are unmarked in this respect – they collocate with nouns indicating large or small quantities. Another system distinguishes between allowing a pattern that includes a benefactor, or not. In pattern or construction terms, this might be expressed as follows:

- The pattern **V n** or the 'acquire something' construction: all three verbs are used with this pattern.
- The pattern **V n *for* n** or the 'acquire something for someone' construction: all three verbs are used with this pattern.
- The pattern **V n n** or the 'acquire someone something' construction: only COLLECT and GATHER are used with this pattern/construction.

In other words, whereas Hasan argues that the features distinguish between verbs, and that verbs that share features are classed together, this approach argues that features distinguish between constructions, and that verbs may occur with several constructions.

The difference in approach can be illustrated in more detail using the semantic field of Creation, described in Chapter 8. The study of this field was inspired by the category of 'creative' material processes in Halliday and Matthiessen (2014: 234), and it is the one that most closely fits a single process type. In Halliday and Matthiessen's account, verbs are divided into Intransitive and Transitive and into General (i.e. less fixed collocations between verb and object) and Specific (i.e. more fixed collocations between verb and object). In the terms used in this study, the transitive/intransitive distinction is one of form, while the general/specific distinction is one of meaning. The intransitive verbs are only general in range of meaning, and include examples such as APPEAR, EMERGE, and OCCUR. Other general verbs are both transitive and intransitive and include FORM and GROW. General verbs that are only transitive are exemplified by CREATE, MAKE, and PREPARE. The specific transitive verbs are grouped according to their meaning; the examples given are:

- ASSEMBLE, BUILD, and CONSTRUCT i.e. make a physical structure;
- COMPOSE, DESIGN, DRAFT, DRAW, FORGE, PAINT, SKETCH, and WRITE i.e. make a creative artefact on paper or other medium;
- BAKE, BREW, and COOK i.e. make food or drink;
- KNIT, SEW, and WEAVE i.e. make fabric or something from it;
- DIG and DRILL i.e. make a hole;
- FOUND and ESTABLISH i.e. make an institution;
- OPEN and SET UP i.e. make an organisation or company.

These look very much like the basis for constructions. However, this is a categorisation of verbs, not constructions. Arguably, in construction terms, a 'make a cake' construction would have the specific meaning of 'create something edible from raw ingredients' and the verb might be a general one, such as MAKE, or a specific one, such as BAKE. In other words, the distinction between 'General' and 'Specific' verbs would be disregarded; instead, it would be argued that a general verb such as MAKE takes on the more specific meaning when it is used with a given collocate such as *cake*.

Halliday and Matthiessen (2014) include only transitive and intransitive uses in their table. Most of the verbs they list could be used ditransitively, if only infrequently. A few verbs occur in a dependency relation with prepositional phrases, that is, they occur with the patterns **V n *in/on* n** or **V n *from/out of* n**. From the SFG perspective, this means that the clause includes an additional participant. A further innovation of this study is that, unlike Halliday and Matthiessen (2014), it makes a distinction between physical and abstract created entities.

Attempting to merge the insights from Halliday and Matthiessen 2014 with the insights from this study yields the following prose description of constructions that extend the specificity of the material: creative process type.

The [material:creative] process type enters into two systems: the number of participants and the nature of the created entity. The number of participants may be one, two, or three. If the number of participants is one, it is the created entity; if it is two, they are the creator and the created; if it is three, two of them are the creator and the created, and the other is either beneficiary, location, or constituents. The created entity may be physical or abstract. An abstract entity may be an event, an organisation or institution, or a situation. Merging these two systems leads to the following taxonomy:

- **One-participant constructions** may be divided into those that relate to a physical entity and those that relate to an abstract entity:
  - One-participant constructions that relate to a physical entity are:
    - The 'physical entity appears' construction, using verbs such as APPEAR and EMERGE. E.g. 'A new theatre appeared on the bank of the Thames'.
    - The 'physical entity grows' construction, using verbs such as DEVELOP, FORM, and GROW. E.g. 'The forest grew slowly'.
  - One-participant constructions that relate to an abstract entity are:
    - The 'abstract entity appears' construction, using verbs such as APPEAR and EMERGE. E.g. 'A new problem emerged'.
    - The 'abstract entity grows' construction, using verbs such as DEVELOP, FORM, and GROW. E.g. 'Several problems developed'.
    - The 'event occurs' construction, using verbs such as HAPPEN, OCCUR, and TAKE PLACE. E.g. 'Three birthday parties took place there'.
- **Two-participant constructions** may be divided according to their specific meaning. Some constructions relate to physical entities, some relate to entities such as organisations, and another relates to abstract entities.

- Examples of two-participant constructions which indicate that a physical entity has been created are:
  - The 'make a physical structure' construction, using verbs such as CREATE, MAKE, ASSEMBLE, BUILD, and CONSTRUCT. E.g. 'They built a castle'.
  - The 'create a creative artefact' construction, using verbs such as CREATE, MAKE, COMPOSE, DESIGN, DRAFT, DRAW, FORGE, PAINT, PUBLISH, SKETCH, and WRITE. E.g. 'She painted a picture'.
  - The 'cook food' construction, using verbs such as MAKE, PREPARE, BAKE, BREW, and COOK. E.g. 'He baked three loaves of bread'.
  - The 'make a garment' construction, using verbs such as CREATE, MAKE, KNIT, SEW, and WEAVE. E.g. 'She knitted a scarf'.
  - The 'drill a hole' construction, using verbs such as MAKE, DIG, and DRILL. E.g. 'They drilled a hole'.
- An example of a two-part construction which indicates that an entity such as an organisation has been created is:
  - The 'found an organisation' construction, using verbs such as CREATE, FOUND, ESTABLISH, OPEN, and SET UP. E.g. 'He founded the greatest university in the world'.
- An example of a two-part construction which indicates that an abstract entity has been created is:
  - The 'make an abstract entity' construction, using verbs such as CREATE and MAKE. E.g. 'Her actions created several problems'.

- **Three-participant constructions** include a beneficiary, a location, or constituents.
  - Three-participant constructions with a beneficiary are:
    - The 'make someone something' construction, using any of the verbs found in the two-participant constructions. E.g. 'Annie made Jerry a cake'.
    - The 'make something for someone' construction, using any of the verbs found in the two-participant constructions. E.g. 'Jerry made a cake for Annie'.
  - Three-participant constructions with a location are:
    - The 'make something in somewhere' construction, using verbs such as CARVE, ENGRAVE, ETCH, and IMPRINT. E.g. 'He carved a message in the tree-trunk'.
    - The 'make a hole in something' construction, using verbs such as BORE, DRILL, MAKE, and PUNCH. E.g. 'She drilled a hole in the board'.

    - The 'write words on something' construction, using verbs such as CARVE, ENGRAVE, INSCRIBE, PRINT, and WRITE. E.g. 'He wrote a message on the whiteboard'.

- Three-participant constructions with constituents are:

    - The 'make something from constituents' construction, using verbs such as MAKE, CONSTRUCT, and MANUFACTURE. E.g. 'They manufacture the biscuits from organic ingredients'.
    - The 'make something out of constituents' construction, using verbs such as MAKE, CONSTRUCT, and MANUFACTURE. E.g. 'They manufacture the biscuits out of organic ingredients'.

Although the constructions are differentiated primarily by the verbs that occur in them, each one has a meaning that is more than the combination of the constituents, that is, in a sense they are non-compositional. For example, the 'cook food' construction means 'make something that can be eaten or drunk, combining ingredients and/or applying specific preparation and/or cooking techniques'. The 'create an artefact' construction means 'use a medium such as ink or paint on paper or canvas to bring into being an artefact such as a book or painting'. The 'make an abstract entity' construction means 'bring situation into being through words or actions'.

The Meaning Network and Systemic Network that together summarise this description of the [material:creative] process type are shown in Figures 9.2 and 9.3.

This discussion demonstrates that an accommodation can be made between the study in this book and the work of Hasan and of Halliday and Matthiessen, replacing the focus on lexis with a focus on constructions. For the most part, however, the semantic fields outlined in Chapters 6–8 do not match the process types identified by Halliday and Matthiessen (2014). The semantic area encompassed by each set of networks derives from semantics rather than from the lexicogrammar and shows the system of lexicogrammatical resources that realise that semantic field. The Communication field, as discussed in Chapter 7, for example, includes the Verbal process patterns of **V that, V n that**, and **V n**, but includes many other patterns, and the constructions associated with them, besides. In focusing on the semantic field, this work has affinities with work in Systemic Functional Linguistics (SFL) that takes meaning rather than the lexicogrammar as its starting point, such as the Appraisal framework (Martin and White 2005). The systems associated with Attitude, for example, can be discussed in terms of constructions based on the complementation patterns of adjectives (Hunston and Su 2019). It might be argued that taking the semantic field rather than the process type as entry point for these

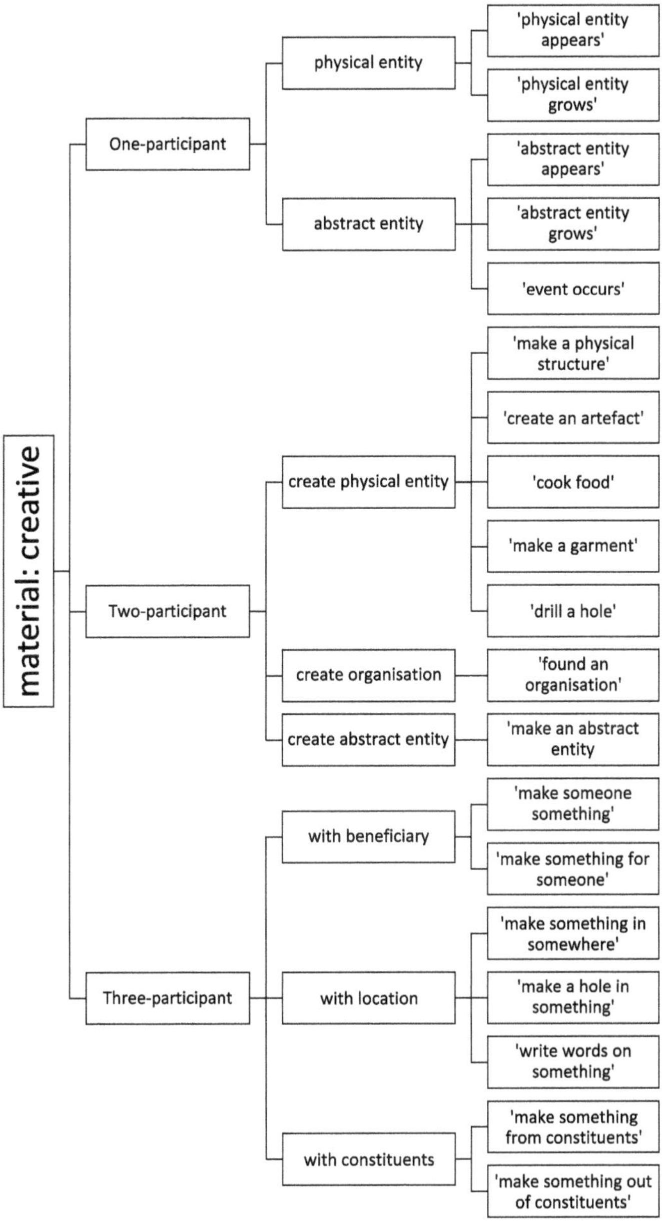

Figure 9.2 Creative process constructions: Meaning Network

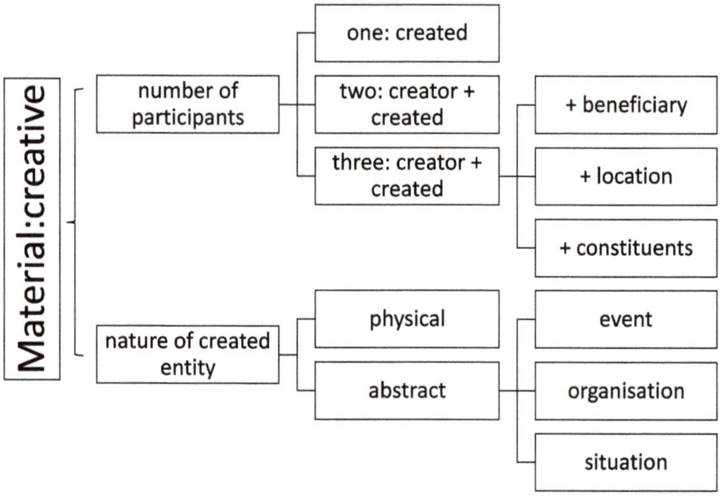

Figure 9.3 Creative process: Systemic Network

systems leads to a more extensive survey of the language resources available. At the very least it offers a complementary perspective.

The final question to be considered here is the 'why does it matter?' question. Systemic Functional Linguistics is an internally consistent account of how language works. Equally importantly, however, it offers significant insights into language as a social construct and demonstrates how choices within the language system contribute to a community's view of the social and physical world. It is therefore the case that many insights from SFL are useful even to researchers who do not draw on the model in its entirety. Their argument might be summarised as 'Given a situation in the social or physical world, what sets of language resources might be used to construe that situation, and how do choices between those resources affect responses to the situation?' Choices in transitivity, for example, have been demonstrated many times to contribute to a view of the world. Thompson (2014: 133–139) shows the difference between two reports of novel medical treatments, one from a newspaper and one from a medical journal. The newspaper uses more material and verbal processes, such as example (2). The journal uses more relational and cognitive processes, such as example (3). Both examples are taken from Thompson (2014).

(2) Dentists have invented a device . . . (material process; newspaper article)

(3) . . . in most cases, symptomatic treatment will be adequate . . . (relational process; journal article)

To simplify somewhat, the newspaper article is about people, their feelings and their actions, whereas in the journal article, people are secondary to abstract nominalisations such as 'treatment'. Nominalisation allows the agent of the process (the person who is responsible for the action) to be deleted and is a key topic in Critical Discourse Analysis (Billig 2008; van Dijk 2008; Martin 2008). Similarly, Fairclough (1989: 50–51) notes that in an example such as (4), the human beings responsible for the unsafe lorry loads do not appear in the text and are therefore not held accountable for causing stones to fall from lorries.

(4) Unsheeted lorries from Middlebarrow Quarry were still causing problems by shedding stones . . .

Semantically based studies such as Appraisal (Martin and White 2005) also exemplify the social significance of choice. An early paper by Martin (1999), for example, shows how two characters in a play are distinguished by their use of Appraisal resources; the more spontaneous, emotionally aware character uses Affect to evaluate entities, while the more repressed character uses Appreciation and Judgement.

Examples such as these challenge the study in this book: can the choices represented in Chapter 6–8 be shown to 'matter', in a social sense? Can they be argued to make a difference to how the world is perceived? To some extent, this argument can be made. It will be illustrated here using the example of the semantic field Causation (see Chapter 6) and specifically the subfield of 'causing (a change in) thought or emotion'. The key distinction made in that figure is the presence or absence or the position of the Cogniser/Emoter. In most constructions, the Cogniser/Emoter is present, as the object of the verb, as in examples (5) and (6) (Cogniser/Emoter underlined).

(5) [The engineer] was able to persuade his masters that the modern Feltham cars might be a good buy. (BNC)
(6) The novel had interested him . . . (BNC)

In a small number of constructions, the Cogniser/Emoter appears obliquely, in a prepositional phrase (example (7), Emoter underlined), or does not appear at all (example (8)).

(7) . . . the abstraction which arouses incomprehension in the ordinary spectator. (BNC)

(8) Results of experiments . . . seem to cast doubt on the usefulness of the categorization . . . (BNC)

This might be interpreted in terms of whether the evaluative meaning is averred or attributed (Hunston 2011) and how open to challenge the evaluation is. In examples (6) and (8) the situation is straightforward: evaluation of the novel in example (6) is attributed to 'him', achieved via Affect, and is open to challenge; evaluation of the categorisation in example (8) is averred, achieved via Appreciation, and less open to challenge. In example (5) evaluation of the cars is attributed to the masters, but the fact that this evaluation is the result of persuasion opens it to challenge. In example (7), evaluation of the abstraction as incomprehensible is both attributed and averred (the spectators do not understand it, and the speaker assesses it as incomprehensible to them). Thus, the degree of challenge is dependent on the construction used.

It is, then, possible to make the case that showing the network relations between constructions highlights the textually significant choices that the language user makes and so contributes to the use of SFG to support ideological interpretations of a text.

9.4 Conclusion

This book began with an approach to lexis and grammar that is purely descriptive. Pattern Grammar adopts only the most general of theories: language is highly patterned, and that patterning suggests that there is no divide between lexis and grammar (Sinclair 1991; Hunston and Francis 2000). It is based on the detailed observation and coding of the thousands of words that comprise the COBUILD dictionary (Sinclair 1995). That coding allows for the most comprehensive account available of the complementation of verbs, nouns, and adjectives in English. It has been argued in this book that this detailed account can be used to inform more theoretically driven accounts of English. Specifically, constructicons of English can be made more complete by taking into account the Verb Argument Construction inventory exemplified in this book and found on the Transitivity-Net website. In turn, constructions can be shown to be an alternative to lemmas as the end-point of transitivity systems in SFG.

It is hoped that the study reported in this book will be followed by others using or adapting the same techniques. One priority area would be to extend the same approach to the complementation patterns of nouns and adjectives (Francis et al. 1998; grammar.collinsdictionary.com/grammar-pattern). This could expand the potential constructicon of English by an estimated further 400 constructions, accounting between them for thousands of nouns and adjectives. A second priority is to undertake quantitative work on the constructions that have been identified. Although such work is more complex than a simple judgement of 'this is what is significantly frequent' (Gries 2019), it offers enormous potential for specifying more exactly what the meaning potential of a given construction is. The quantitative information, together perhaps with empirical studies of language users, could either corroborate or challenge the status of the potential constructions shown in this book and on the Transitivity-Net website.

It is hoped too that the possibility of incorporating constructions into descriptions based on SFG will be of benefit to that model of Linguistics. At the very least, it offers the opportunity of designing networks that bridge the gap between grammatical and lexical perspectives. If quantitative information can be added to the taxonomies of constructions, it will provide the information needed to specify what is marked or unmarked in the expression of a given semantic field and thereby add to our knowledge of what is distinctive in a given register. This suggests that the work reported in this book could be of value to discourse studies. For this to be undertaken fully, the semantic fields exemplified in this book would need to be added to, extending the coverage. While semantic fields are not discrete, identifying a more systematic way of enumerating such fields would make them more useful to discourse studies.

This book began with the observation that three traditions of language description share a perspective on language but rarely attempt to accommodate one another. The book has shown that, taking Corpus Linguistics as a starting point, the three perspectives can be unified, arguably to the benefit of each.

References

Aarts, B. 2023. Oblique predicative constructions in English with *for* and *as*: *qua* vs *qualitate qua*. *English Language and Linguistics* 27(4): 773–788.

Andor, J. 2015. Trains of thought on the issue of syntax, the lexicon, and pragmatics: An interview with Noam Chomsky. *International Review of Pragmatics* 7(1): 145–155.

Barlett, T. and O'Grady, G. (eds.) 2017. *The Routledge Handbook of Systemic Functional Linguistics*. London: Routledge.

Barnbrook, G. 2002. *Defining Language: A Local Grammar of Definition Sentences*. Amsterdam: Benjamins.

Barnbrook, G. and Sinclair, J. 1995. Parsing COBUILD entries. In J. Sinclair, M. Hoelter, and C. Peters (eds.) *The Languages of Definition: The Formalization of Dictionary Definitions for Natural Language Processing*. Luxembourg: Office for Official Publications of the European Communities. pp. 13–58.

Barnbrook, G. and Sinclair, J. 2001. Specialised corpus, local and functional grammars. In M. Ghadessy, A. Henry, and R. Roseberry (eds.) *Small Corpus Studies and ELT: Theory and Practice*. Amsterdam: Benjamins. pp. 237–278.

Bender, E. and Kathol, A. 2001. Constructional effects of 'just because … doesn't mean'. *Proceedings of the Annual Meeting of the Berkeley Linguistics Society* 27(1): 13–26.

Biber, D., Johansson, S., Leech, G., Conrad, S., and Finegan, E. 1999. *Longman Grammar of Spoken and Written English*. London: Longman.

Billig, M. 2008. The language of critical discourse analysis: The case of nominalization. *Discourse and Society* 19(6): 783–800.

Boas, H. 2008. Determining the structure of lexical entries and grammatical constructions in Construction Grammar. *Annual Review of Cognitive Linguistics* 6: 113–144.

Charles, M. 2006. The construction of stance in reporting clauses: A cross-disciplinary study of theses. *Applied Linguistics* 27(3): 492–518.

Cheng, W. and Ching, T. 2018. 'Not a guarantee of future performance': The local grammar of disclaimers. *Applied Linguistics* 39(3): 263–301.

Chrispin, L. 2021. A Cognitive Functional Account of Pure Intransitive Classification. Unpublished PhD thesis, Cardiff University.

Croft, W. and Cruse, A. 2004. *Cognitive Linguistics*. Cambridge: Cambridge University Press.

Davidse, K. 2017. Systemic functional linguistics and the clause: The experiential metafunction. In Barlett and O'Grady (eds.) *The Routledge Handbook of Systemic Functional Linguistics*. London: Routledge. pp. 79–95.

Diessel, H. 2020. A dynamic network approach to the study of syntax. *Frontiers in Psychology* 11: 604853.

Diessel, H. 2023. *The Constructicon: Taxonomies and Networks*. Cambridge: Cambridge University Press.

van Dijk, T. 2008. Critical discourse analysis and nominalization: Problem or pseudo-problem? *Discourse and Society* 19(6): 821–828.

Ellis, N., Römer, U., and O'Donnell, M. 2016. *Usage-Based Approaches to Language Acquisition and Processing: Cognitive and Corpus Investigations of Construction Grammar*. London: Wiley.

Fairclough, N. 1989. *Language and Power*. London: Longman.

Fawcett, R. 2017. From meaning to form in the Cardiff Model of language and its use. In Barlett and O'Grady (eds.) *The Routledge Handbook of Systemic Functional Linguistics*. London: Routledge. pp. 56–76.

Fillmore, C. 1976. Frame semantics and nature of language. *Annals of the New York Academy of Sciences* 280(1): 20–32.

Fillmore, C. 2013. Berkeley Construction Grammar. In T. Hoffman and G. Trousdale (eds.) *The Oxford Handbook of Construction Grammar*. Oxford: Oxford University Press. pp. 111–132.

Fillmore, C. 2014. Frames, constructions, and FrameNet. In T. Herbst, H.-J. Schmid, and S. Faulhaber (eds.) *Constructions Collocations Patterns*. Berlin: De Gruyter Mouton. pp. 121–166.

Fillmore, C., Kay, P., and O'Connor, M. 1988. Regularity and idiomaticity in grammatical constructions: The case of 'let alone'. *Language* 64(3): 501–538.

Fillmore, C., Johnson, C., and Petruck, M. 2003. Background to Framenet. *International Journal of Lexicography* 16(3): 235–250.

Fillmore, C., Lee-Goldman, R. and Rhomieux, R. 2012. The FrameNet constructicon. In I. Sag and H. Boas (eds.) *Sign-Based Construction Grammar*. Stanford: CSLI. pp. 283–322.

Fontaine, L. 2017. Lexis as most local context: Towards an SFL approach to lexicology. *Functional Linguistics* 4(1): 1–17.

Fontaine, L. (2025). Lexicogrammar: The powerhouse of language. In A. Sellami-Baklouti, F. Benelhaj, S. Choura and N. Abid (eds.) *SFL: Power and Empowerment in SFL: Papers from the 48th International Systemic Function Congress*. Sfax, Tunisia: University of Sfax. Special issue of *Academic Research: Revue d'études littéraire, linguistique et de science humaines* 1(19). pp. 10–30.

Francis, G. 1993. A corpus-driven approach to grammar: Principles, methods and examples. In M. Baker, G. Francis and E. Tognini-Bonelli (eds.) *Text and Technology: in Honour of John Sinclair*. Amsterdam: Benjamins. pp. 137–156.

Francis, G., Hunston, S., and Manning, E. 1996. *Collins COBUILD Grammar Patterns 1: Verbs*. London: HarperCollins.

Francis, G., Hunston, S., and Manning, E. 1998. *Collins COBUILD Grammar Patterns 2: Nouns and Adjectives*. London: HarperCollins.

Gilquin, G. 2010. *Corpus, Cognition and Causative Constructions*. Amsterdam: Benjamins.

Goldberg, A. 1995. *Constructions: A Construction Grammar Approach to Argument Structure*. Chicago: University of Chicago Press.

Goldberg, A. 2006. *Constructions at Work*. Oxford: Oxford University Press.

Goldberg, A. and Jackendoff, R. 2004. The English resultative as a family of constructions. *Language* 80(3): 532–568.

Goldberg, A. and Herbst, T. 2021. The *nice-of-you* construction and its fragments. *Linguistics* 59(1): 285–318.

Götz-Votteler, K. 2007. Describing semantic valency. In T. Herbst and K. Götz-Votteler (eds.) *Valency: Theoretical, Descriptive and Cognitive Issues*. Berlin: Mouton de Gruyter. pp. 37–50.

Gries, S. 2019. 15 years of collostructions: Some long overdue additions/corrections (to/of actually all sorts of corpus-linguistics measures). *International Journal of Corpus Linguistics* 24(3): 385–412.

Gries, S. and Stefanowitsch, A. 2004. Extending collostructional analysis: A corpus-based perspective on 'alternations'. *International Journal of Corpus Linguistics* 9(1): 97–129.

Gross, M. 1993. Local grammars and their representation by finite automata. In M. Hoey (ed.) *Data, Description, Discourse*. London: HarperCollins. pp. 26–38.

Halliday, M. 1961. Categories of the theory of grammar. *Word* 17(3): 241–292.

Halliday, M. 1970. Language structure and language function. In J. Lyons (ed.) *New Horizons in Linguistics*. Harmondsworth: Penguin. pp. 140–165. Reprinted in Halliday MAK. 2002. *On Grammar* (edited by J. Webster) London: Continuum. pp. 173–195.

Halliday, M. 1973. *Explorations in the Functions of Language*. London: Edward Arnold.

Halliday, M. 1978. *Language as Social Semiotic: The Social Interpretation of Language and Meaning*. London: Edward Arnold.

Halliday, M. 1985. *An Introduction to Functional Grammar*. 1st ed. London: Edward Arnold.

Halliday, M. 1991/2007. The notion of 'context' in language education. In J. Webster (ed.) *Language and Education: Collected Works of MAK Halliday Volume 9*. London: Continuum. pp. 269–290.

Halliday, M. 1993. Quantitative studies and probabilities in grammar. In M. Hoey (ed.) *Data, Description, Discourse: Papers on the English Language in Honour of John McH Sinclair*. London: HarperCollins. pp. 1–25.

Halliday, M. 1994. *An Introduction to Functional Grammar*. 2nd ed. London: Edward Arnold.

Halliday, M. 2013. *Collected Works of M.A.K. Halliday. Vol 11: Halliday in the 21st Century*. J. Webster (ed.). London: Bloomsbury.

Halliday, M. and James, Z. 1993. A quantitative study of polarity and primary tense in the English finite clause. In J. Sinclair, M. Hoey, and G. Fox (eds.) *Techniques of Description: Spoken and Written Discourse*. London: Routledge. pp. 32–66.

Halliday, M. and Matthiessen, C. 2014. *Halliday's Introduction to Functional Grammar*. 4th ed. London: Routledge.

Hanks, P. 2004. Corpus pattern analysis. In G. Williams and S. Vessier (eds.) *Proceedings of the 11th Euralix International Congress*. Lorient: UBS. pp. 87–98.

Hanks, P. 2013. *Lexical Analysis: Norms and Exploitations*. Cambridge, MA: MIT Press.

Hasan, R. 1996/1984. The nursery tale as genre. *Nottingham Circular* 13: 71–102. Reprinted in R. Hasan. *Ways of Saying: Ways of Meaning: Selected Papers of Ruqaiya Hasan* (C. Cloran, D. Butt, and G. Williams eds.) London: Cassell. pp. 51–72.

Hasan, R. 1996/1987. The grammarian's dream: Lexis as most delicate grammar. Published 1987 in M. Halliday and R. Fawcett (eds.) *New Developments in Systemic Linguistics: Volume 1*. London: Pinter. pp. 184–212. Republished in C. Cloran, D. Butt, and G. Williams (eds.) *Ways of Saying: Ways of Meaning: Selected Papers of Ruqaiya Hasan*. London: Cassell. pp. 73–103.

Haspelmath, M. 2023. On what a construction is. *Constructions* 15(1): 1–15.

Herbst, T. 2007. Valency complements or valency patterns? In T. Herbst and K. Götz-Votteler (eds.) *Valency: Theoretical, Descriptive and Cognitive Issues*. Berlin: Mouton de Gruyter. pp. 15–36.

Herbst, T. 2024. From learner's dictionaries to construction. Paper given at PhrasaLex III: Phraseological approaches to Lexicography. Universität Innsbruck July 2024.

Herbst, T., Heath, D., Roe, I., and Götz, D. 2004. *A Valency Dictionary of English*. London: Mouton de Gruyter.

Herbst, T. and Götz-Votteler, K. (eds.) 2007. *Valency: Theoretical, Descriptive and Cognitive Issues*. Berlin: Mouton de Gruyter.

Herbst, T. and Uhrig, P. 2019. Towards a valency and argument structure constructicon of English: Turning the valency patternbank into a constructicon. *Lexicographica* 35(1): 87–104.

Hilpert, M. 2014. *Construction Grammar and Its Application to English*. Edinburgh: Edinburgh University Press.

Hiltunen, T. 2010. *Grammar and Disciplinary Culture: A Corpus-Based Study*. Helsinki: University of Helsinki.

Hoey, M. 2005. *Lexical Priming: A New Theory of Words and Language*. London: Routledge.

Hoffman, T. 2016. Construction Grammars. In B. Dancygier (ed.) *The Cambridge Handbook of Cognitive Linguistics*. Cambridge: Cambridge University Press. pp. 310–329.

Hunston, S. 1995. A corpus study of some English verbs of attribution. *Functions of Language* 2(2): 133–158.

Hunston, S. 2008. Starting with the small words: Patterns, lexis and semantic sequences. *International Journal of Corpus Linguistics* 13(3): 271–295.

Hunston, S. 2011. *Corpus Approaches to Evaluation: Phraseology and Evaluative Language*. London: Routledge.

Hunston, S. 2013. Systemic functional linguistics, corpus linguistics, and the ideology of science. *Text and Talk* 33(4): 617–640.

Hunston, S. 2019. Patterns, constructions, and applied linguistics. *International Journal of Corpus Linguistics* 24(3): 324–353.

Hunston, S. 2022. *Corpora in Applied Linguistics*. 2nd ed. Cambridge: Cambridge University Press.

Hunston, S. 2024. Coming to terms with success. *Journal of Corpora and Discourse Studies* 7: 63–76.

Hunston, S. and Sinclair, J. 1999. A local grammar of evaluation. In S. Hunston and G. Thompson (eds.) *Evaluation in Text: Authorial Stance and the Construction of Discourse*. Oxford: Oxford University Press. pp. 75–100.

Hunston, S. and Francis, G. 2000. *Pattern Grammar: A Corpus-Driven Approach to the Lexical Grammar of English*. Amsterdam: Benjamins.

Hunston, S. and Su, H. 2019. Pattern, construction and local grammar: The case of evaluation. *Applied Linguistics* 40(4): 567–593.

Hunston, S. and Sui, X. 2024. Modelling the Output from Concordance Lines. Paper given at ICAME45, University of Vigo, Spain, June 2024.

Katamba, F. 1993. *Morphology*. London: Macmillan.

Kay, P. and Fillmore, C. 1999. Grammatical constructions and linguistic generalizations: The 'what's X doing Y' construction. *Language* 75(1): 1–33.

Khachatryan, R. 2009. Ways of expressing causation in Modern English. *Armenian Folia Anglistika* 5(1–2): 125–133.

Kress, G. and van Leeuwen, T. 2006. *Reading Images: The Grammar of Visual Design*. 2nd ed. London: Routledge.

Laffut, A. 2006. *Three-Participant Constructions in English*. Amsterdam: Benjamins.

Levin, B. 1993. *English Verb Classes and Alternations: A Preliminary Investigation*. Chicago: University of Chicago Press.

Lin, F. Y. and Peng, A. X. 2006. Systemic Functional Grammar and Construction Grammar. In Barbara, L. and Berber Sardinha, T. (eds.) *Proceedings of the 33rd International Systemic Functional Congress*. São Paulo: Pontifícia Universidade Católica de São Paulo. pp. 331–347.

Lyngfelt, B., Borin, L., Ohara, K., and Torrent, T. (eds.). 2018. *Constructicography: Constructicon Development across Languages*. Amsterdam: Benjamins.

Matthews P. 2007. The scope of valency in grammar. In T. Herbst and K. Götz-Votteler (eds.) *Valency: Theoretical, Descriptive and Cognitive Issues*. Berlin: Mouton de Gruyter. pp 3–14.

Martin, J. 1999. Beyond exchange: Appraisal systems in English. In S. Hunston and G. Thompson (eds.) *Evaluation in Text: Authorial Stance and the Construction of Discourse*. Oxford: Oxford University Press. pp. 143–175.

Martin, J. 2008. Incongruent and proud: De-vilifying 'nominalization'. *Discourse and Society* 19(6): 801–810.

Martin, J. and White, P. 2005. *The Language of Evaluation: Appraisal in English*. Basingstoke: Palgrave Macmillan.

Matthiessen, C. 1999. The system of transitivity: An exploratory study of text-based profiles. *Functions of Language* 6(1): 1–51.

Matthiessen, C. 2006. Frequency profiles of some basic grammatical systems: An interim report. In G. Thompson and S. Hunston (eds.) *System and Corpus: Exploring Connections*. London: Equinox. pp. 103–142.

Matthiessen, C. 2014. Extending the description of process type within the system of transitivity in delicacy based on Levinian verb classes. *Functions of Language* 21(2): 139–175.

Matthiessen, C. 2023. *System in Systemic Functional Linguistics: A System-Based Theory of Language*. Sheffield: Equinox.

McEnery, T. and Hardie, A. 2012. *Corpus Linguistics*. Cambridge: Cambridge University Press.

Michaelis, L. 2004. Type shifting in construction grammar: An integrated approach to aspectual coercion. *Cognitive Linguistics* 15(1): 1–67.

Michaelis, L. 2024. Staying terminologically rigid, conceptually open and socially cohesive: how to make room for the next generation of construction grammarians. *Constructions and Frames* 16(2): 278–310.

Moon, R. 2007. Sinclair, lexicography, and the COBUILD project: The application of theory. *International Journal of Corpus Linguistics* 12(2): 159–181.

Moon, R. 2009. Sinclair, lexicography, and the COBUILD project: The application of theory. In R. Moon (ed.) *Words, Grammar, Text: Revising the Work of John Sinclair*. Amsterdam: Benjamins. pp. 1–22.

Mumford, S. and Anjum, R. 2013. *Causation: A Very Short Introduction*. Oxford: Oxford University Press.

Neale, A. 2002. More Delicate Transitivity: Extending the Process Type System Networks for English to Include Full Semantic Classifications. Unpublished PhD thesis, Cardiff University.

Neale, A. 2006. Matching corpus data and system networks: Using corpora to modfy and extend the system networks for Transitivity in English. In G. Thompson and S. Hunston (eds.) *System and Corpus: Exploring Connections*. London: Equinox. pp. 143–163.

Neale, A. 2017. Transitivity in the Cardiff Grammar. In Bartlett and O'Grady (eds.) *The Routledge Handbook of Systemic Functional Linguistics*. London: Routledge. pp. 178–193.

O'Grady, G. 2019. SFL and critical discourse analysis. In G. Thompson, W. Bowcher, L. Fontaine, D. Schönthal (eds.) *The Cambridge Handbook of Systemic Functional Linguistics*. Cambridge: Cambridge University Press. pp. 462–484.

Perek, F. 2021. Constructions Grammar in action: The English constructicon project. *Cognitextes* 21.

Perek, F. 2005. Beyond evocation: Frames and constructional meaning in the English Constructicon. In A. Ziem, A. Willich, and S. Michel (eds.) *Constructing Constructicons: Issues, approaches and cross-linguistic perspectives*. Amsterdam: Benjamins.

Perek, F. and Patten, A. 2019. Towards an English constructicon using patterns and frames. *International Journal of Corpus Linguistics* 24(3): 354–384.

Ruppenhofer, J., Ellsworth, M., Petruck, M., Johnson, C., and Schffczyk, J. 2016. *FrameNet II: Extended Theory and Practice*. Berkeley: ICSI.

Sass, B. 2024. Identifying Constructicon Entries in Query Text. Paper presented at the International Conference on Construction Grammar 13, University of Gothenburg, Sweden, August 2024.

Semino, E. and Short, M. 2004. *Corpus Stylistics: Speech, Writing and Thought Presentation in a Corpus of English Witing*. London: Routledge.

Sinclair, J. (ed.) 1987. *Looking Up: An Account of the* COBUILD *Project in Lexical Computing and the Development of the Collins* COBUILD *English Language Dictionary*. London: Collins.

Sinclair, J. (ed.) 1990. *Collins* COBUILD *Student's Dictionary*. London: HarperCollins.

Sinclair, J. 1991. *Corpus Concordance Collocation*. Oxford: Oxford University Press.

Sinclair, J. (ed.) 1995. *Collins* COBUILD *English Dictionary*. London: HarperCollins.

Sinclair, J. 2004. *Trust the Text: Language, Corpus and Discourse*. London: Routledge.

Song, J., Yang, C., Sun, Y., et al. 2024. Quantitative research on Chinese sentences structure based on Pattern Grammar. *Sage Open* July–September14: 1–16

Stefanowitsch, A. and Gries, S. 2003. Collostructions: Investigating the interaction of words and constructions. *International Journal of Corpus Linguistics* 8(2): 209–243.

Su, H. 2018. 'Thank bloody God it's Friday': A local grammar of thanking. *Corpus Pragmatics* 2(1): 83–105.

Su, H. 2020. Local grammar and diachronic speech analysis: A case study of apology in the history of American English. *Journal of Historical Pragmatics* 21(1): 109–136.

Su, H. and Wei, N. 2018. 'I'm really sorry about what I said': A local grammar of apology. *Pragmatics* 28(3): 439–462.

Su, H., Zhang, Y., and Chau, M. H. 2022. Exemplification in Chinese English-major MA students' and expert writers' academic writing: A local grammar based investigation. *Journal of English for Academic Writing* 58: 101120.

Taverniers, M. 2021. Modelling interfaces with context in SFL: Stratification, instantiation, metafunctions. *Functions of Language* 28(3): 291–314.

Thompson, G. 1994. *Collins* COBUILD *English Guides 5: Reporting*. London: HarperCollins.

Thompson, G. 2014. *Introducing Functional Grammar*. 3rd ed. London: Routledge.

Thompson, G., Bowcher, W., Fontaine, L., and Schönthal, D. (eds.) 2019. *The Cambridge Handbook of Systemic Functional Linguistics*. Cambridge: Cambridge University Press.

Tucker, G. 1998. *The Lexicogrammar of Adjectives: A Systemic-Functional Approach to Adjectives*. London: Cassell.

Webster, J. 2019. Key terms in the SFL model. In G. Thompson, W. Bowcher, L. Fontaine, and D. Schönthal (eds.) *The Cambridge Handbook of Systemic Functional Linguistics*. Cambridge: Cambridge University Press. pp. 35–54.

West, M. 1953. *A General Service List of English Words*. London: Longman, Green.

Wible, D. and Tsao, N. L. 2020. Constructions and the problem of discovery: A case for the paradigmatic. *Corpus Linguistics and Linguistic Theory* 16(1): 67–93.

Yang, Y. 2023. The diachronic analysis of resultative constructions: A systemic functional framework. *Language, Context and Text* 5(1): 80–107.

Yu, D., Li, L., Su, H., and Fuoli, M. 2024. Assessing the potential of LLM-assisted annotation for corpus-based pragmatics and discourse analysis: The case of apology. *International Journal of Corpus Linguistics* 29(4): 534–561.

Zhang, L., Jiang, R., and Zhang, J. 2024. 'Table 1 shows that . . . ': A local grammar of graphic data commentary in discourse of Economics. *English for Specific Purposes* 74: 68–81.

Zhang, Y. and Su, H. 2023. (Mis)use of definition in Chinese EFL postgraduate students' academic writing: A local grammar based investigation. *Journal of English for Academic Purposes* 65: 101283.

Ziem, A., Flick, J., and Sandkühler, P. 2019. The German constructicon project: Framework, methodology, resources. *Lexicographica* 35(1): 15–40.

Index

For EU product safety concerns, contact us at Calle de José Abascal, 56–1°, 28003 Madrid, Spain or eugpsr@cambridge.org.

www.ingramcontent.com/pod-product-compliance
Ingram Content Group UK Ltd.
Pitfield, Milton Keynes, MK11 3LW, UK
UKHW022030120925
462840UK00007B/74
9781009629027